About This Book

Why is this topic important?

It is estimated that more than half of all e-learning is being created with PowerPoint®. Those using PowerPoint as an authoring tool—from front-line trainers to instructional designers—need help making their PowerPoint-based e-learning programs more engaging and more effective while maximizing use of simple approaches, tricks, and tools.

What can the reader achieve with this book?

Jane Bozarth, e-learning coordinator for the state of North Carolina and author of *e-Learning Solutions on a Shoestring: Help for the Chronically Underfunded Trainer,* brings you solid ideas for transforming bullet-based content into engaging, interactive online learning programs. From finding compelling approaches for programs, to creating interactive games, to utilizing add-on quiz and tracking tools, this book will help the reader take simple PowerPoint-based e-learning to a level on par with programs created with long-learning-curve higher-end products, custom art, and approaches dependent on programming expertise. The book focuses more on basics of effective, engaging design than on technical specifications; where appropriate, however, instructions and tutorials are provided.

How is this book organized?

Readers will take a chronological tour through the process of creating good e-learning with PowerPoint, from developing objectives and creating a storyboard to developing a user-friendly interface, choosing and developing meaningful art and animation, adding interactivity, narration, and multimedia, and uploading programs for use by learners. The accompanying CD offers step-by-step instructions, narrated tutorials, and working examples of many items described in the book.

Who is this book for?

This book is meant for anyone using PowerPoint to create online learning programs, from front-line trainers to instructional designers, and even those who may be familiar with other programming-based approaches. It's also meant for those already using PowerPoint or PowerPoint-based authoring products (such as Articulate or Adobe Presenter) who want to move from storing content to building more interesting, engaging programs. This book is especially meant for those who not only want to create e-learning with PowerPoint but to create *good* e-learning with PowerPoint.

About Pfeiffer

Pfeiffer serves the professional development and hands-on resource needs of training and human resource practitioners and gives them products to do their jobs better. We deliver proven ideas and solutions from experts in HR development and HR management, and we offer effective and customizable tools to improve workplace performance. From novice to seasoned professional, Pfeiffer is the source you can trust to make yourself and your organization more successful.

Essential Knowledge   Pfeiffer produces insightful, practical, and comprehensive materials on topics that matter the most to training and HR professionals. Our Essential Knowledge resources translate the expertise of seasoned professionals into practical, how-to guidance on critical workplace issues and problems. These resources are supported by case studies, worksheets, and job aids and are frequently supplemented with CD-ROMs, websites, and other means of making the content easier to read, understand, and use.

Essential Tools   Pfeiffer's Essential Tools resources save time and expense by offering proven, ready-to-use materials—including exercises, activities, games, instruments, and assessments—for use during a training or-team-learning event. These resources are frequently offered in looseleaf or CD-ROM format to facilitate copying and customization of the material.

Pfeiffer also recognizes the remarkable power of new technologies in expanding the reach and effectiveness of training. While e-hype has often created whizbang solutions in search of a problem, we are dedicated to bringing convenience and enhancements to proven training solutions. All our e-tools comply with rigorous functionality standards. The most appropriate technology wrapped around essential content yields the perfect solution for today's on-the-go trainers and human resource professionals.

Pfeiffer
www.pfeiffer.com   *Essential resources for training and HR professionals*

For my dad.

Pfeiffer™

Better **Than Bullet Points**

Creating Engaging e-Learning with PowerPoint®

JANE BOZARTH

BICENTENNIAL
1807
WILEY
2007
BICENTENNIAL

John Wiley & Sons, Inc.

Published by Pfeiffer
An Imprint of Wiley
989 Market Street, San Francisco, CA 94103-1741
www.pfeiffer.com

Library of Congress Cataloging-in-Publication Data

Bozarth, Jane.
    Better than bullet points: creating engaging e-learning with PowerPoint®
/ Jane Bozarth.
      p. cm.
    Includes bibliographical references and index.
    ISBN 978-0-7879-9245-3 (pbk.)
     1. Employees—Training of—Computer-assisted instruction. 2. Computer-assisted instruction. 3. Microsoft PowerPoint (Computer file) 4. Presentation graphics software. 5. Internet in education. I. Title.
  HF5549.5.T7B6196 2007
  658.3'12404—dc22

                          2007033650

Acquiring Editor: Lisa Shannon
Director of Development: Kathleen Dolan Davies
Production Editor: Dawn Kilgore

Editor: Rebecca Taff
Editorial Assistant: Marisa Kelley
Manufacturing Supervisor: Becky Morgan

Printed in the United States of America
Printing   10 9 8 7 6 5 4 3

CONTENTS

CONTENTS OF THE CD-ROM

ACKNOWLEDGMENTS

So it turns out that, while the first book is an exciting adventure, subsequent books are *work*. I am indebted to the dozens of people and organizations who contributed screenshots and other materials, and continue to be amazed at the remarkable and quick generosity of others. There is always danger in singling out particular entities, but I really must comment on the extraordinary help and extra effort from the folks at http://ferl.becta.org.uk, the Royal Veterinary Cottage, Professor Danton O'Day, and Tom and Alice Atkins of Right Seat Software, makers of Vox Proxy.

I am especially appreciative of the most generous Adam Warren of Southampton University, who contributed tutorials to the CD and graciously loaned me his design for the instructional screens herein.

Thanks, too—as usual—to Pfeiffer Acquisitions Editor Lisa Shannon (how delightful to have an editor who just gives me whatever I want!). Thanks to Cindy Epps, Cindy Thacker, and Teri Armstrong for their help with Chapter 2. And thanks to my extended training family and author support system: Jennifer Hofmann, Kassy LaBorie, Patti Shank, Karl Kapp, and Nanette Miner. Because I can find no more public place to thank him, I want to mention my favorite narrator Michael Telesca, whose good humor and patience are as valuable as his golden tones. Also: many thanks to the world's best neighbor, Colleen O'Connor Grochowski, Ph.D. As always, much appreciation to the world's most supportive employers, Thom Wright and Ann Gillen Cobb. Thanks for letting me work.

Finally, and it is not enough: very special thanks to my dear husband, Kent Underwood, who in supporting my books and The Dissertation has never complained about having not eaten at our dining room table since the last millennium.

Getting the Most from This Resource

What Will This Book Do for You?

There is so much more to e-learning, and to PowerPoint®, than bullets and animated text. This book will show you how to use PowerPoint to create engaging, successful e-learning programs.

Why PowerPoint?

With so many authoring tools available, why would a trainer choose to stick with PowerPoint? A better question might be, "With PowerPoint so intuitive, familiar, and easy to use, why would a trainer choose to buy an expensive authoring tool?"

- PowerPoint allows for rapid development and deployment of e-learning.

- PowerPoint provides for easy addition of graphics and simple animation.

- Many training shops have libraries of PowerPoint presentations, originally developed for classroom use, ripe for updating and rethinking as online programs.

- The advent of motion path animation gives PowerPoint users animation options previously only available to users of higher-end graphics programs.

- Even novice PowerPoint users will find the learning curve shorter than that associated with other tools (and often downplayed in the sales pitches for those tools).

- e-Learning created with PowerPoint brings with it none of the licensing fees or per-user costs associated with other tools.

- Those new to e-learning may be unaware of the time and costs attached to updating online training content; using PowerPoint can make maintenance much easier.

- And odds are, if you're a trainer, you already own PowerPoint.

Really, you may find that you never need much more for creating engaging, compelling e-learning.

According to Brian Chapman of Brandon Hall Research (2005), Power-Point is the most popular e-learning tool on the market. Used by itself or in conjunction with a PowerPoint-based add-on authoring tool (such as Articulate Presenter), PowerPoint is being used for e-learning purposes by many small firms as well as large organizations like Nestle, John Deere, the State of North Carolina, Deloitte Touche Tohmatsu, the American Society for Prevention of Cruelty to Animals, and Dade Behring.

Who This Book Is For

This book is primarily for the trainer wearing several hats, including that of instructional designer and, now, e-learning expert. As many readers are likely making the shift from classroom to online training approaches, there is a good deal of coverage on instructional design for e-learning. The book is intended for those with minimal (or who have no interest in) programming and coding skills, who wish to use PowerPoint partly due to its user-friendly, programming-free capabilities.

What This Book Covers

This book is not about how to use PowerPoint. It's about how to use PowerPoint's features—such as animation and hyperlinking—to create good online instruction. After a decade as a classroom trainer, I returned to graduate school and, on completing a degree with a major in technology in training, set out to implement a new statewide e-learning initiative. Shocked at both the ineffectiveness and outrageous expenses associated with the e-learning programs available then, my goal was to develop sound, cost-effective approaches to online training. I found, more often than not, that PowerPoint was my tool of choice and that nearly all good online training programs I encountered used approaches easily replicable with PowerPoint. After years of providing workshops on creating good e-learning, particularly with PowerPoint, and working with participants on their own solutions, I want to make this information accessible to a broader audience: you. You've probably created (and seen) plenty of PowerPoint shows that consist mostly of bulleted text supplemented by some clip art and some simple animation. But have you ever considered using PowerPoint to create an online art history course designed to look like a *noir* mystery movie? An online interactive simulation featuring audio clips of angry customers? A "Hollywood Squares"-type game with characters based on your organization's top managers? You can do all this, and much more, with nothing more than PowerPoint.

Throughout the book, I frequently repeat my mantra, "It's about design, not software," and offer many examples of ways to make online content more interesting and engaging. These are "real" examples, found from web searching or from submissions from workshop participants. They were chosen for inclusion here due to their unique approach, unusual treatment, or especially compelling use of material. Even though all were not necessarily developed with PowerPoint, they all use approaches that could be replicated with PowerPoint. This book will help you see how to do that.

A suggestion: look at as many e-learning programs as you can. Search www.google.com for "e-learning showcase," "e-learning demo," "e-learning samples," and "e-learning gallery." (See especially Jane Knight's site www.e-learningcentre.co.uk for the excellent "showcase" section.) Also try substituting "distance learning" and "online learning" in the search phrases. When you see something you especially like, ask, "How did they do that?" "Can I do that?" and "Can I do that with PowerPoint?" Often the answer will be, "Yes!"

Things to Look For

Watch for the "Lesson Learned" boxes for tips on saving time, energy, and frustration, These are all things that I, or a colleague, learned the hard way. Look, too, for the CD icon,

as the CD accompanying this book provides printable tools, some quick tutorials, and examples of working animations and interactions described in the book, along with instructions for creating them. As site addresses and products are prone to change, and as new products are always being launched, I often suggest searching the Internet for additional information or ideas. The "search" icon

suggests search terms to help guide you; with most searches, while you may end up with hundreds of hits, I'd pay most attention to the first few pages.

Note: This book includes dozens of screenshots taken from e-learning programs. For the sake of clarity, and to ensure images would print clearly, these have sometimes been modified from their original form. Often the example has been stripped of additional elements such as logos, template features, textured backgrounds, and so forth, so that it appears in "bare bones" form. Other times changes have been made to color, particularly gradient or shaded colors, to ensure that the images would print correctly in black and white for use in this book. In most cases the examples shown are accompanied by links to the original programs so that you can see them in their entirety and in their original format. See also the "Other Resources" section at the end of the book.

Technology Skills

This book is written for the trainer or instructional designer who has basic PowerPoint skills. If you can create a simple slide show, add and resize clip art and photographs, make some use of Word Art, and know how to make a line of text fly in, then this book should be appropriate for you. The Appendix provides a quick overview of PowerPoint tools. Those with very rudimentary skills might want to practice basic tasks or seek out additional training.

 Searching www.google.com for specific tasks, such as "how to create animations in PowerPoint," will take you to any number of tutorials.

While this is not a "how to use PowerPoint" text, I have in some cases included step-by-step instructions for several operations. Decisions about when to do this were driven by questions I most frequently am asked during workshops or during consultations. Most often, questions arise not from how to use a particular built-in feature but from how to manipulate something in a way that may not be evident. For instance, most participants understand the basics of hyperlinking, but have never considered how to use that capability to create a simulation or game-show-type game. Similarly, most people grasp the idea of simple animation—it's available through drop-down menus—but few have explored the possibilities of editing clip art. Questions also arise about functions that are beyond those typically associated with using Power-Point for classroom presentations—for instance, adding narration or uploading to the Web. Instructions have been included for these pursuits.

In writing this book, I have assumed that most users have PowerPoint 2002 (XP includes the 2002 version) or 2003, and that some have upgraded to Vista/2007. Readers with earlier versions will find most of this book relevant to them; the biggest difference will be the more limited animations available to those using older versions. PowerPoint 2007 introduced a new interface, and where the difference is noticeable, instructions have been included for both 2007 and 2002XP/2003. Otherwise, changes brought with 2007 are, for the purposes of developing e-learning, minimal.

How to Use This Book

As this book offers a chronological tour through the process of creating e-learning with PowerPoint, I recommend reading chapters in order, then returning to sections as need be. The book does sometimes reference material covered earlier, so familiarity with the content will help. It seems that every PowerPoint user, regardless of level, has a particular area of interest and skill. Those with an artistic bent may know a great deal about creating from-scratch illustrations, while having no experience with adding narration; others may have extensive experience with complex animations while knowing nothing about compressing images. So skim where you feel you should, but please look out for new ideas, examples, and tips, even in areas where you feel you are fluent.

What This Book Covers

Chapter 1 provides an overview, with many examples, of the possibilities of using PowerPoint for developing e-learning. We then begin a chronological tour of creating good PowerPoint-based e-learning programs. Chapter 2 discusses the basics of instructional design for e-learning, with particular attention paid to setting clear goals, reducing cognitive load, and practical applications of the research on multimedia learning. This chapter also walks through the process of transforming former classroom content for online delivery and ends with ideas on choosing an appropriate treatment and examples of creating a basic program layout. Chapter 3 deals with developing a good user interface, creating navigation, and making decisions about learner control. Chapter 4 addresses the issue of choosing graphics and text that are meaningful, rather than decorative, and examines the impact the right images can have. In Chapter 5 we extend this discussion to creating and editing images for use in e-learning programs. Chapter 6 offers a look at effective animations and, as with the discussion of images, the focus is on animations that teach rather than entertain. Chapter 7 provides extensive examples of creating interactions, from quizzes and games to simulations with branching decision making. Chapter 8 provides examples of some add-ons, such as animated talking characters, and discusses ways of extending programs through blended learning and collaborative experiences. Examples of performance support tools, job aids, and ideas for "nice to know" content are included. Chapter 9 covers the final step of development, adding narration and multimedia. And in Chapter 10 we look at ways of distributing our e-learning programs to our learners. The Appendix offers a quick overview of basic PowerPoint features and commands. Finally, the References and Resources are meant to provide more than just citations for material: please visit sites listed or take a look at authors quoted for inspiration and further education.

Disclaimer

This book references a number of websites and particular products. There is always danger when talking about Web technologies: site addresses change, companies merge, and products disappear. Please check my website, www.bozarthzone.com for updates, information about changes, or revised links.

Foundations

CHAPTER 1

Creating e-Learning with PowerPoint

There's an old urban myth that humans use only 2 percent of their brains. While that's never been substantiated, the idea does seem to bear out in regard to PowerPoint: most users employ just a fraction of PowerPoint's capabilities. Those of us in training know that an awful lot of classroom PowerPoint shows are just mind-numbing screen after screen of bulleted text. Adventuresome trainers may add some decorative elements like spinning slide transitions, pretty clip art, or animated text. In its worst application, poorly designed PowerPoint shows are uploaded to the web and called "e-learning." But they aren't "e-learning" programs. They are e-presentations or e-lectures or e-reading, but there's no learning there anywhere. Likewise, those who think PowerPoint can't be used to create good e-learning programs have likely only seen PowerPoint at its worst: slide after slide of bulleted lists, dizzying irrelevant animation, and decorative rather than meaningful graphics. (For that matter, many e-learning programs, regardless of the authoring tool used, suffer from the same problems. Search www. Google.com for a common topic like "online safety training" and see what you get.)

> "In user testing, Microsoft found that nine out of every ten features that customers wanted to see added to Office products were already in the program."
>
> **Ina Fried, www.CNETnews.com, September 2005**

It's a shame that PowerPoint is so often badly used or underused, because it can be so much more than a presentation tool. For those interested in e-learning, it can often replicate what is otherwise done with expensive authoring tools. With PowerPoint, some imagination, and some patience, you can create interesting, engaging online courses with meaningful interactivity. Figures 1.2 through 1.9 show some examples of PowerPoint's potential.

Examples

Multiple-Choice Quizzes

Figure 1.1. Multiple-Choice Quiz

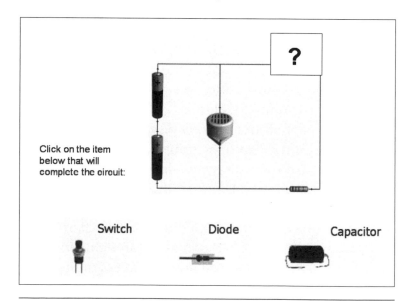

Source: Simon Drane. Component images. www.crocodile-clips.com.

Matching Exercises

Figure 1.2. Matching Exercise

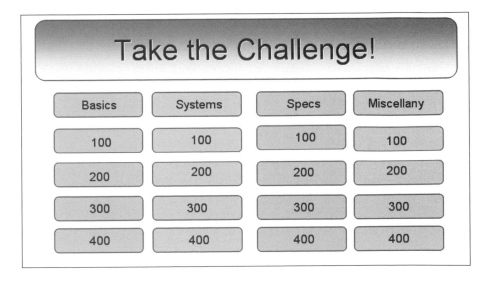

Game-Show-Type Games

Figure 1.3. Jeopardy-Type Game

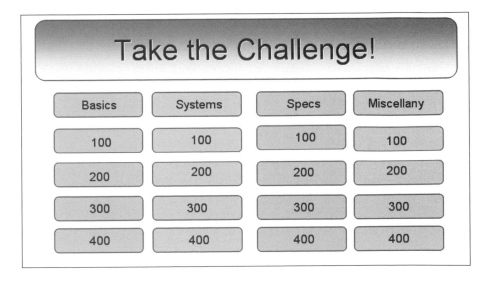

Word Search Puzzles

Figure 1.4. Word Search Puzzle

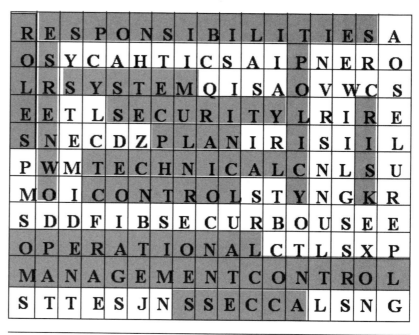

Source: Marirose Coulson and Donna Ebling, Booz Allen Hamilton

Mazes

Figure 1.5. Maze

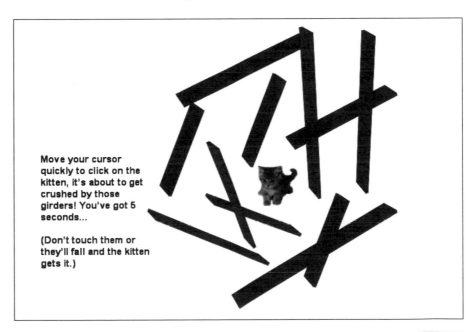

Source: From online PowerPoint manual available at www.agsci.utas.edu.au/ppmultimedia/.

Authored by Nicholas D'Alessandro, Simon James, Anna McEldowney, and Ruth Osborne, University of Tasmania. Copyright: Commonwealth of Australia. Copyright Regulations 1969. This material has been reproduced and communicated to you by or on behalf of the University of Tasmania pursuant to Part VB of the Copyright Act 1968 (the Act). The material in this communication may be subject to copyright under the Act. Any further reproduction or communication of this material by you may be the subject of copyright protection under the Act.

Case Studies

Figure 1.6. Case Study

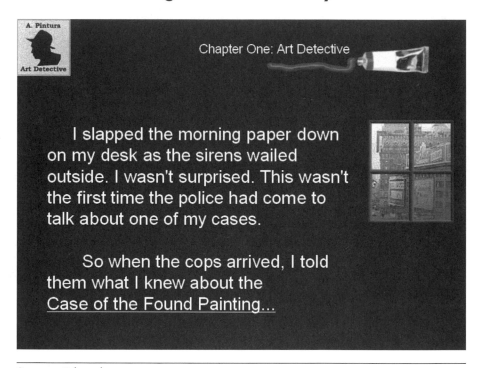

Source: Eduweb

Simulations with Branching Decision Making, with Embedded Audio and Video Clips

Figure 1.7. Simulation with Branching Decision Making

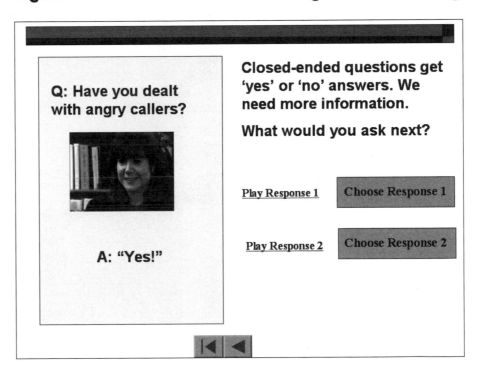

Animations That Teach

Figure 1.8. Animation Illustrating Concept

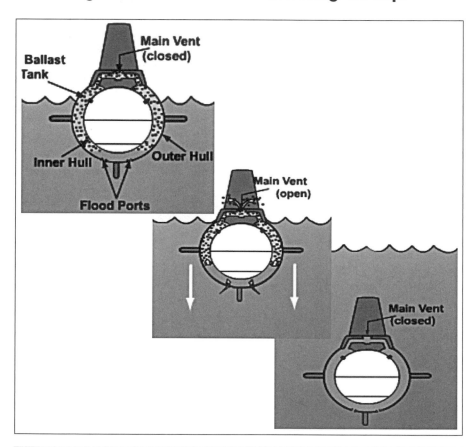

Source: www.onr.navy/mil

Let's Get Started

The rest of this book takes you on a step-by-step walk through the process of developing e-learning with PowerPoint. Chart 1.1 provides an overview of the basic process for creating an e-learning program with PowerPoint, while Table 1.1 offers a checklist (there's a printable version on the CD accompanying this book) of the process in more detail.

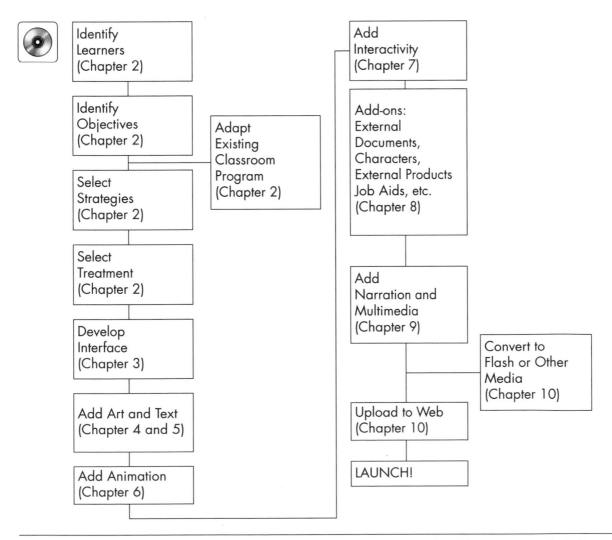

Table 1.1. Checklist for Creating an e-Learning Program with PowerPoint

❑ Identify your learners.
❑ Determine objectives.
❑ Adapt existing classroom program (if applicable).
❑ Choose strategies.
❑ Choose treatment.
❑ Create main file folder and subfolders for images, media, etc.
❑ Develop storyboard.
❑ Create Graphic User Interface (GUI) and slide and title masters. Include "how to use this program" information for new learners.
❑ Add art and text.
❑ Add animation.
❑ Add interactivity.
❑ Add narration and multimedia.
❑ Save everything!
❑ Add other elements: documents, characters, external quizzes and sites, pre- and post-work, "blended" components, job aids.
❑ Add a site map.
❑ Save everything!
❑ Convert to Flash or other media (optional).
❑ Upload to web or LMS.
❑ Test.
❑ Launch.

Better Than Bullet Points. Copyright © 2008 by John Wiley & Sons, Inc. Reproduced by permission of Pfeiffer, an Imprint of Wiley. www.pfeiffer.com

Lesson Learned

Use Chart 1.1 as your guide. Along the way, be sure to test, test, test! Check your objectives with your stakeholders. Have some of your learners try out your interface. See how interactions work in different versions of browsers. A key to rapid training development is to "pilot as you go", rather than wait to launch a product only to have it see extensive revision.

The accompanying CD offers narrated explanations, "you try" tutorials, examples of items such as working animations and interactions, and templates for game design.

Summary

This book will help you move "beyond the bullets" to new ways of thinking about PowerPoint-based e-learning. Success in applying this material isn't a matter of technical wizardry. It takes patience and creativity and a willingness to experiment and learn, as we often do, through some trial and error. I hope you enjoy this journey.Source: Nick D'Alessandro, University of Tasmania. © Commonwealth of Australia.

It's About Design, Not Software

"Begin with the end in mind."

Stephen Covey, *The Seven Habits of Highly Effective People*

n breaking out of the bulleted-text box, ask: Who are your learners? What is it you're trying to accomplish, how can you do it in an engaging, effective way, and which strategies will support the goals of the training? When developing meaningful instruction, it's vital to stay focused on desired outcomes. Even those with strong skills in developing classroom-based training will find still more challenges in designing for the online environment. This chapter looks at the basics of instructional design for e-learning and offers guidelines for transforming classroom content for online delivery.

Who Are Your Learners?

Understanding your target audience will help you choose appropriate treatments and useful interactions. You cannot build credible, effective scenarios, cases, story-based experiences, and simulations without a clear understanding of your learners and their reality. What do most of them do on the job? What do the rest do? Why are they accessing this e-learning course? Is it required? By whom? What do they already know about this topic? What reactions might they have to this topic/content? Do they have a history with this topic? What is it?

A big advantage of e-learning is "scalability," that is, a program can be delivered to many learners at once. This brings with it, though, the temptation of trying to create a program that is all things to all people, while relevant to none. Consider the issue of a company's "infection control" update. The instruction that will be effective for the general office staff will likely not be useful for the company nurses. The level of prior knowledge, tasks carried out during the work day, and expectations of performance are very different. For instance, the first group might benefit from some simple reminders about hand washing, perhaps in the form of the PowerPoint-based "Bacteriopoly" game shown in Chapter 8. Nurses, however, might need much more in-depth information. Be very clear about the needs of your target audience, and be prepared to create perhaps two levels or different versions of a program.

Objectives and Strategies

The learning objectives of your program will drive the design. What are the desired performance outcomes? It can be hard to keep these in sight when caught up in designing. And it can be challenging to develop objectives that support real-world performance. "Academic" objectives, such as, "the participant will list, define, describe. . ." are easy to write, and they're easy to teach to (lecture, bulleted slides), and they're easy to test (matching, multiple choice). But is any learning taking place that will be of any use in the workplace? My supervisor has never, *ever*, asked me to "list" anything.

> The problem with most learning objectives is that they "tend not to relate to anything anyone will actually be able to do in this world."
>
> **Roger Schank,** *Lessons in Training, Learning, and e-Learning*

I'm guessing that readers involved in training and instructional design have at least a passing knowledge of Benjamin Bloom's taxonomy of objectives, which describes learning in terms of level of abstraction. If you envision Bloom's ideas as a ladder moving up through levels of sophistication, the lowest level, knowledge, addresses only recall and provides training that asks learners to do little more than recite a series of steps in a process or memorize some definitions of terms. The remaining climb up the ladder would include, in order, comprehension, application, analysis, synthesis, and evaluation. (This is an extremely truncated explanation, meant as a quick reminder for those with a background with Bloom; those unfamiliar with his work are encouraged to search

 www.google.com for "Bloom's taxonomy".) Table 2.1 outlines levels of the taxonomy and offers ideas for strategies and activities appropriate for each.

Bloom further refined his thinking to include the concept of learning domains. He identified three: cognitive, psychomotor, and affective. In the training vernacular this is often restated in terms of objectives: What do you want learners to know? What do you want them to do? And how do you want them to feel? What might look like a very straightforward topic could very well include all three domains. Consider, for instance, a program on using fire extinguishers. You want the learners to know where the extinguisher is located as well as other basic fire-safety procedures. You want them to do by using the extinguisher correctly. And you want them to feel confident that this is a task they can handle without panicking. Other topics may involve only one domain: learning to use a new office copier very similar to the old one may involve only the psychomotor domain, while using a very different model might touch the cognitive as well as the psychomotor. Leadership

Table 2.1. Matching Outcomes to Strategies

OUTCOME if you want learner to. . .	SOME STRATEGIES then try. . .	RATIONALE because this will encourage. . .	SPECIFICS (and here are some ideas; all can be done online)
Knowledge List, define	Text presentation; Simple test	Recall	Matching terms to definitions; Ordering in correct sequence; Simple multiple-choice quiz; Printable worksheet; List the four steps in defusing an angry customer; Given choices, correctly choose phrase most likely to defuse angry customer
Comprehend Explain, predict, describe	Restate; Paraphrase; Translate	Deeper understanding; Connection between verbal description and behavior	Given choices, predict outcomes of different phrases in defusing angry customer; Given choices, rank order phrases used to defuse angry customer, from most effective to least effective
Application Solve, experiment	Practice; Determine; Get a "feel" for it	Experiential learning; Trial and error	Given simple scenario, utilize four-step process in defusing angry customer; Given brief description of angry customer, practice using defusing phrases in a skill practice or role play
Analysis Connect, infer	Taking it apart to see how it works; Isolate "precursors" to end results	Careful examination of complicated behaviors	Given complex scenario, break into component parts to identify underlying factors; Given "script" of unsuccessful customer interaction, identify phrases or words that made the situation worse

OUTCOME if you want learner to. . .	SOME STRATEGIES then try. . .	RATIONALE because this will encourage. . .	SPECIFICS (and here are some ideas; all can be done online)
Synthesis Debate, contrast distinguish; Compile, pull together, accumulate	Structured case studies; Worked examples	Connect prior experience to new learning; Facilitate transfer	Given complex scenario, work to identify root of customer complaint and utilize four-step process in defusing customer's anger
Evaluate Judge, choose course of action, evaluate data	Less structured case studies, simulations	Opportunity to self-correct; Provide practice; Encourage reflection; Facilitate transfer	Given complex less-structured scenario, generate own effective response to angry customer

training may employ a good many strategies aimed at the cognitive and affective domains, but require little in the way of psychomotor skills. A failing of many learning programs (and live training, too, in my experience) is focusing exclusively on the cognitive domain. It's where we encounter hours and hours of lecture in the classroom, and screen after screen of content online. Again: Talking is easy. Presenting bullet points is easy. Figuring out how to reach the other domains—to provide psychomotor practice or to elicit an emotional response—is your challenge in developing effective PowerPoint-based e-learning.

Along with other development decisions, you will need to estimate time it will take to create your e-learning program. Here is a list of typical considerations:

- Nature of the training

- Complexity of the training

(*continued*)

- Existing training materials (Amount/Type/Quality)

- Knowledge and experience of the project manager

- Interest and attitude of the project manager

- Interest and attitude of the practice development/sales person

- Knowledge and experience of the instructional developers

- Interest and attitude of the instructional developers

- Client knowledge of development process

- Client attitude toward the project and project team

- Evaluation and pre-testing requirements and procedures

- Media elements

- Degree of learner versus system control of learning

- Materials approval process

- Number of iterations

- Development methodology

- Development and programming tools and systems

- Explicit design, development, and documentation standards

- Number and nature of mid-project changes

- Experience of the programming staff

- Experience and capabilities of the media product staff

- Requirements to interface with other systems and technology

- Existing hardware and software architecture

Thanks to Richard M. Cavagnol, Principal, Technology Applications Group, Inc.

Cognitive Load

Many e-learning programs (and many classroom PowerPoint shows, for that matter) simply ask too much of learners. The tendency toward decorative fonts, busy templates, bright background colors and textures, branding elements like company logos, and too much text can be overwhelming. Consider the example shown in Figure 2.1, from a program someone brought to me and asked if I would narrate, so it could be "e-learning." What is the "learning" here? There are several ideas, represented by text of equal size, with unclear connection. The template is unrelated to the content, and the graphic suggests profit rather than the productivity the text beside it mentions. It gets worse: while you can't view it here, the font of the last lines uses a blaring icy-blue shadowed text, the middle lines of text spiral and bounce while the

Figure 2.1. Example of Cognitive Overload

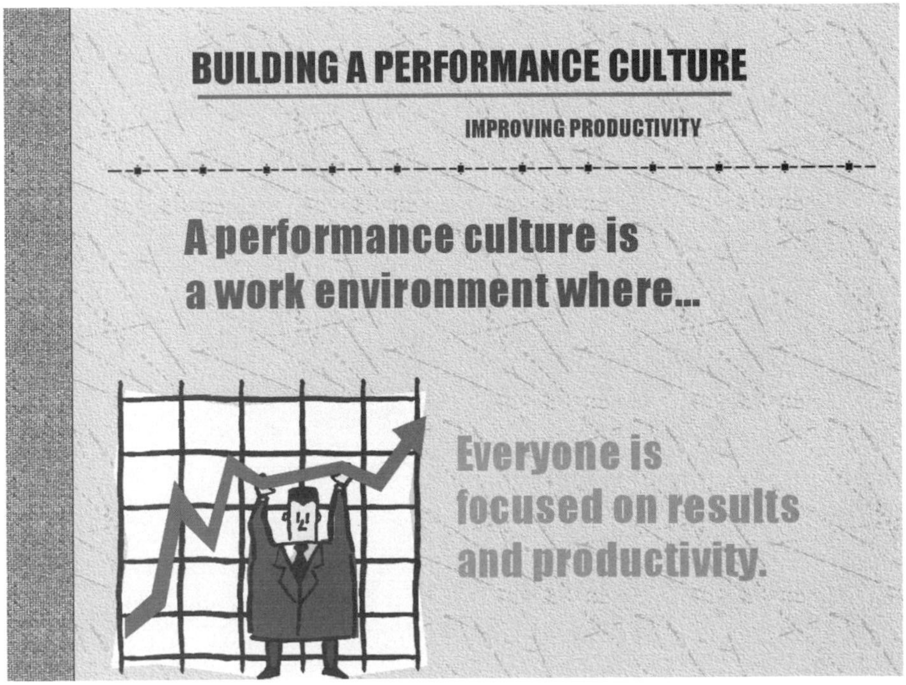

BUILDING A PERFORMANCE CULTURE

IMPROVING PRODUCTIVITY

A performance culture is
a work environment where...

Everyone is
focused on results
and productivity.

slide loads, and every slide change is accompanied by a chiming sound effect. The learner doesn't have a chance!

While some simple editing—cutting out extraneous information, cleaning up the look, finding more relevant graphics—could correct many of these problems, psychology professor Richard Mayer, famous for his research on multimedia learning, offers his "Select—Organize—Integrate" (SOI) model as a rubric for approaching the issue of cognitive load. How can we help learners know and acquire what matters? Table 2.2 offers some suggestions.

Mayer has also conducted extensive research on the effectiveness of multimedia learning (see the "References" section for studies) and has

Table 2.2. Mayer's "SOI" Model

Select	Remove interesting but extraneous information
	"Chunk" information into smaller pieces
	Use font size, colors, and highlighting to indicate importance
	Be concise
	Use white space for emphasis
Organize	Advance organizers
	Graphic organizers
	Relevant graphics
	Flow charts and diagrams
	Process maps
	Steps or sequence flows
Integrate	Cases
	Simulations
	Self-assessments
	Elaborative questions
	Activities that encourage processing

developed a number of principles useful for those of us working to develop e-learning programs. Mayer's **principles of multimedia learning** especially relevant to the purposes of this book are:

1. *Multimedia principle:* Learning is enhanced by the presentation of words and pictures rather than words alone. Figures 2.2 and 2.3 show an example.

Figure 2.2. Before: Text List of Required Items

Written Warning

Definition:
A detailed disciplinary notice for conduct or performance

A Written Warning Must:
State that it is a warning
State the reason for the warning
Detail the improvements required
Indicate length of time allowed for improvement
State the consequences if improvements are
not made
Outline the appeal process

Figure 2.3. After: Sample Letter Shows Items in Realistic Context

MEMORANDUM
To: Jessica Jones, Office Assistant
From: Steve Smith, Office Manager
Date: October 20, 2007
Subject: Written Warning—Unsatisfactory Job Performance

State that it is a warning

The purpose of this letter is to give you written warning for unsatisfactory job performance. The specific unsatisfactory performance for which you are being warned is excessive tardiness. On August 19, September 15, and October 5 I talked with you about the importance of starting work promptly. During our last conversation we discussed the consequences of Reason prove in this area.

2. *Coherence principle:* Learning is enhanced when extraneous material is omitted. Figures 2.4 and 2.5 show another before-and-after example.

Figure 2.4. Before: Slide with Extraneous Material

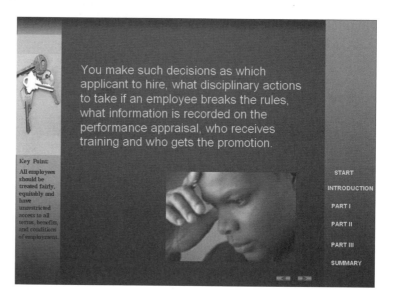

Figure 2.5. After: Slide with Extraneous Information Removed

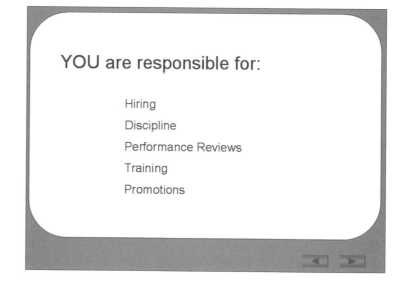

3. *Split attention principle:* This is a common problem with narrated e-learning courses. Designers add word-for-word audio voiceover to match the on-screen text. Different parts of the brain process visual and auditory information at different speeds (we usually read faster than a narrator talks); splitting attention this way causes the material to compete for the learner's attention, creates overload for the learner, and greatly reduces the learner's ability to take in the information.

4. *Redundancy principle:* Similar to the split attention principle. Mayer found that presenting animation with narration was more effective than animation plus narration *and* on-screen text.

5. *Contiguity principle:* Learners learn better when on-screen text and visuals are integrated rather than placed apart. The valley images shown in Figures 2.6 and 2.7 illustrate this.

The final product? As I said at the beginning of the chapter, begin with the end in mind. You will need to make some predictions about how you will distribute your e-learning program; these decisions could affect program design. Chapter 10 discusses this at length, but briefly, you have several options in saving the file you will upload to the web:

- Save as a PowerPoint file (.ppt). This will ensure that all animations, narrations, timings, etc. will remain intact. Users will need a compatible version of PowerPoint or the free PowerPoint viewer. Note that this will require the upload of enormous files, which will consume bandwidth and will likely take a long time to load so learners can view the program. Learners will also be able to download and edit the show.

- Save as a PowerPoint slideshow (.ppt). This is more tamperproof but also brings problems with file size.

- Save as a Web page (.html). This creates many separate files. Animations, sound effects, and narration will not survive the upload.

Figure 2.6. Before: Text Separated from the Image Increases Cognitive Load

Photos used with permission of Debbie Milton

- Save as a Flash file (.swf). While this requires purchase of an additional product (these start at about US $300), PowerPoint-to-Flash converters can be an excellent investment for those wanting to develop programs with extensive animation and narration. The product will significantly reduce the file size and will ensure play back on virtually any machine. One drawback: at press time few, if any, converter tools support trigger animation effects, although that could change.

Choosing a Treatment

In developing e-learning with PowerPoint, it's crucial that you consider not just developing interactivity but also ways of approaching the content. The right treatment—your overall approach—is often what

Figure 2.7. After: Text Integrated into Image Helps Learners Acquire Information

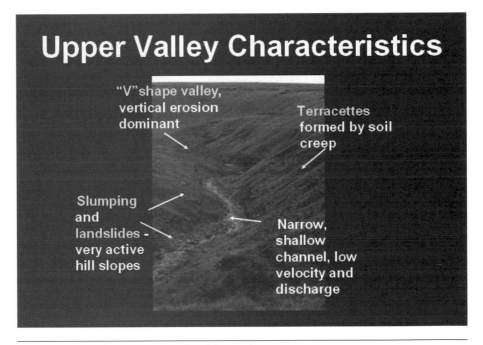

Photos used with permission of Debbie Milton

moves a program from "e-presentation" to "e-learning." Bullet-ridden, content-based programs rarely get past the cognitive domain, and remain at the lowest levels of Bloom's taxonomy. No authoring tool will magically create "relevant, engaging" learning on its own—and making it "pretty" doesn't make it more effective.

Rather than ask, "How can I teach this?" ask, "How can my participants learn this?"

Nanette Miner, Ed.D., *The Accidental Trainer*

Figures 2.8 through 2.12 show several before-and-after examples of possible treatments.

Figure 2.8. Treatment for Program for Art Museum

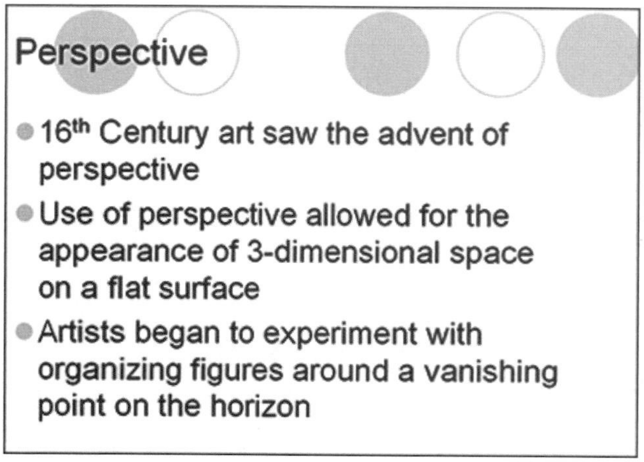

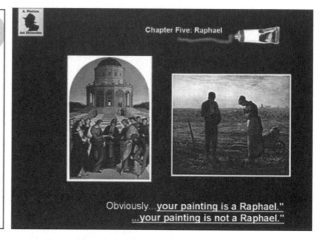

Before: List of facts

After: Interactive mystery "The Case of the Found Painting"

Source: Eduweb

Figure 2.9. Treatments for Ethics Program for New Veterinarians

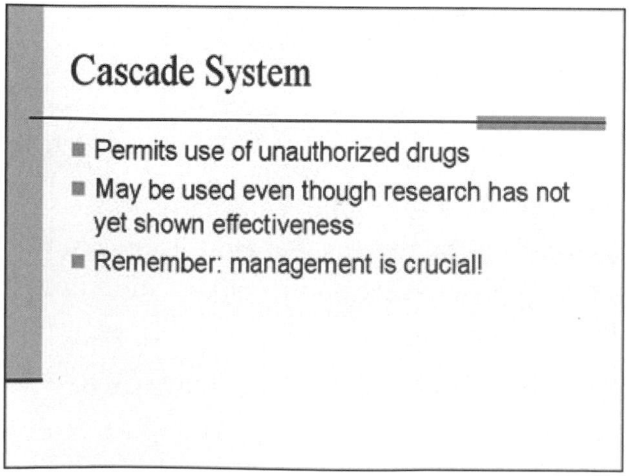

Before: List of facts

After: Interactive decision-making simulation

Source: Royal Veterinary College

Figure 2.10. Treatment for Electrical Circuitry Program

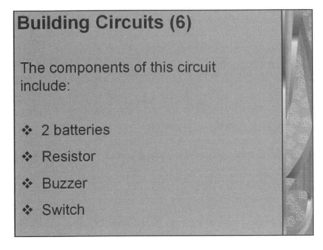

Before: Presentation of content   After: Realistic practice

Source: Simon Drane

Figure 2.11. Treatment for Sexual Harassment Course

Before: "Wall of words" text content   After: Case study using photos and voice clips

Source: www.brightlinecompliance.com

Figure 2.12. Treatment for Equal Employment Opportunity Course

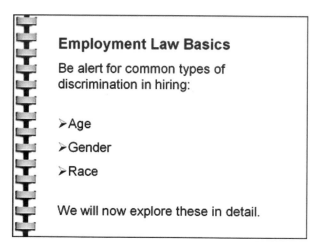

Before: Bulleted content

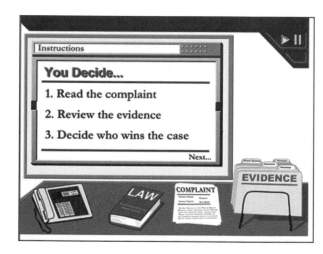

After: Interaction with elements of a case

Writer's Block?

We've just looked at various treatments for e-learning programs: a film noir mystery, a veterinary case simulation, and a job skill training practice. Finding the right approach and an interesting treatment can be challenging. There's nothing wrong with looking around to see how others have approached a topic or type of content. And brainstorming, free-writing, and free-association exercises can help. Try sitting down with a blank sheet of paper and jotting down every word you can think of associated with a topic. Figure 2.13 shows a list of words I came up with when designing a module on the organization's complex employee discipline process. The word that popped out at me was "maze"; this ended up forming a metaphor for the treatment, a simulation that took a supervisor on an online walk through the "maze" of the process.

Figure 2.13. Free-Association

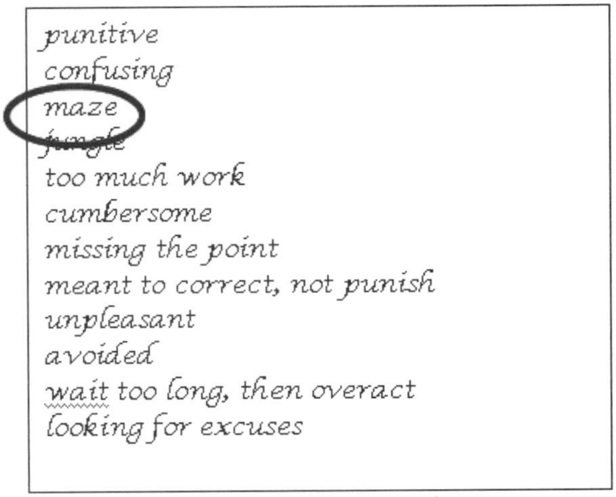

punitive
confusing
maze
jungle
too much work
cumbersome
missing the point
meant to correct, not punish
unpleasant
avoided
wait too long, then overact
looking for excuses

Source: www.eduweb.com/pintura/

A free-writing exercise can also provide inspiration. Take a blank sheet of paper and set a timer for three minutes. Start writing, and keep writing, about the topic until the time is up. Grammar, spelling, and logic don't matter—just keep writing and see what ideas surface. Another strategy is to make a list of possible different approaches to see what treatments they might suggest. Table 2.3. provides an example.

Can You Find a Story?

Cliff Atkinson's *Beyond Bullet Points* (2005) vouches for the effectiveness of a good story to enhance presentations. Many of his ideas can be applied to e-learning programs as well. In using stories in online learning, think of good storytellers you know and good stories you've heard. You'll usually find some interesting characters, a problem to be handled, and a resolution—often with a "happy ending." In online programs

Table 2.3. Possible Approaches to "Sharks"

If Your Intent Is:	Then Here Are Some Possible Approaches
Shark: Killer of the Seas	Case of scuba diver alone battling beast
	Facts about how much sharks can eat an hour, how strong their jaws are, the history of terrifying attacks
	Learners will watch "Jaws" and write a report
Sharks are misunderstood	Video clips of children swimming with sharks
	Facts: great proportion of shark species no threat to humans
	Shark attacks very rare but get lots of press
Shark is the victim; it's man who's the killer	Facts about shark species now endangered/ extinct
	Facts about decline

such stories often take the form of case studies or simulations, such as the art history mysteries of "A. Pintura, Art Detective" (Figure 2.14) and the impossible decisions faced by the characters struggling for survival in "Hunger Banquet" (Figure 2.15). You will see more examples of these two stories in the book.

Figure 2.14. Story: "A. Pintura, Art Detective"

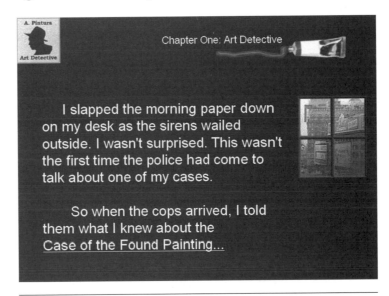

Source: Eduweb

Figure 2.15. Story: "Hunger Banquet"

You are Gloria Narua

You live in the southern African nation of Mozambique, where you grow crops on a small plot of land. Most years you can produce enough maize, eggplant, carrots, and kale to feed your three children.

You'd like to send your oldest son to school but you can't afford it. He is 9 years old and desperate to learn to read and write. Besides, this year, you'll need his help in the field. Your husband died last spring. People say it could have been AIDS but you can't be sure.

As you look toward the harvest you are worried. The rains were not good this year. This could make for a tough year to come...

≫ **Continue**

› **Manhemé, Mozambique**

≫ **Does Gloria have AIDS?**

Source: www.hungerbanquet.org

From Classroom to Online: Think "Transform," Not "Transfer"

Converting an existing (and presumably successful) classroom course to an online format can be a tricky, time-consuming undertaking. The easy way out—simply moving the content and lecture portions to an electronic means—is what leads to e-"learning" at its worst: slide after slide of bulleted content. Engaging activities and the contributions of individual instructors are lost. Look for ways to capture the richness that a good instructor brings to the classroom, such as responsiveness, a sense of humor, engagement, interesting stories and examples, and immediate feedback. Also, when considering moving a classroom course online, approach it not just as converting one form to another, but as an opportunity to improve the existing product. This is a chance to cull the extraneous, nice-to-know information, to improve what's already there, and to leverage technology for what it can do: for instance, a plain-vanilla paper-and-pencil classroom quiz can be reborn as a dazzling, engaging, seductive online test.

Cut-n-chunk

This is a good time to reexamine purpose, intent, and objectives. What are the intended outcomes of the program? In order to "work" online, a full-day classroom program must be distilled to its essential elements. Cut out extraneous, "nice-to-know" information. Is some information population-specific? Is some information tangentially relevant to most but really relevant to none? Every element of the online program should be relevant to most learners. Another issue to consider: How old is the classroom program? How recently was it updated? Is content still current? Are there newer means of delivering the same content, perhaps through electronic aids or other performance support tools?

An ongoing challenge for e-learning designers is the need to cut, then cut some more. In choosing what to keep and what to edit out, remember the learners first: If they don't use it—lose it!

What's Working? What's Not?

Find out which aspects of the classroom program are most successful—and which fail. Talk with learners and the classroom instructors, and review any evaluation or follow-up data they are able to provide. Are learners leaving the classroom fully prepared to perform successfully back on the job? If not, where are there gaps? Where do instructors feel they need to provide additional explanation? What concepts are difficult to explain? What questions or misunderstandings come up time and again? What opportunities for practice exist in the classroom session? Does the classroom use cases, simulations, and scenarios for practice? What do good individual instructors add to the experience?

Inventory Your Assets

In examining the existing classroom program don't overlook the assets associated with it. Assemble everything—handouts, PowerPoint shows, videos, case studies, evaluation forms—*everything* associated with the program. There are likely many paper documents—outlines, worksheets, quizzes—that might be repurposed for the online version. Likewise, slide shows, video clips, case studies, and role play information may, too, be useful as part of the e-learning program. Take care not to reinvent the wheel. You may find that much can be adapted for your new purpose.

Converting from Classroom to Online: The Process*

1. Analyze the current state of the classroom program.

2. Update and cut 'n' chunk material.

---

*Model adapted from an online presentation, "Successfully Transitioning Classroom Content to Online Interactivity," by Roni Viles and Katherine Stevens, offered by the E-Learning Guild (www.elearningguild .com) on July 14, 2006.

3. Identify ways of adding interactivity and capturing richness added by good instructors.

4. Articulate new future state of the (online) program.

5. Storyboard the new online program.

Example: Equal Employment Opportunity Training Program

1. Analyze the current state of the program.

   - Classroom program taught by subject-matter experts (SMEs) in two half-day sessions

   - Extensive lecture-based review of case law

   - Long (two-page) detailed cases focusing on past court issues: learners asked to discuss, but then told "right" answer per the court decision

   - Too much information on laws, little on how to apply

   - "Smile sheet" evaluation only; despite fifteen years of providing program, no research on application back on the job, data as to whether incidents/lawsuits have decreased, etc.

   - SMEs authoritarian, law- and content-focused

   - Learners provided with 110-page spiral-bound manual, no workbook-type activities or exercises, no quick references (FAQs, tabs, color coding, etc.), due to spiral binding, no discretion in reorganizing or adding to manual

   - Much content provided elsewhere, as with mandatory unlawful harassment training and hiring programs; many learners already familiar with key ideas/content

   - Heavy emphasis on fact that program is mandated, resulting in many learners as "prisoners"

2. Update and cut–n-chunk.

- Provide test-out sections so those with prior knowledge can go straight to new learning.

- Seek evaluation beyond smile-sheet level to ascertain effectiveness of components.

- Change focus to practical application and desired behavior.

- Move legal details to optional links.

- Eliminate portions that replicate other training.

- Downplay mandate and look for ways to gain interest and voluntary attendance.

- Offer optional supplemental classroom session or provide other mechanism for questions and answers—Web meeting, discussion board, etc.

- Provide questions and situations that provoke reflection on implications, repercussions, etc.

3. Take inventory of assets associated with the classroom program.

- Manual

- Video clips (available online for free from a government site)

- Case studies

4. Identify ways of developing interactivity and capturing contribution of instructors.

- Use scenarios to teach concepts.

- Provide practical application and exercises.

- Use "What would you do?" scenarios instead of past court decisions.

- Provide interactive activities for reinforcement.

- Incorporate relevant "war stories" into the online material.

5. Articulate the "future state" of the online program.

- Possible treatments: "day in the life" of a manager; judge as narrator/character leading through info; first-person characters explaining their situations; simulation with "what would you do?" scenarios

- Choose treatment and create outline.

6. Storyboard the new program.

- The final step in transforming classroom training to Power-Point-based e-learning is to create a storyboard from which to work. This is further discussed in the next section.

Why Storyboard?

The key to making dynamic, effective, interactive PowerPoint-based e-learning is careful planning. Storyboarding and creating mockups of your program will help you organize your thoughts and ensure that your ideas flow logically, without gaps or overkill. It's also a quick, inexpensive way to "test drive" and experiment with your ideas. While you can storyboard in a number of ways, even by sketching on a sheet of paper, PowerPoint is itself a great storyboarding tool. Using the slide sorter view will help you get a "bird's eye view" and see the whole program at once, not just a screen at a time. You might notice that six consecutive screens are text heavy, or there are no opportunities for interaction for a long while. Using the "notes" format (click "view," then "notes page") gives you room below each slide for capturing ideas about navigation, multimedia, and narration and can provide guidelines for instructional designers or graphic artists with whom you might work. The only drawback: if many people will be reviewing or editing the program, you might want to instead choose a tool like Word that allows for tracking changes.

Storyboarding in PowerPoint has another advantage: it can also support your efforts in communicating with other stakeholders connected to your e-learning efforts. Apart from helping you express your vision to graphic designers, the format is usually familiar to clients and helps them to envision the final product better than, say, a long text-only script.

> "Remember, the goal of storyboarding is to plan as much as possible before you begin to actually create your online materials. It's much easier to erase or throw away and create new drawings and slides than it is to redesign a completed program!"
> **Dede Nelson, Instructional Designer, NC State University**

Types of Storyboards

Let's take a look at different ways of doing storyboards, using a "shark" example, intended for use as an educational program in a museum. (Thanks to Ken Loge for the shark materials.)

A simple storyboard may just provide a quick overview of your program. Figure 2.16 shows a storyboard drawn by hand; Figure 2.17 illustrates a storyboard created in PowerPoint using the Insert-Picture-Organizational chart command.

Placing ideas on separate slides, then looking at the program in the slide sorter view, allows you to drag and drop slides to easily rearrange and see how the flow works with different approaches. Figure 2.18 shows the entire program at once in the slide sorter view.

Figure 2.16. Simple Hand-Drawn Storyboard

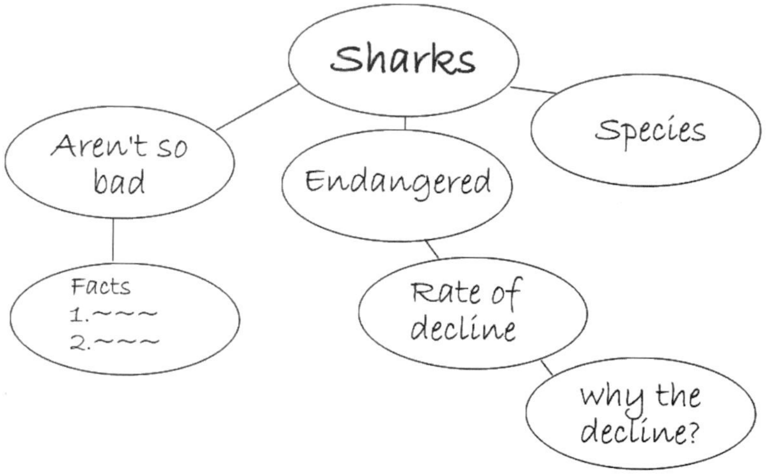

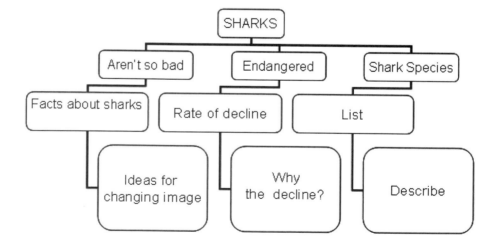

Figure 2.17. Storyboard Created with PowerPoint Flow Chart

Figure 2.18. PowerPoint Slide Sorter View

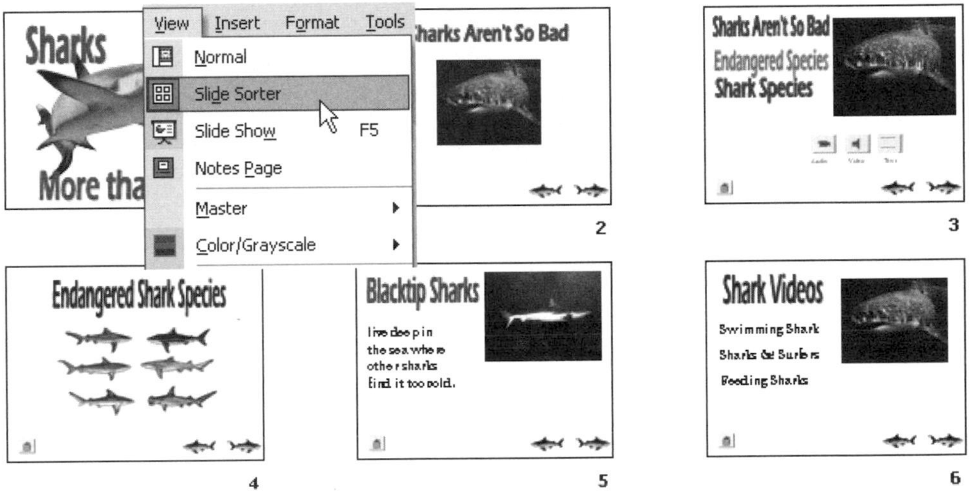

Source: www.dreamsteep.com

A more detailed storyboard includes notes regarding programming, links, multimedia, etc. Figure 2.19 was created in PowerPoint "normal" view using the text area for speaker notes.

Rather than print out the separate notes pages, I prefer to work from a side-by-side plan; this also provides a convenient script for narrators. To create it, choose "File—Send To—Microsoft Word," as shown in Figure 2.20.

Figure 2.19. Using Speaker Notes Area to Create Storyboard

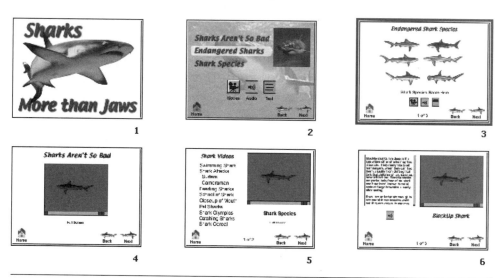

Source: www.dreamsteep.com

Figure 2.20. Send PowerPoint File to Word to Create Side-by-Side Storyboard

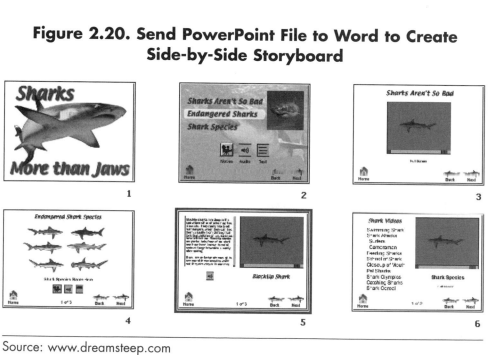

Source: www.dreamsteep.com

The resulting Word document will look like the one shown in Figure 2.21.

"Learning objectives is where you're going; the *storyboard* is your road map. There is a big difference between a well laid out resource with clear learning objectives and a jumble of badly linked slides."

Dr. Simon James, Lecturer and Multimedia Expert,
University of Tasmania

For those doing initial brainstorming, or those working with graphic designers or other team members, another strategy is to leave the Power-Point slides blank pending choosing graphics, inserting media, etc., as shown in Figure 2.22.

Figure 2.21. PowerPoint Storyboard Sent to Word

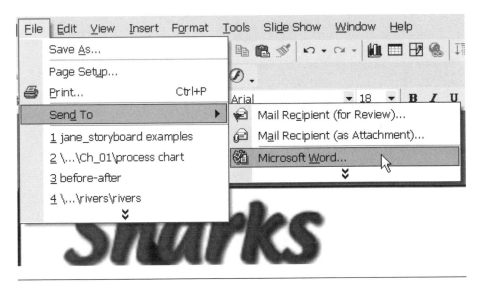

Source: www.dreamsteep.com

Figure 2.22. Text Storyboard

Slide 1

Title
Shark swims back and forth. Silly "Jaws"-type music plays.
Hitting any key or clicking the mouse jumps to "Main" screen. After 1 minute of no activity, the program auto-advances to "Main".

Slide 2

Main
"Home" always goes to this screen.
Clicking the shark image goes to the "Title" screen.
Shark icons set to "next" and "previous"

Slide 3

Sharks Aren't So Bad
Will need captioning for those with auditory impairments

Source: www.dreamsteep.com

Summary

An effective e-learning program grows out of careful identification of learners, articulation of objectives, and an approach that supports the instructional goals. While it's tempting when working with PowerPoint to just open a new slide show and start adding content, the time spent in specifying outcomes and storyboarding will pay off in ease of development and reduction of rework and piloting time. If you are working to transform an existing classroom program to an online format, this phase of development is a good time to examine what's working—or not—with the classroom sessions, and ensure that the new program provides opportunities for learning, rather than just parroting the content of the classroom program. Being mindful of the principles of good instruction, and especially the new considerations of multimedia that e-learning demands, will help to ensure the success of your program.

Now that you have some understanding of the basics of instructional design for e-learning purposes, we'll move on into development issues. The next chapter covers the learner's relationship with your program: look, feel, navigation, and the graphic interface.

SECTION 2

Interface and Content

The Graphic User Interface and Course Architecture

In developing your e-learning program, it is vital that you create a user-friendly interface with clear information on how to navigate the course. Additionally, your program will need a unified look and feel in terms of colors and any branding elements that your organization requires. In designing an interface you'll also need to consider the overall structure of your course. Is this a single, short, standalone topic, or will instruction be provided in several modules? Will learners need to access material in a particular sequence, or can they skip around the subtopics within a program. Use your storyboard as a tool for identifying manageable chunks, modules, and basic ideas about organizing the final program.

This chapter covers concepts related to the GUI, navigation, course architecture, and considerations of learner control. There is also information on setting up overall course architecture as well as an introduction to the use of action buttons and hyperlinking.

The CD accompanying this book includes tutorials for several tasks covered in this chapter, including working with slide masters, inserting action settings, and using navigation tools.

The Graphic User Interface

A critical factor in the success of an e-learning program is the learner's view of it. Known as the "graphical user interface" (the GUI, or "gooey," and now sometimes shortened to just UI), it establishes the user's relationship with the program or the dialogue between the learner and the training. Think of the GUI as, essentially, the e-learning program's dashboard, containing links, icons, buttons, and other navigational tools, and any of the branding elements associated with the program. As with most things related to e-learning, less is more: your goal should be to create an attractive, clean interface that gives the learner clear direction about what to do next (see Figure 3.1). The carefully designed GUI supports the learner; the poor one can cause the learner to give up in frustration.

Figure 3.1. Clean, Clear Interface

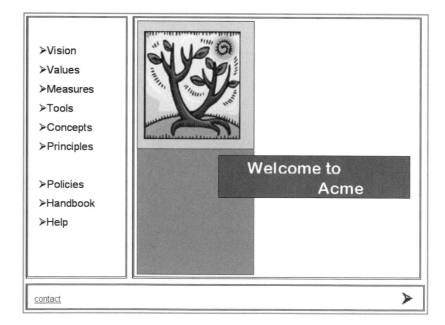

GUI Basics

In designing the GUI, keep in mind that online learners need to *always* know four things:

1. What to do next

2. How to get home

3. What's going on

4. How to get out

Some tips for a good interface include:

- Be consistent and clear. Don't use an arrow on one screen and a "next" link on another.

- At minimum, the program should include navigational information indicating next screen, previous screen, home screen, and links to help and/or contact information. Learners need to know how to exit, although, depending on how you choose to distribute the course (see Chapter 10), you may just instruct them to close the browser. PowerPoint has transparent navigation already built in; that is, any mouse click will take the learner to the next screen. (If you don't want learners just clicking along, you can disable this feature by clicking "slide show-slide transition" and unchecking the option to "advance on mouse click" and choosing "apply to all slides."

- Use clear, consistent icons. Don't assume that learners will understand that a white flag icon means "help." Labeling the icons on the first screen never hurts.

- Most programs contain a menu to an outline of different topics, segments, or modules (an example is shown in Figure 3.1). Short, single-topic programs may be the exception. Some programs also have an opening table of contents screen.

- You may also link to other tools, a glossary, contact information, or set an email link for submitting questions or asking for help.

- If you are using audio or video, include information for learners so they will know how to adjust the volume on their computers.

- Consider including a screen counter or progress bar to indicate to learners how much of the program has been completed/how much is left.

- Tell learners what's happening. Often video clips take a moment to load, or there may be a delay as documents open. Advise learners of this so they don't assume something's wrong. Include information such as, "Click here to open a Word document. . ." or "This link will take you to an online quiz." Figure 3.2 shows an example.

Figure 3.2. Slide Counter and "What's Happening"

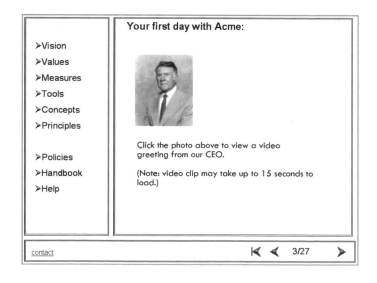

The overall structure of your course may determine how you design the GUI. The "Acme" example in the figure works much like a Web page, allowing learners to click on links to access information on particular topics. The GUI in Figure 3.3, from a simulation requiring learners to move in a more linear manner, offers a "forward" button with directions explicitly stated in the text (circled here for readers). The "x" at the top right corner allows learners to exit the program, while the small upward arrow returns learners to the home screen.

Other GUIs might be developed around a theme or the chosen treatment. The "A. Pintura: Art Detective" program, introduced earlier in the book and shown again in Figure 3.4, is developed as a noir-type mystery. The overall look is a black screen, with plain white text, and simple underlined navigation links. Most screens ask the learner to make a choice about where to go next, rather than just prompting them to move to the following slide.

Figure 3.3. Simple GUI

Source: Royal Veterinary College

Figure 3.4. GUI from "A. Pintura: Art Detective"

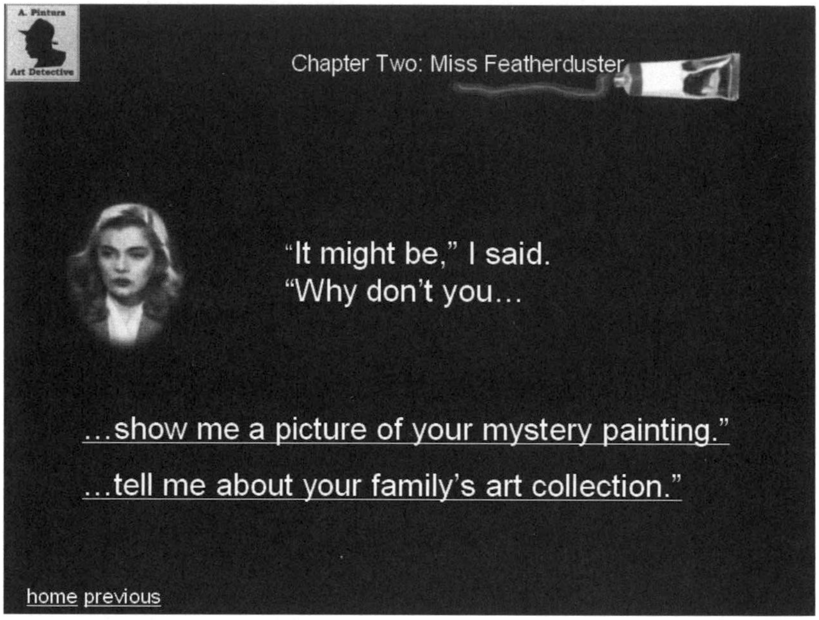

Source: www.eduweb.com

Colors

When thinking about the overall look of your program, remember that color has meaning:

- RED: warning, danger, heat, stop

- GREEN: go, money

- BLUE: calm

Color may also have cultural implications: in the United States, for instance, white indicates purity. In Asian cultures it is the color of death.

Learner Control: Some Decisions

As the trainer/designer you will need to make some decisions about the degree of control your learners will have. Often, e-learning programs include a navigation button that indicates "last" screen. Providing such an option means that a learner could, if he or she wanted, just skip to the end of the e-learning program from any other screen. It's up to you whether you want to give learners that much discretion. Likewise, if your program is modular or arranged by topics, will you allow the learner to visit sections as he or she likes, or will you force some sort of sequence? Realize, too, that learners likely have experience surfing the Web and are used to making choices about where to go next and what content they wish to view.

On a philosophical note: it is the nature of e-learning to require discretion and self-direction on the part of learners, and at some point we must learn to trust them. Consider the learner in a "live" class who leaves the room for three minutes to take a phone call. Do we say that person is not "complete"? Why is it that skipping a screen of an e-learning program is considered so much more serious? Similarly, unless the content of the e-learning program is teaching a step-by-step procedure, why shouldn't the learner be allowed to choose the order in which to view topics? While you don't want learners getting "lost" in your program, engagement and persistence are supported by learners feeling a sense of control.

Navigation Tools and Action Buttons

For basic navigation, PowerPoint will let the learner advance to the next slide just by clicking the space bar or "Enter" key, but you will need to be sure to communicate this to the learner. An e-learning program more often will have buttons, arrows, or other symbols indicating "next" to the learner. An easy solution here is inserting PowerPoint's customizable action buttons (shown in Figure 3.5).

Figure 3.5. Action Buttons Included with PowerPoint

PowerPoint Action Buttons

▶ Next

🏠 Home

◀ Back

❓ Help

◀| Return to first slide

ⓘ Information

▶| Advance to last slide

Custom button

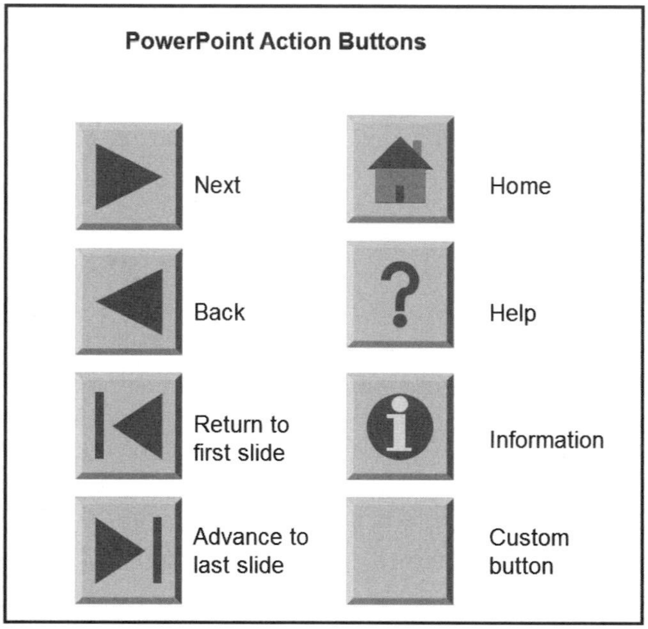

 See the CD for an Action Settings Tutorial on working with action settings and navigation.

Action buttons are preprogrammed for actions such as "next slide" and "first slide," but can easily be reset to link to any other slide, file, or even external site and can provide the learner with visual cues for moving through the program. To insert the action buttons included with PowerPoint 2002 and 2003, look at the menu bar at the top of the PowerPoint screen and choose "slide show" and then "action buttons"; in PowerPoint 2007, the action buttons can be found in the "shapes" tools (see Figure 3.6). (*Note:* throughout the rest of the book, instructions for accessing a particular command or tool will be noted simply as "slide show—action buttons.") After choosing a button, browse for the destination link (Figure 3.7).

Figure 3.6. Accessing Action Buttons

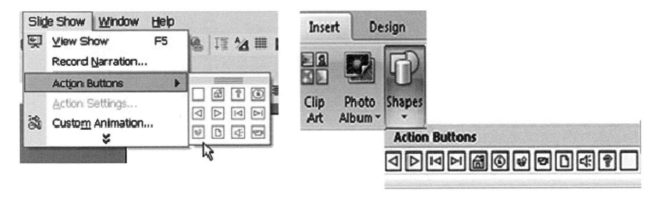

2002/XP/2003   2007

Figure 3.7. Use Preset, or Reset, PowerPoint's Action Buttons

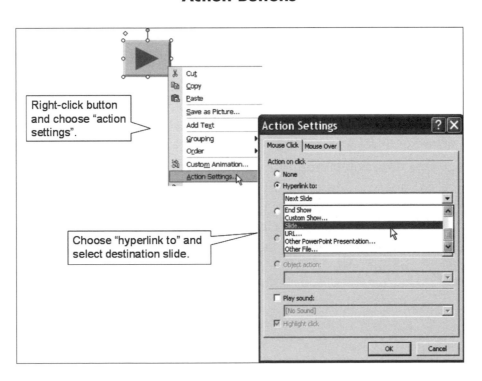

Figure 3.8. PowerPoint's Action Buttons Can Be Customized

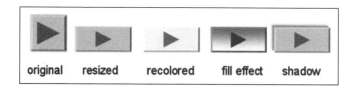

The action buttons included with PowerPoint can be further customized by resizing and/or recoloring them as shown in Figure 3.8.

PowerPoint also allows for much more sophisticated navigation through the use of hyperlinks. The designer can create hyperlinks from text boxes, graphics, and other elements placed on a slide. These will take the learner from this selected "hotspot" or "hot object" (or whole slide) to another slide within the same show, another PowerPoint show, a website, or a document such as a Word or PDF file. A hyperlink to an email address will, when clicked, open an already-addressed email window on the learner's computer screen.

Hyperlinks within a program can be inserted in one of two ways: by selecting an object and giving it an action setting, as shown with the button in Figure 3.7, or by inserted by right-clicking on the object, choosing "hyperlink," and selecting the link's destination. Figure 3.9 shows an example of a program's outline page. When viewed in slide show mode, clicking on the "what" box will take the learner directly to the "what" slide. See Figure 3.10 to see how this interaction was created. (*Note:* as shown in Figure 3.10, the options for hyperlinking to an existing file or Web page, to another slide within the current PowerPoint show, or to an email address.)

Figure 3.9. Box on Table of Contents Hyperlinks to Corresponding Slide

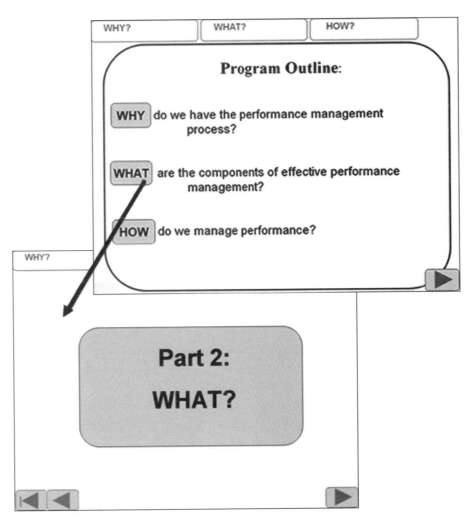

Figure 3.10. Choose "Insert-Hyperlink" and Browse for Destination Slide

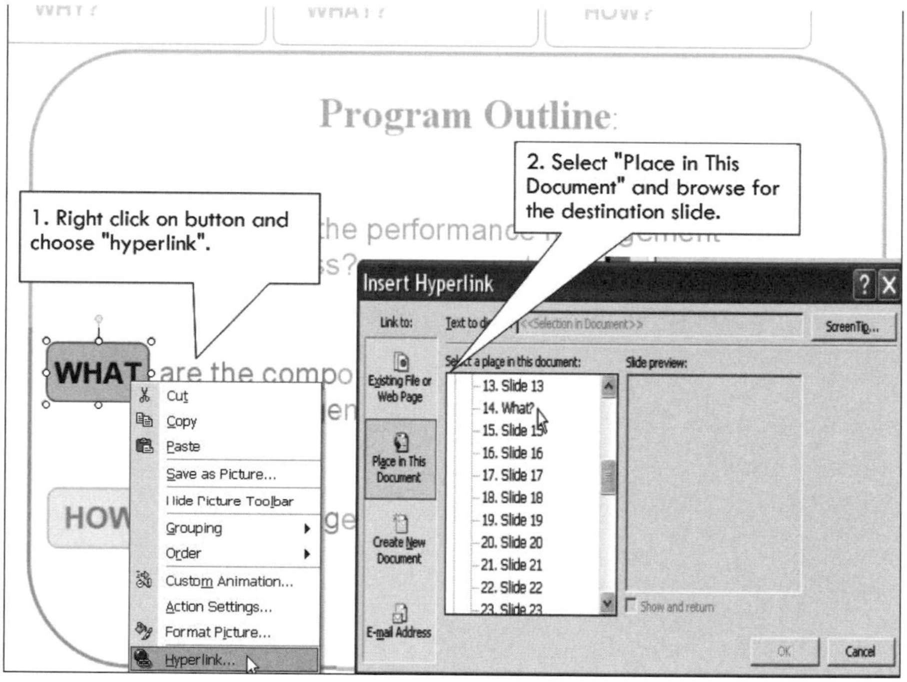

You may also find that the action buttons or shapes included with PowerPoint do not meet your design needs. Navigation symbols can be created from other objects, arrows, words, or simple linked text. Programming is done by highlighting the item and clicking "insert-hyperlink," as shown above in Figure 3.10. Figure 3.11 shows an array of choices for navigational tools found during a simple search of www.google.com for "free navigation buttons and icons"; the shark icons are from the storyboarding examples in Chapter 2.

"Interface design has nothing to do with instructional design but has everything to do with effective e-learning. Proper placement of buttons, navigational aids, and screen tools can make or break your e-learning project, no matter how effective the instructional design."

Thomas Toth, *Technology for Trainers*

Figure 3.11. Varied Options for Navigation Tools

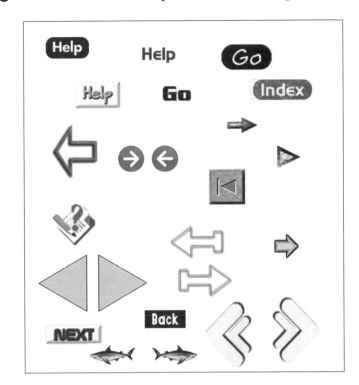

Eye Movement and Placement of Items

In designing the GUI for your program, it's important that you understand the basics of eye movement. Think about reading: when you read a page, your eyes move across the top line from left to right, then drop down to the second line at the far left, and then continue left to right again. This "Z" movement is the most natural and intuitive for learners. A good GUI makes use of this Z movement to support clarity, ease of use, and emphasis. Figure 3.12 shows a GUI created to accommodate the eye's natural Z movement. Important content is given "center stage," while supporting information, like links and navigation icons, are placed in positions of less emphasis. Information across the top of the screen communicates the learner's location in terms of subject, topic,

Figure 3.12. Good GUI Recognizes "Z" Eye Movement

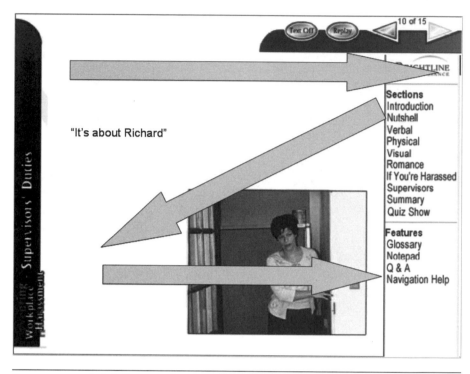

Source: www.brightlinecompliance.com

segment, or chapter. Also note how the placement of the "next" arrow pointer button naturally leads the eye off the screen and toward the next one.

You are probably already aware of some unspoken standards of designing for the Web, although you may not have given it much thought. Most designers know to develop with the Z in mind, and users are, generally, accustomed to looking to the left side of the screen for links. Note how uncomfortable the layout of Figure 3.13 seems when compared to Figure 3.12.

Figure 3.13. Counterintuitive Layout

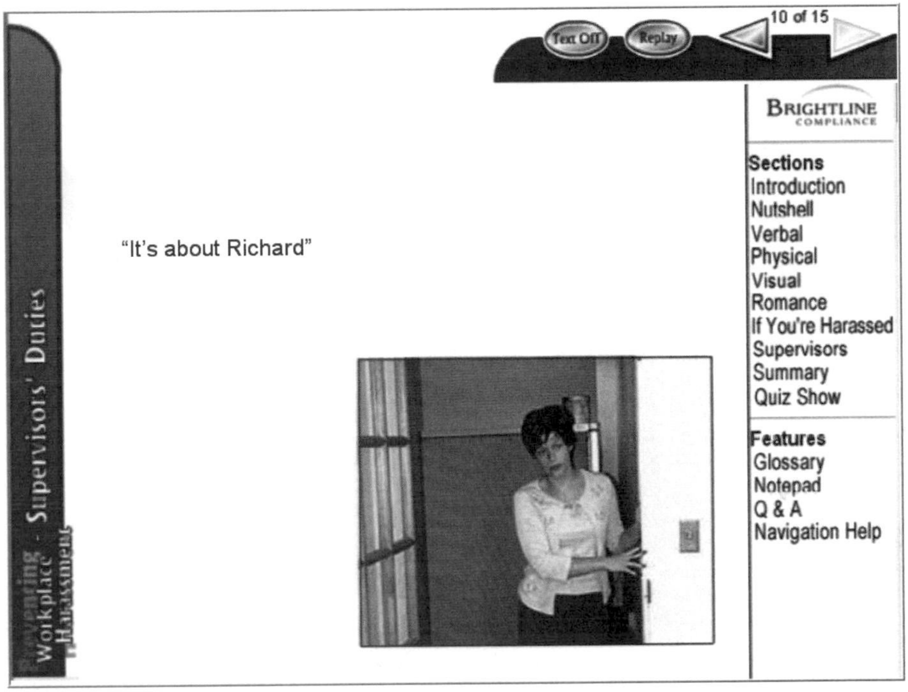

Source: www.brightlinecompliance.com

Working with Z eye movement in mind supports what is known in the Web world as maximizing your screen "real estate." Figure 3.14 illustrates the real estate concept. How long does it take to even notice the line that says "nearly invisible"?

Figure 3.14. Value of Screen "Real Estate"

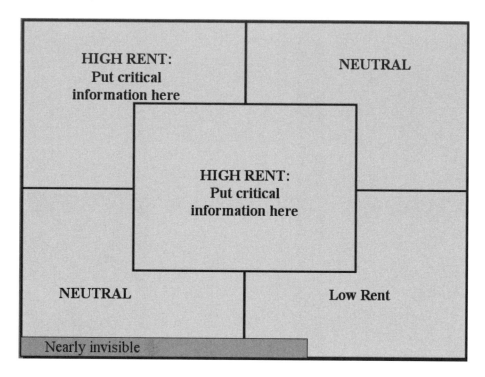

Lesson Learned

In maximizing your screen real estate, watch out for how much space logos and other branding elements consume. Consider placing logos and similar items only on the first and last slides rather than on all slides.

Figures 3.15 through 3.18 show additional problems with GUIs.

Figure 3.15. Common Problems with GUIs

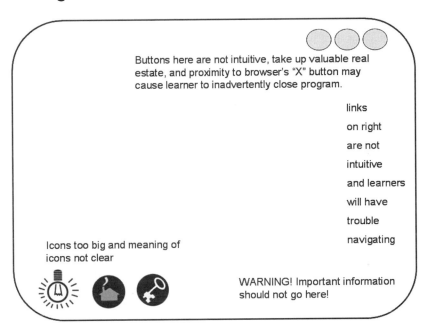

Figure 3.16. Background Makes Text Hard to Read

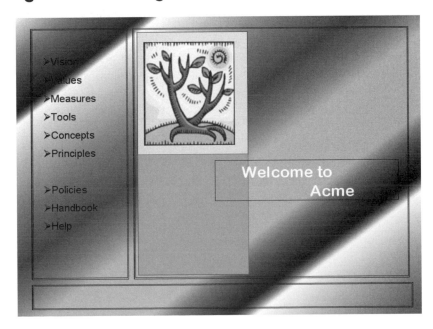

Figure 3.17. Fonts Are Hard to Read

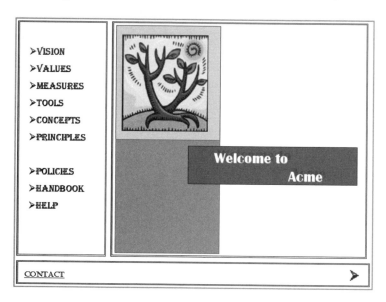

Figure 3.18. Font Color Does Not Sharply Contrast

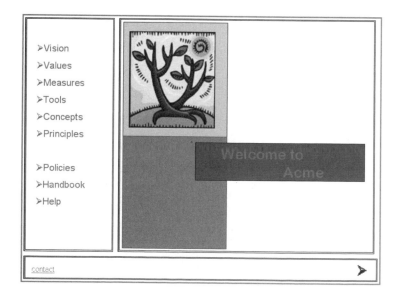

Lesson Learned

As you develop your e-learning program, see how it displays on other computer screens. Different monitors display colors differently; what looks like good contrast on your screen may look like faded text on another.

Building the GUI

Again, think of the GUI as a template defining the look, feel, and navigation basics for your e-learning program. This is a matter of creating slide masters by adding elements that will make up your new interface.

Create a Slide Master

Using a slide master will make your job much easier. Slide masters make for consistent, professional appearance: insert objects that will appear on each slide, including any branding elements, navigation items, etc. The slide master functions, essentially, as a template for the screens in your e-learning program. Open the slide master by clicking "view—master—slide master," as shown in Figure 3.20. Note that the master is set up for text-based basic presentation slides; you can highlight and delete slide areas you don't need (such as the title running across the near-center of the screen), although they will not, unless you add to them, appear on the final slides. Figures 3.19 through 3.22 show steps in creating a slide master for use in an e-learning program.

Also see the CD for a tutorial on working with slide masters.

Figure 3.19. Access the Slide Master View

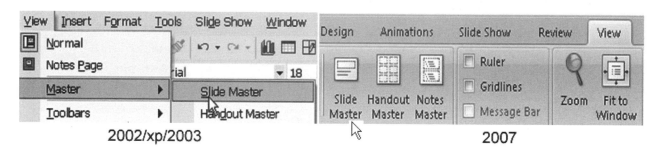

2002/xp/2003   2007

Figure 3.20. Blank Slide Master

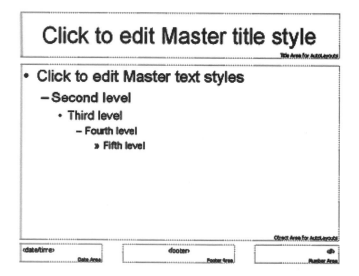

Figure 3.21. Add Navigation Elements Such as Buttons

Figure 3.22. Completed Program

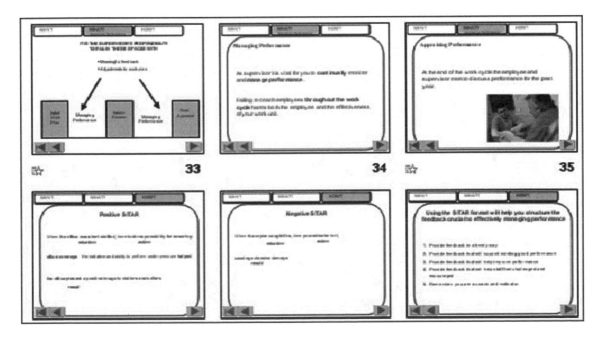

If for some reason you want a slide within the same program to differ from others—for example, if you need a title or "home" slide or module introduction slides different from the rest of the program—you can achieve this by creating multiple slide masters (in PowerPoint versions 2002/XP and newer). Click "view—master—slide master." When the master toolbar appears, click "insert new."

> **Lesson Learned**
>
> When developing a long program or one with several modules, create separate PowerPoint shows rather than one long show. This will make editing, managing, and updating materials much less cumbersome and will help keep file sizes to reasonable levels.

Examples: Creating the GUI

Figures 3.23 through 3.27 show different styles of GUIs and how they were created.

Figure 3.23 uses PowerPoint's autoshapes to create a basic framework.

Figure 3.23. Slide Master for Program Uses Autoshapes

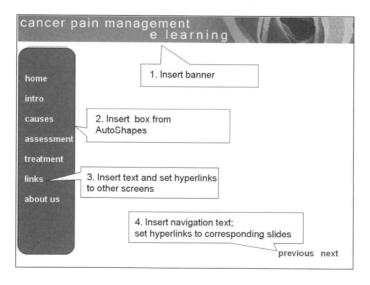

Figure 3.24. Each Screen Will Look Like This

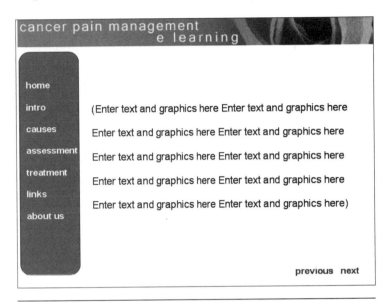

The "Cancer Pain Management" interface is adapted from an existing online program and is used here with the generous permission of Dr. Mahibur Rahman, Director, Emedica. The program can be accessed in full, for free, at www.emedica.co.uk. Click the "e-learning" link.

Figures 3.25 and 3.26 show a main screen with tabbed navigation; subsequent screens have links to topics. Figure 3.27 shows how tabs were created with autoshapes.

The CD includes a narrated explanation of how this GUI was created with tabbed navigation.

Figure 3.25. GUI with Tabbed Navigation

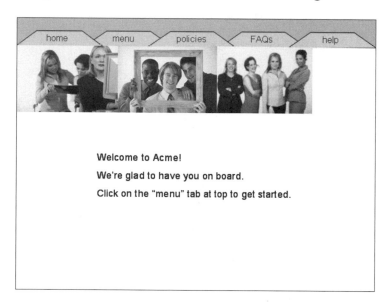

Figure 3.26. Subsequent Slides Contain Links to Topics

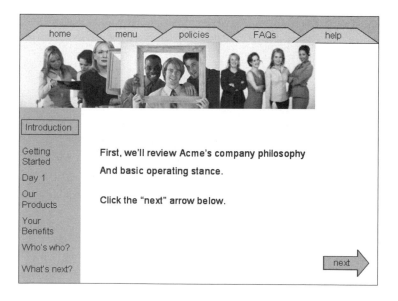

Figure 3.27. Steps in Creating Screen, Including Tabs for Navigation

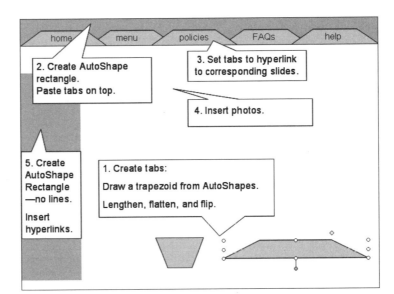

Figure 3.27 shows how to create this screen.

In developing the GUI it's okay to be creative provided that learners have clear guidance. Figure 3.28 shows navigation based on icons: images link to the corresponding topics.

The example in Figure 3.29 is also icon-based but uses none of the traditional navigational markers (arrows, "next," even words indicating topics) but it's easy enough to tell that the program is linear, and determine the order in which screens should be viewed.

Figure 3.28. Icon-Based Navigation

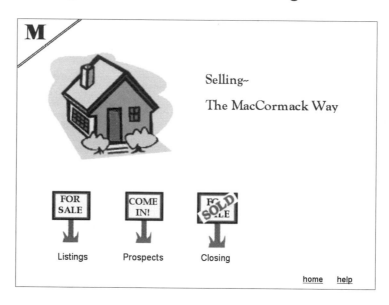

Figure 3.29. Icon-Based Navigation

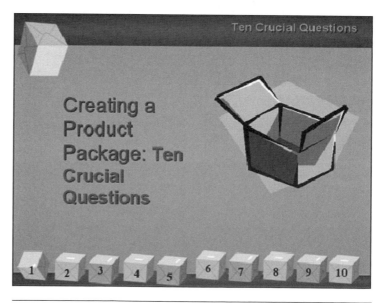

Adapted from program by Laura Bergell, www.maniactive.com

Lesson Learned

When testing your e-learning program, actually sit and watch learners going through it. What seems intuitive or clear to you may not be clear to them—and watching them interact with the material will give you ideas about how to fix it. This will also give you a sense of how much time different screens, quizzes, or interactions may take to complete.

Architecture

Although there are no hard-and-fast rules (see next text box), most e-learning courses will contain some similar elements. These usually include:

- A title and/or "welcome" slide

- An advance organizer. As noted in Richard Mayer's "SOI" model discussed in Chapter 2, it's important to provide learners with a course outline, statement of objectives, or explanation of course structure. Figure 3.30 shows an example.

Figure 3.30. Advance Organizer

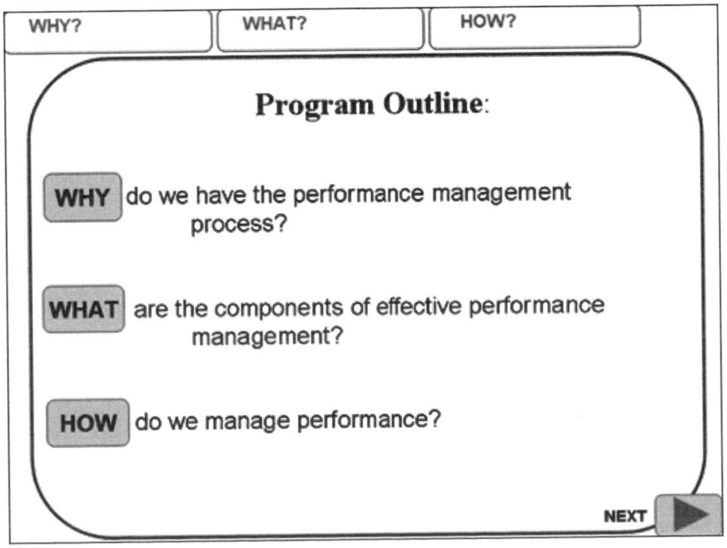

- An explanation of how to use the course, as shown in Figure 3.31. The words "home," "previous," and "next" do not appear on subsequent screens. If you are using media, you may want to add information about controlling the volume of audio or video clips.

- A glossary of terms and acronyms

- A site map is especially important with modular programs created with PowerPoint. As PowerPoint does not support bookmarking, learners cannot leave a program and subsequently return to the same screen. A site map allows them to get back to the general area at which they left off. The site map also lets learners search a program and return to parts they wish to review. Figure 3.32 shows an example of a site map.

Figure 3.31. Explanation of Navigation

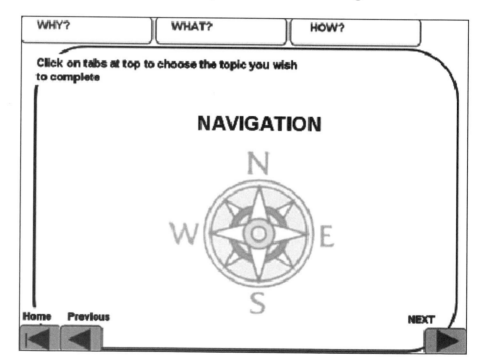

Figure 3.32. Example of Site Map

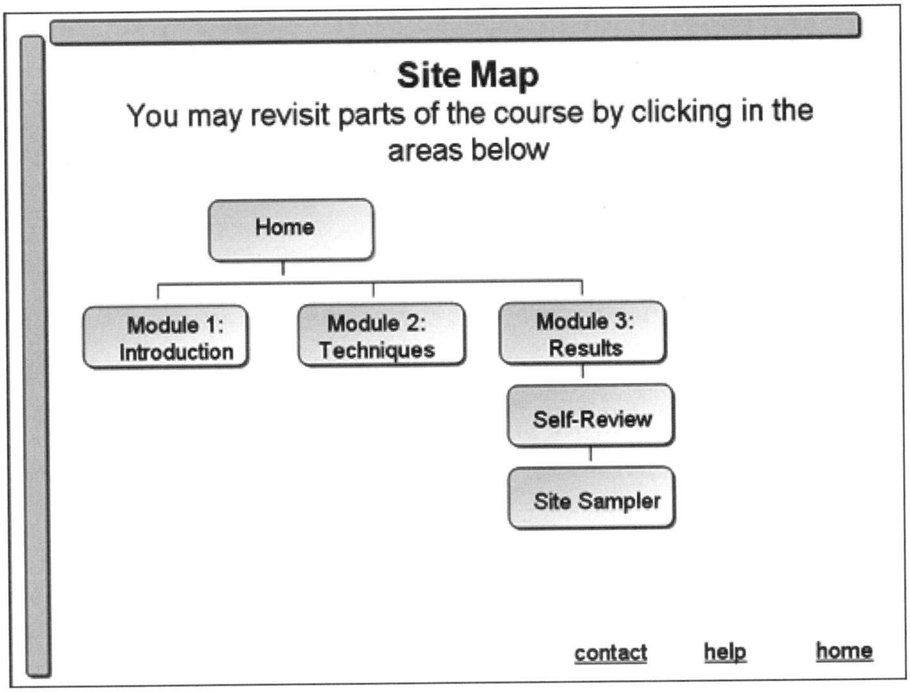

Other architectural elements—such as the sequence of slides, the placement of modules, and the layout of branching interactions, can be pulled from your program storyboard.

Excuse My Rant

While I receive many requests for it, I will not provide, do not advocate, and do not use, a single course "template," and I am wary of vendors offering such things. While all courses need some basic elements—such as a home page—the concept of a single multi-slide template appropriate to all e-learning programs supports the erroneous notion that e-learning can be created by simply dumping

(continued)

content onto slides. And it creates the temptation to do just that. Such templates might be fine for informational presentations, but are anathema to good training. Examples of engaging e-learning programs like the "A. Pintura: Art Detective" mystery and the "Gamekeeper's Conundrum" simulation came from solid, creative design and would never have been developed had the designers started by trying to shovel content into predetermined screens or worked from some preconceived notion of how courses should look. Be brave! Be creative!

Summary

Although it may seem tedious, creating a good GUI and a clear organizational structure will save work (and rework) in the long run. Now the real fun starts: adding the content to your e-learning program. Chapter 5 offers guidelines for creating and editing art and text.

CHAPTER 4

Designing for Impact

Use Graphics with Soul

In choosing images that will support your instructional message, give real thought to what will help you convey intent and support your learners. There are a number of excellent, extensive clip art, photo, and sound galleries, among them the Microsoft Office gallery (http://office. microsoft.com/en-us/clipart/default.aspxs), iStockphoto (www. istockphoto.com), and Clipart.com (www.clipart.com); the trick, however, is not in choosing an image but in choosing the right one. Jamie McKenzie, editor of *From Now On: The Educational Technology Journal,* rails against what he calls "mulitmediocracy" and encourages us to look beyond first glances at clip art galleries to find graphics with *soul.* The example on the next page illustrates the problem of choosing the right graphic for a quick online tutorial on email etiquette, designed to convey the fact that email is not private. A quick search of clip art galleries provides many images, such as those shown in Figure 4.1, but most are too cutesy, too busy, or just indecipherable for the purpose of the tutorial.

Figure 4.1. Images from Clip Art Gallery Search for "email"

Figure 4.2. Graphic with Soul for the Email Etiquette Program

Thanks to www.indezine.com for free background template

Compare this to Figure 4.2, which puts a human (implicitly, the learner) into the message. Additionally, the grayscale effect suggests the seriousness of the topic.

What Conveys the Message?

As with the topic above, some programs implicitly demand graphics that are serious and authoritative. This is especially important with most medical, legal, and compliance-related programs. Looking at Figure 4.3, with photos taken from the same clip and photo art gallery, which doctor would you want to perform your open heart surgery?

As we discussed in Chapter 2, it is crucial that you be clear, before you begin developing your e-learning program, about what you are trying to accomplish. The right graphic can set the tone, establish a mood, and support the instructional message. Look at these examples.

Figure 4.3. Choose Your Heart Surgeon

Example 1: Civil Rights Timeline

The first image of this timeline, shown in Figure 4.4, presents data about civil rights legislation. Figure 4.5 shows how the addition of the right photograph supports the data in conveying a sense of history and the struggles behind those rights.

Figure 4.4. Civil Rights Timeline

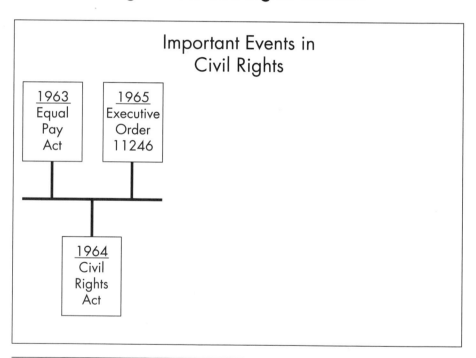

Courtesy of Paige Dosser

Figure 4.5. 1964 Harlem Riot Photo

Used with permission of UPI/Corbis

Example 2: Vietnam Vets*

In the second example, the designer wanted to create an awareness of the need—and support for—funding for treatment for aging veterans. The typical approach, shown in Figure 4.6, would likely include a title slide, bar chart showing data about the problem, then a bulleted list of possible solutions. Figure 4.7 shows the same topic, revised to begin with just the image of the Vietnam Memorial. The updated program opens with a long silence, then a narrator saying, "Our vets need us now. . ."

*Thanks to Seth Godin (www.sethgodin.com) for the "Vietnam vet" example

Figure 4.6. Typical Approach to Request for Support

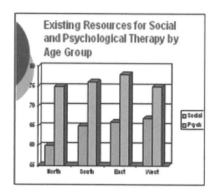

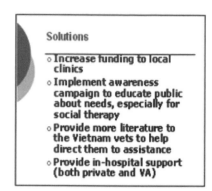

Figure 4.7. Information from Figure 4.6 Provided as Voiceover to This Image

"Let Me Show You What I Mean"

The just-right image conveys the message, "Let me show you what I mean." What is the essence of what you are trying to say? Try to distill your message and intent. A good exercise is to take any text-based slide and try to re-create it with images. The figures below illustrate the difference this can make with a program on "cubicle etiquette." The first slide, shown in Figure 4.8, shows a text-only version of one screen. Figure 4.9 shows the same message distilled into images drawn from a clip art gallery. Even before the addition of voiceover explanation, the second slide is much more effective, engaging, and memorable.

Figure 4.8. Text-Only Slide

Get Some Exercise

- Resist the urge to ask your colleague a question over the cubicle.
  - Get up and ask your questions.
  - Or send an email or instant message, or call on the phone to ask if your colleagues are available.
- Besides disturbing your colleague, you will be disturbing everyone else by blurting out your query or comment.

Source: "Cubicle Etiquette" by Gary Michael Smith, *Intercom* magazine, November 2000

Figure 4.9. Same Slide Re-Created with Graphics

Source: "Cubicle Etiquette." Thanks to Patricia Delaney

The example in Figures 4.10 through 4.12, screens from an online program teaching learners to read diagrams of electrical circuits, shows how simple graphics with minimal clutter can make a complex idea understandable. In this case, the designer moved from images of a completed circuit to a legend explaining each image, then finally a "textbook" diagram of the circuit.

Figure 4.10. Slide 1 Shows the Completed Circuit

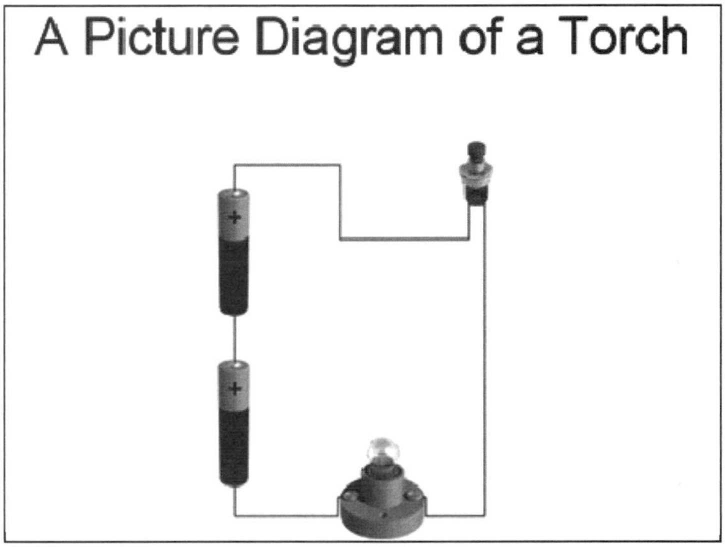

A Picture Diagram of a Torch

Source: Electric circuit program copyright Simon Drane; electric circuit component images are from www.crocodile-clips.com

Figure 4.11. Slide 2 Explains the Symbols

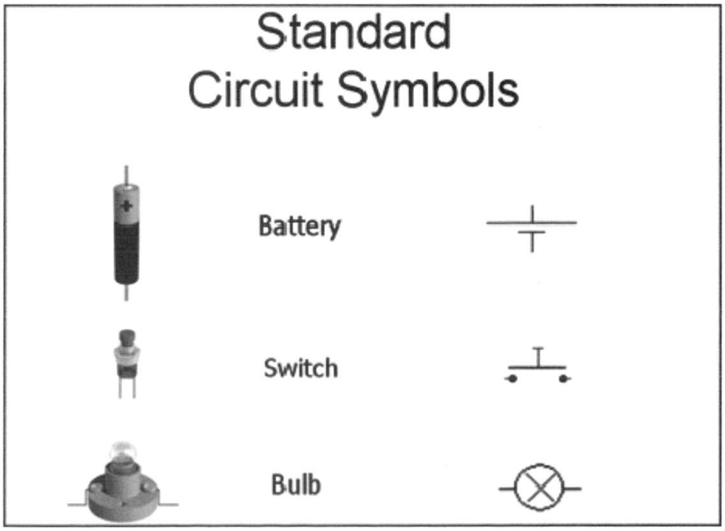

Standard Circuit Symbols

Battery

Switch

Bulb

Source: Electric circuit program copyright Simon Drane; electric circuit component images are from www.crocodile-clips.com

Figure 4.12. Slide 3 Provides Schematic of the Circuit

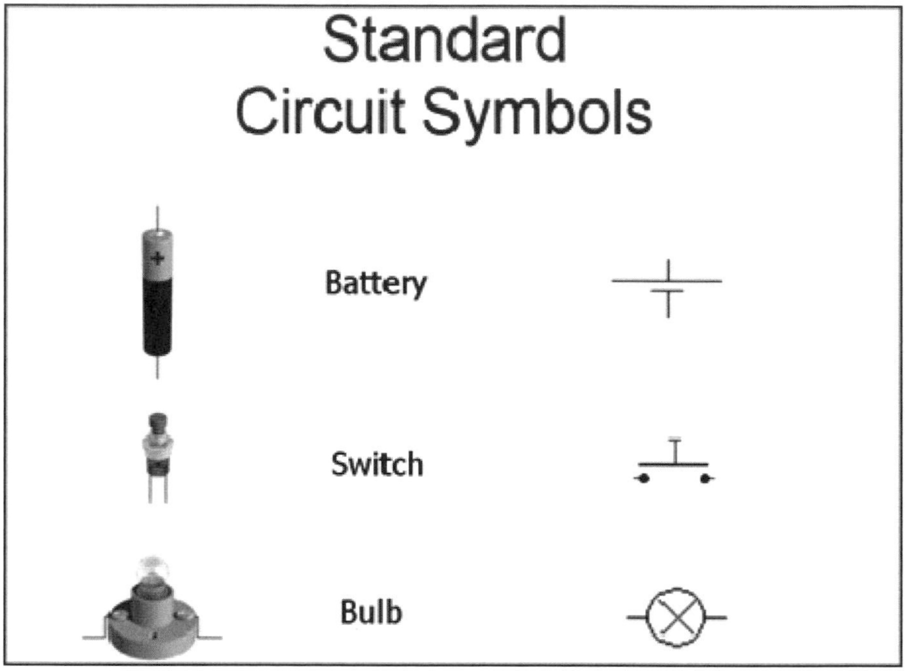

Source: Electric circuit program copyright Simon Drane; electric circuit component images are from www.crocodile-clips.com

In some cases it may be that a diagram, rather than an image, is worth a thousand words. Use of the right diagram—such as a flowchart or a pyramid showing hierarchical relationships—proves invaluable in clarifying information and supports per Mayer's (Chapter 2) guidelines on providing instruction in ways that will help the learner organize it. Diagrams can easily be created with PowerPoint's diagramming features, shown in Figure 4.13.

Figure 4.13. PowerPoint's Diagram Gallery

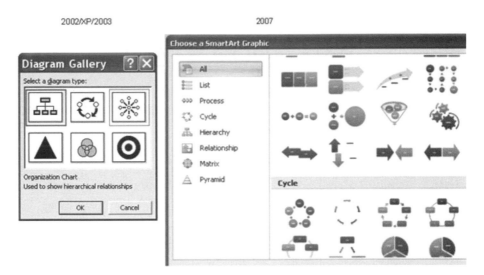

Is There a Visual Here?

Sometimes we get so caught up in explaining a concept that we forget to take a step back and look for a visual of the idea. Figure 4.14 shows a screen with details about the content required for a disciplinary warning letter. Figure 4.15 shows the same information, but in a realistic—and more memorable—context.

Figure 4.14. Before: Text List of Required Items

Written Warning

Definition:
    A detailed disciplinary notice for conduct or
    performance

A Written Warning Must:
    State that it is a warning
    State the reason for the warning
    Detail the improvements required
    Indicate length of time allowed for improvement
    State the consequences if improvements are
        not made
    Outline the appeal process

Figure 4.15. After: Sample Letter Shows Items in Realistic Context

MEMORANDUM
To: Jessica Jones, Office Assistant
From: Steve Smith, Office Manager
Date: October 20, 2007
Subject: Written Warning—Unsatisfactory Job Performance

State that it is a warning

The purpose of this letter is to give you written warning for unsatisfactory job
performance. The specific unsatisfactory performance for which you are being
warned is excessive tardiness. On August 19, September 15, and October 5 I
talked with you about the importance of starting work promptly. During our last
conversation we discussed the consequences of | **Reason** | prove in this area.

Blunders

It is easy to be seduced by galleries of entertaining images and interesting fonts. Some common mistakes are illustrated below.

Dreadful Design

The slide shown in Figure 4.16 shows many of the most typical design flaws, from too much content to illegible text to space-hogging template elements.

Figure 4.16. Example of Design Mistakes

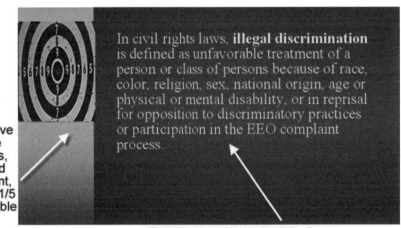

Decoration

Figure 4.17 makes use of a cute graphic that has nothing to do with the training or the message on the screen. Learners will wonder, "What does loyalty have to do with a bee lifting weights?"

Figure 4.17. Decorative Graphic

Noisy

"Noise" refers not only to sound but to clutter and extraneous information on a screen. If I want, for instance, to discuss the details of just one slide, I need to show only that. Figure 4.18 shows the slide, but includes a view of my whole desktop screen, opened to a full view of the Power-Point program, while Figure 4.19 shows just the slide with no other information around it.

Figure 4.18. Too Much Extraneous Information

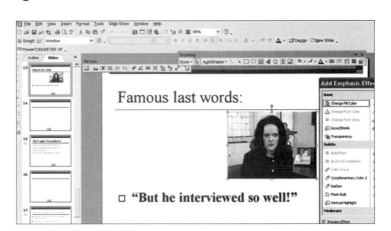

Figure 4.19. Extraneous Information Removed

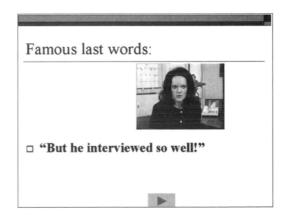

Figure 4.20. This Screen Is Far Too "Noisy" to Be Effective

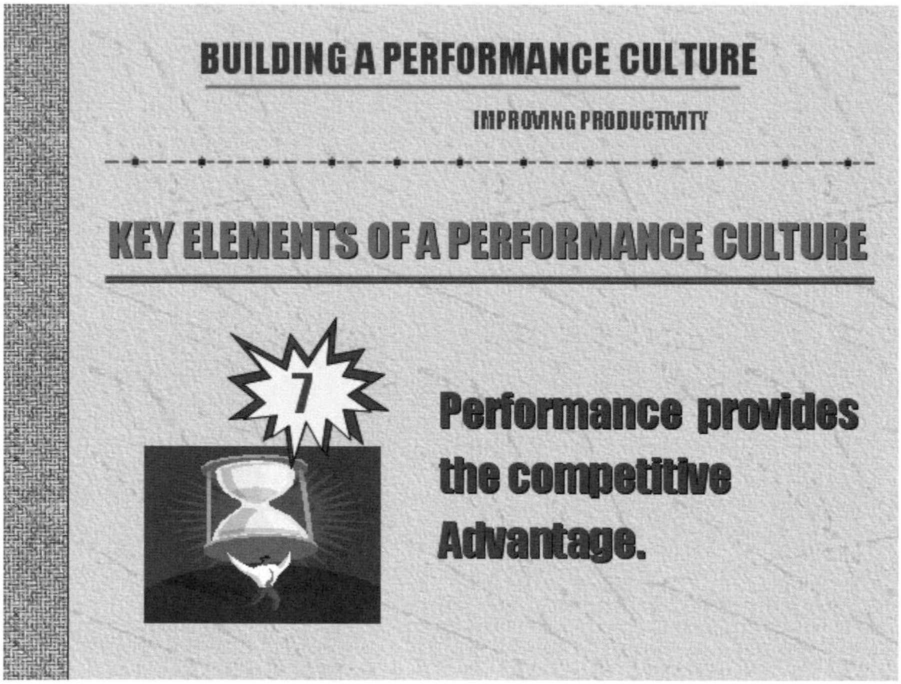

Figure 4.20 shows problems with noise on a single slide. The preset template is cluttered with items unrelated to the content, including a sidebar, decorative dotted line, and a heavy line below the heading. The cute clip art image only tangentially relates to the concept. The callout star is distracting and due to brightness appears to be the most important element on the screen. The shadowed text and crowded font make the letters run together. Finally, all the lines of text of similar size compete with each other. One wonders: What is this slide about?

Demeaning

Sometimes the temptation to use a cute piece of art overrides good judgment. The designers of Figures 4.21 and 4.22 probably meant well, but ended up with images that are insulting to learners.

Figure 4.21. Insulting Approach

Figure 4.22. Insulting Approach

Text

In adding text-based content to your e-learning program, remember Mayer's "Select—Organize—Integrate" model discussed in Chapter 2. Provide clearly organized materials with strong headings and transitions, chunk material into manageable bites, and use plenty of white space. Also use text as a tool: employ bold, color, and highlighting for emphasis (remember, though, not to overuse—the emphasis is lost if every other word is bold). Additionally, remember the two critical rules about using text in an e-learning program:

1. Cut it in half.

2. Cut it in half again.

Figure 4.23 shows an example of ruthlessly editing text.

Figure 4.23. Edit

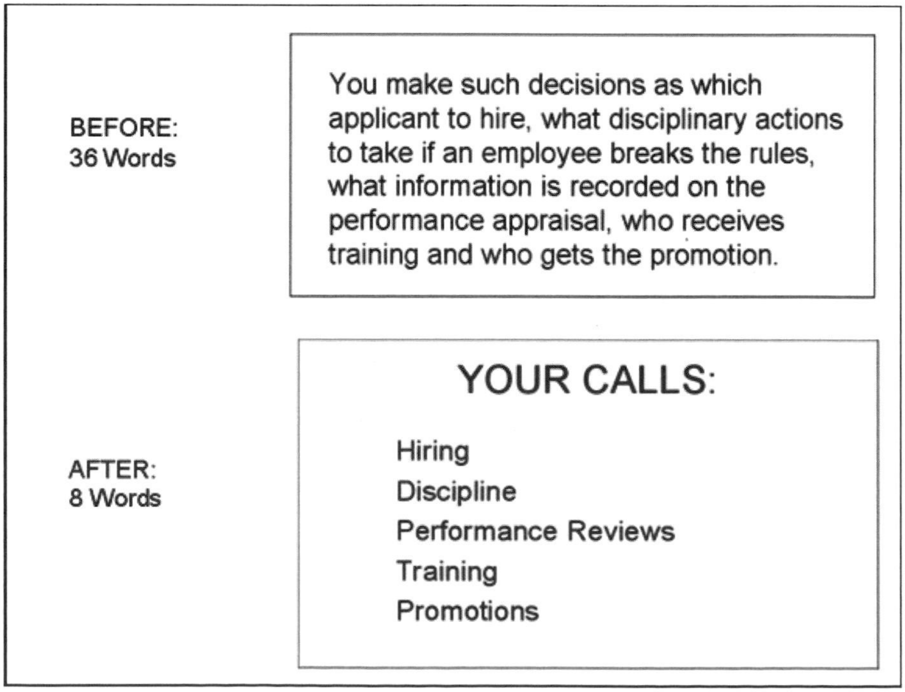

BEFORE:
36 Words

You make such decisions as which applicant to hire, what disciplinary actions to take if an employee breaks the rules, what information is recorded on the performance appraisal, who receives training and who gets the promotion.

AFTER:
8 Words

YOUR CALLS:

Hiring
Discipline
Performance Reviews
Training
Promotions

(An aside: We know from the research of Mayer and others that learning is enhanced if narration and on-screen text don't match. The first slide here might serve well as the voiceover to accompany the second slide.)

Lesson Learned

Use standard fonts. If you are distributing your e-learning program in a PowerPoint file format, unusual fonts may not display properly on learner machines.

Arial and Verdana are both readable non-serif fonts, and Times New Roman and Georgia are popular serif fonts. See the comparisons of 16-point fonts below, noting the difference in relative size and the space between letters:

Arial 16-point

Verdana 16-point

Times New Roman 16-point

Georgia 16-point

Take care using *italicized* text. it can be difficult to read, and learners may mistake it —and <u>underlined</u> text—for a hyperlink.

Chunk Content and Use White Space

Break content down into manageable "bites" for learners. Creating more screens is preferable to overloading fewer. This will reduce cognitive load for learners, thereby supporting the acquisition of new learning.

Summary

In creating effective e-learning from PowerPoint, be judicious in choosing meaningful art. The right image can illuminate, elucidate, and help to create the "ah-ha" moment that will make the online learning experience so worthwhile to learners. The wrong image—apart from being distracting—can actually hurt learning. The next chapter discusses ways of creating and editing art that will have an impact.

Creating and Editing Art

ow that we've taken a look at using graphics with meaning and text that supports learning, let's move on to actually creating and editing art. As we saw in the discussion of graphics with soul, the just-right image can make all the difference in making a program effective and engaging. Too many e-learning programs suffer from the dreaded "wall of words," due more to lack of creativity than lack of resources. PowerPoint itself provides means for creating and editing clip art, but it seems few users make much use of this capability. Additionally, the MS Paint program that loads with Windows (go to Start—Programs—Accessories—Paint) provides additional capability at no cost. In this chapter we'll review some basics of creating your own art, editing existing art and photos, and saving images for use in e-learning programs.

Bitmap or Vector?

There are two kinds of images: bitmap and vector. *Bitmaps,* also called rasters, are made up of pixels, or small blocks of color assembled to create the image. The icons on your desktop are bitmaps. As you can see from Figures 5.1 and 5.2 below, enlarging the image tends to distort it and make edges appear jagged. Although bitmaps are difficult to resize (going smaller gains considerably better results than enlarging), you may at some point find the need to work with them. Scanned images, images taken with digital cameras, and photographs are bitmaps.

Vector images, on the other hand, are made up of what we might consider drawing objects: lines, curves, and fonts are all vector graphics. Objects are resizable and retain their quality no matter how large. Figure 5.2 shows a simple vector image created with a PowerPoint AutoShape. Notice that enlarging it does not affect the quality: the outside line stays crisp.

Figure 5.1. Bitmap Images Are Made Up of Pixels

Figure 5.2. Enlarging a Vector Graphic Does Not Affect the Quality

Because vector images are large filled blocks of color, they do not, however, display subtle shading or gradation well; for this reason, photographs do not work well as vector images, and it's why most clip art tends to look "cartoony." An advantage, though, to working with clip art vector graphics is that images can be ungrouped and edited individually; that is, each object in the clip art graphic can be enlarged, recolored, removed, duplicated, etc.

It's important to understand the basic differences between vector and bitmap graphics, as you will likely be working with both in the course of creating e-learning with PowerPoint.

Working with AutoShapes and Clip Art

Sometimes an idea can be very effectively conveyed with nothing more than simple shapes. Figure 5.3 was created entirely with PowerPoint AutoShapes.

Figure 5.3. Effective Image Created with AutoShapes

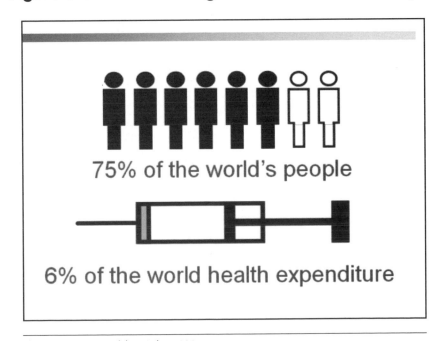

Source: Designed by Adam Warren

PowerPoint allows you to move, recolor, crop, and make other changes to clip art and to photographs. Clip art images are vector graphics so they can be modified in many ways. The figures below were created entirely with clip art and PowerPoint AutoShapes.

 The CD accompanying this book contains a tutorial on working with shapes, colors, and fills and provides a narrated tutorial on creating the images in the example below.

Figure 5.4. Image Created with Clip Art and Drawn Shapes

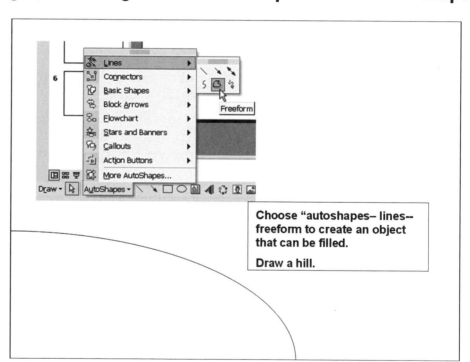

Figures 5.5 through 5.12 show how the image was created. Instructions are contained on the screen—as suggested by Mayer's theory—rather than written out in the captions below the figures.

Figure 5.5. Create Hill with Autoshapes

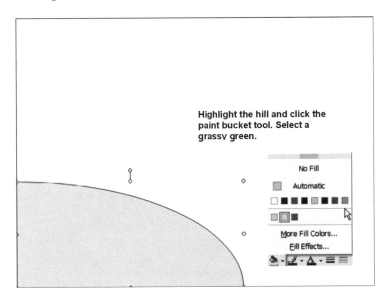

Figure 5.6. Color the Hill Green

Figure 5.7. Insert Clip Art Tree and Cloud

Figure 5.8. Add Water and Fill with Blue

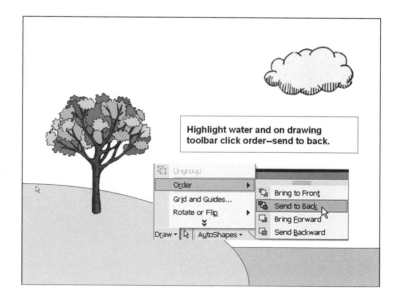

Figure 5.9. Send Water Back Behind Hill

On drawing toolbar highlight water and click order—send to back.

Ungroup

Order
- Bring to Front
- Send to Back
- Bring Forward
- Send Backward

Grid and Guides…

Rotate or Flip

Draw • AutoShapes •

Figure 5.10. Create Condensation Lines

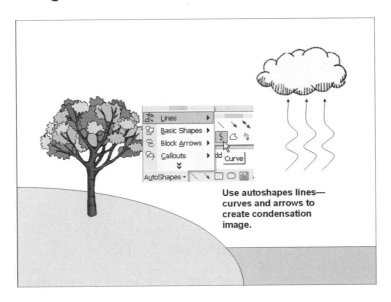

Lines

Basic Shapes

Block Arrows

Callouts

Add Curve

AutoShapes •

Use autoshapes lines—curves and arrows to create condensation image.

Figure 5.11. Create Waves

Figure 5.12. Completed Image

Adapted from R. Mayer (2002). "How condensation works."
In Cognitive theory and the design of multimedia instruction: An
example of the two-way street between cognition and instruction. *New Directions for Teaching and Learning, 89,* 55–71.

Recoloring Clip Art

Versions of PowerPoint prior to 2007 allow you to recolor clip art with the Picture Toolbar. In the instance above, the tree could be changed from spring greens to autumn colors. To recolor clip art:

1. Select the image and choose the "recolor picture" icon on the Picture Toolbar. A box will be displayed with drop-down menus for each color in the image.

2. Make your choices and click "OK."

Figure 5.13 shows a red apple recolored to green. The drop-down menu shows that the apple image has four colors: black outlining, green stem, red skin, and white core. Each of the colors can be changed.

Figure 5.13. Use Picture Toolbar to Recolor Clip Art

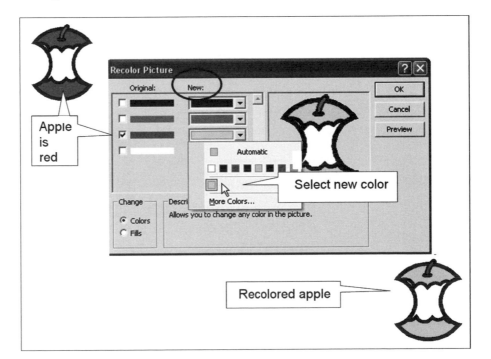

The one-click "recolor picture" tool has been taken away in PowerPoint 2007. In order to recolor clip art with 2007, the image must be ungrouped, as shown in Figure 5.17. Individual image elements can then be edited.

Set Transparent Color

While most clip art from galleries comes with a transparent background, you may sometimes want to use a picture that has background included. You can remove backgrounds from images using PowerPoint's picture toolbar. Figure 5.14 shows a key image that came with a white background; the designer wants to place this on a darker slide so needs to remove the white area from around the key image. To achieve the effect, choose "set transparent color," then click the tool inside the area you wish to change. This can also be used to remove backgrounds from photographs.

Figure 5.14. Use Picture Tools to Set Transparent Areas

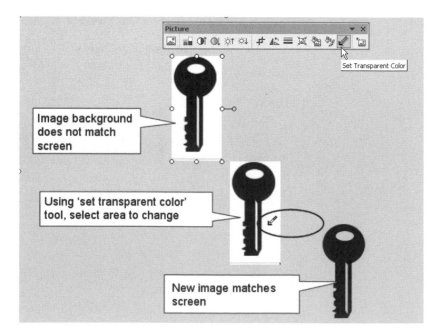

Transforming Clip Art

The next example shows how to ungroup clip art to modify only segments of it. The designer has chosen to use a harvest metaphor for a program introducing learners to the basics of collaboration. A quick search of a clip art gallery for "farm" offers a number of choices. By clicking the gallery's link to "show by style" or "show all in this design," the designer can view all the available pieces of art with the same overall look and feel.

Figure 5.15. Farm Images from the Same Style Gallery

The designer likes the barn image (top center in Figure 5.15), but wants something in the foreground. She finds the image of a haystack (Figure 5.16) and wants to add several to the barn image, so needs to remove the rake. As this is a vector graphic, the components of the image can be ungrouped and individually edited. That is, each of the elements can be removed, resized, recolored, or otherwise modified.

Figure 5.16. Clip Art Image of Haystack

Figure 5.17. Right Click and Select "Grouping—Ungroup"

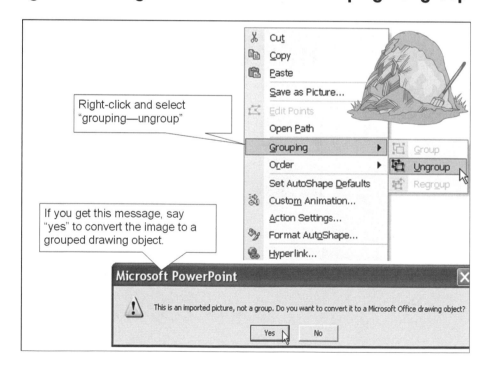

Figure 5.18. Editable Areas Will Appear. Regroup and Delete Pieces of Rake

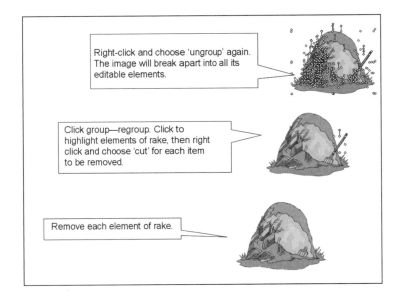

Figure 5.19. Create Copies of Haystack

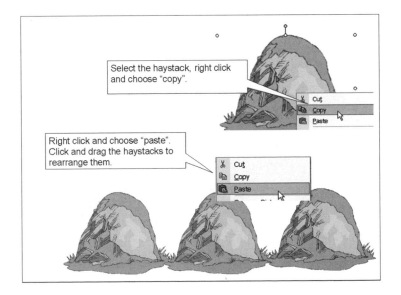

**Figure 5.20. Copy Haystack and Paste onto Screen
to Create Finished Image**

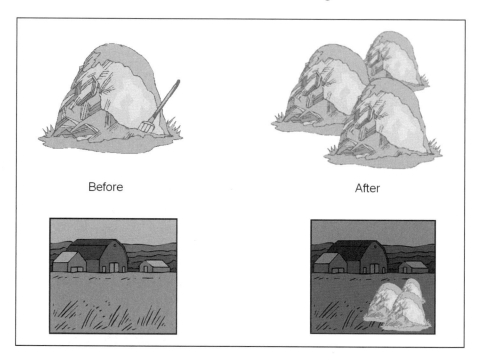

Before   After

Is it e-learning, or is it just text information?

Just using "e-learning" as a way to deliver enormous amounts of
text makes is very expensive in terms of time and effort and will
result in an inferior product. If your e-"learning" program can be
printed out as a Word document, then it should just be delivered
that way.

Editing Photos in PowerPoint

PowerPoint's picture tools offer many option for working with photographs. Figures 5.21 through 5.23 show the changes in a photo—this one was originally in color—when grayscale, washout, and black and white actions are applied. PowerPoint 2007 additionally offers a "sepia" option as well as the choice of "washing" photos with many other colors. To access photo editing tools in 2007, click on the image; the tools will display at the top of the screen. Click "Recolor—Color Modes." In older versions, click "View—Toolbars—Picture."

Figure 5.21. Color Photo Modified with Grayscale Effect

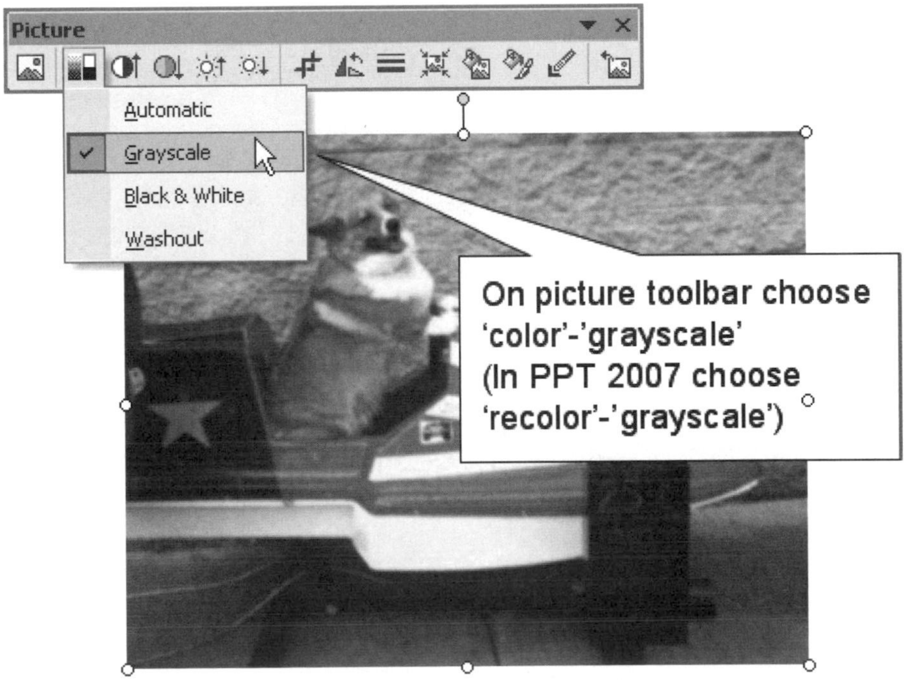

Figure 5.22. Color Photo with Washout Effect

Note in Figure 5.23 that the "Black & White" option creates just that, resulting in a final product resembling an image as it might appear when faxed.

Photos can be enhanced by adding simple elements. The example in Figure 5.24, from a program on therapeutic restraints for clients in a residential treatment facility, shows PowerPoint circle and line added to highlight a section of the photograph. This allows the learner to see both the full position as well as the specifics of hand placement.

Figure 5.23. Color Photo with Black and White Effect

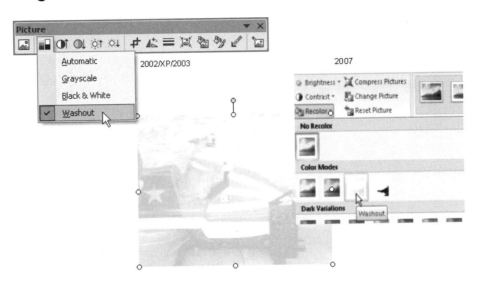

Figure 5.24. PowerPoint Autoshapes Emphasize Important Points of Photo

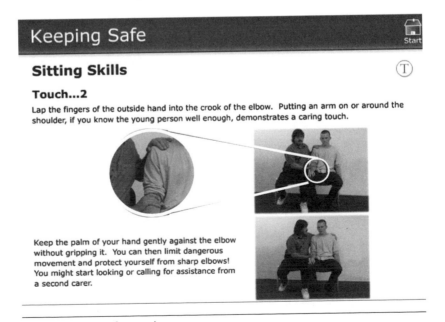

Photo courtesy of www.kwango.com.

All monitors are different

When testing your e-learning program, be sure to take a look at it on monitors other than your own. Colors, especially anything with subtle shading, may display differently on different screens.

MS Paint

Occasionally you may want to make changes to an image beyond PowerPoint's capabilities. You may, for instance, want to add custom effects that are not offered by PowerPoint, erase part of an image, or work with a bitmap image.

You may not realize that you have access to a free graphics program, MS Paint, that is already loaded on computers with the Windows operating system. Click Start—Program—Accessories—Paint, as shown in Figure 5.25.

Figure 5.25. Paint Is in the "Accessories" Folder

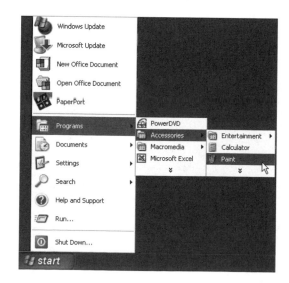

Paint comes with a number of tools for creating and editing art and photographs, as shown in Figure 5.26

Figure 5.26. Tools Available in MS Paint

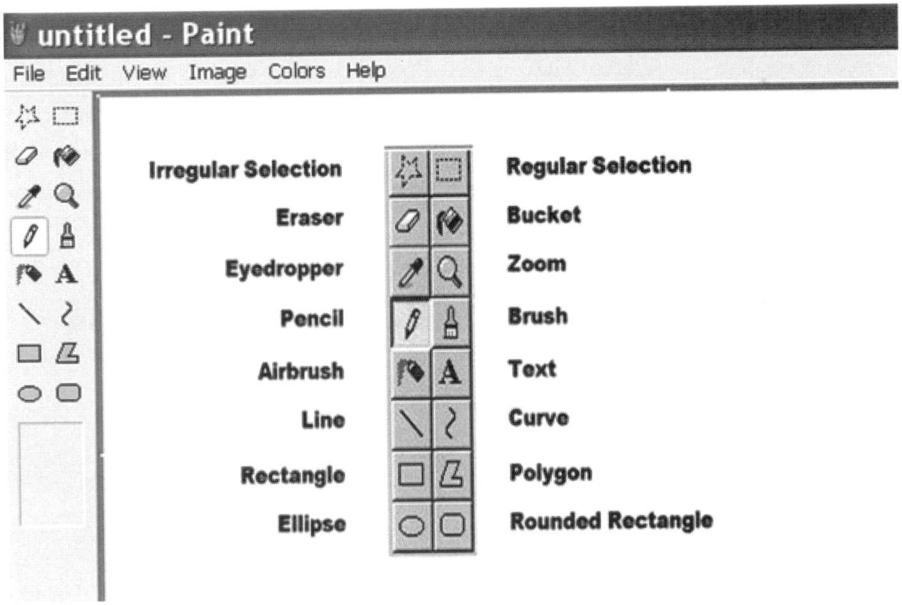

Using Paint to Create and Edit Art

Figure 5.27 shows the effects you can obtain by applying different tools to the same clip art image.

Figure 5.28 shows how MS Paint was used to remove an object. Unlike the image of the rake in the "haystack" in Figures 5.16 through 5.20, I found when I ungrouped this image that removing the man with the chainsaw would actually take away a large part of the tree trunk. So rather than use PowerPoint's ungroup feature, I instead used MS Paint's selection tool to outline the part of the image I wanted to remove, deleted the man with the chainsaw, then used the Color Picker tool to match the color, and finally the Paint Brush tool to repaint the missing part of the image.

Figure 5.27. MS Paint Allows You to Edit and Customize Clip Art

Spray Can Tool   Ellipse Tool

Polygon Tool   Paintbrush Tool

Thanks to Alex Papadimoulis

Figure 5.28. Use Paint to Remove Man with Chainsaw, Then Touch Up Area

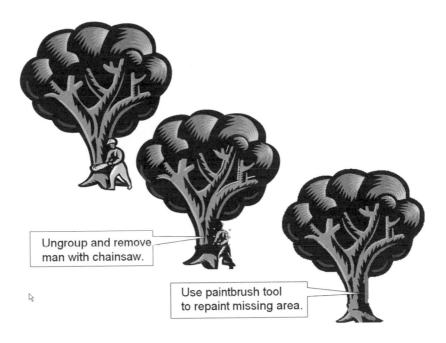

Figure 5.29. Edited Tree Copied and Pasted to from Orchard

Once the image is edited, copy and paste (right click "copy," right click "paste") to create an orchard or forest.

About Screen Shots (aka Screen Captures)

About screen shots: You can capture images of your computer screen—for instance, showing your company's website home page, demonstrating an example in Excel or illustrating how to access the MS Paint program, by using the "Function" + "Print Screen" command that you can then paste into Paint. This will, however, provide you with a shot of your entire desktop, which you'll likely then need to edit with Paint.

The excellent "SnagIt" screen capture software from www.techsmith .com makes this task considerably easier, as it will let you select only the portion of a screen or image, then copy it, save it, add a border, etc. The newest versions include editing tools similar to MS Paint. SnagIt costs approximately US $35 and is a very good investment.

Editing Photos with MS Paint

The Paint tools can also be used for editing photos. I wanted to use the image of a dog, taken on a child's ride-on toy in front of a department store, in a program I was working on. (You first saw this image earlier in the chapter, when we changed it from color to grayscale and black and white.) As shown in Figure 5.30, I used the Selection tool to outline the coin box, the Delete key to remove it, and then the Paintbrush tool to recolor the lines on the area the coin box had previously blocked. Finally, I used the irregular selection tool to outline the dog and rocket, then the delete key to remove the background.

Figure 5.30. MS Paint Allows You to Edit and Customize Photos

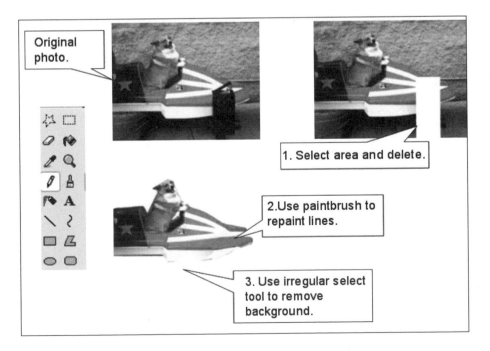

Original photo.

1. Select area and delete.

2. Use paintbrush to repaint lines.

3. Use irregular select tool to remove background.

File Size: Compressing Images

A challenge in developing e-learning is being mindful of file size. The bigger the file, the more server space required, the more bandwidth necessary to distribute the file over the Internet to learners, and the slower the download time. There are a number of simple things you can do to reduce file size, particularly in regard to art and photographs.

 The CD accompanying this book contains a tutorial on inserting and compressing images.

1. You can use MS Paint or the MS Photo Editor or Photo Manager (Start—Programs—Office Tools) to crop art and photos. The crop tool in the PowerPoint Picture Toolbar does *not* actually eliminate the parts of the image that are cut—they are "hidden" and stored with the file. As an example, the element that still remains, even after cropping, is shown in Figure 5.30 as a shadow.

2. You can compress photos by using the Photo Editor (PowerPoint 2002) to resize and change the resolution of photos or the MS Photo Manager (2003 and later) to compress photos. In PowerPoint, the "compress picture" tool will also reduce image size. Compressing photos does require some decisions on your part about what you consider acceptable for your project, as compression does reduce quality.

If using the "compress" tool from PowerPoint's Picture Toolbar, be sure to check the "delete cropped areas of picture" so the cropped parts will be eliminated rather than hidden (as shown in Figure 5.31). Figures 5.32 and 5.33 show reduced quality from reduction and the Compress Pictures tool.

Figure 5.31. Cropping with PowerPoint Crop Tool Does Not Reduce Size

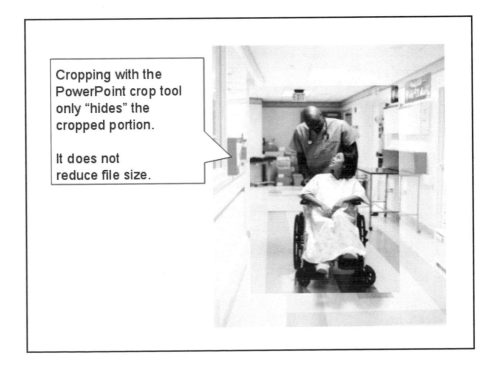

Figure 5.32. Smaller Files Show Reduction in Quality

175 KB   60KB   10KB

Figure 5.33. Compressing Pictures

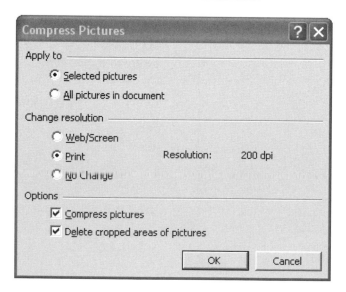

Images that are copied and pasted into PowerPoint are larger than those that are inserted. Use the "Insert—Clip Art" and "Insert—Pictures" commands.

When considering file size, consider your overall plan for your e-learning project.

Video, music, animation and narration also increase file size.

Next Stop: Animation

Making full use of PowerPoint's AutoShapes, drawing tools, and picture tools, supplemented with the MS Paint program, gives you considerable power in creating art that supports your instructional goals. Now that we've covered using graphics with soul, let's move on to creating animation that matters.

CHAPTER 6

Animation

Entire books are available on creating animation with PowerPoint. *This book* attempts to show how animations created with PowerPoint can support instructional objectives. A number of instructional animations are illustrated in this chapter and are meant as inspiration sources and idea-starters.

The CD contains an "Animation Basics" narrated explanation and tutorial as well as working examples of many animations shown in this chapter. While developing skill at creating animations doesn't necessarily require a great deal of specialized training, it does require work, patience, a tolerance for trial and error, and possibly time spent in workshops and/or in reading instructional materials.

A great deal on the specifics of creating animation can be found by visiting www.google.com and searching "creating animations with PowerPoint" or "animating PowerPoint." Whether live, by book, or online, though, the lessons will likely tell you how to use the animation features to do things like animate text or make pictures fly around. It will still be up to you to generalize that information to your ideas for creating effective e-learning. This chapter is intended to help you adapt these basic animations from entertainment to instructional purposes and provides an overview of animation basics, creating animations that teach, using animation to annotate graphics, using triggers to offer learner control over animation, and combining animations.

Animations can be applied to objects, photos, and text in several ways:

- Entrance—item appears on the slide

- Emphasis—may or may not involve motion, for instance, emphasis may involve changing color or size

- Exit—item disappears from the slide

- Motion Path—objects are set to move around the screen

Each of the animation effects is associated with variables: start (on click, on mouseover, per set timing), delay, speed, repeat, and trigger. The order of animations can be changed and can be set to include sound effects and narration.

Animation Should Support Instruction

> "Do not think of animation as an aesthetic concern—do not use it because you think it might make your presentation prettier or more engaging."
>
> **Rick Altman, President, Rick Altman Digital Communications**

It's common to see PowerPoint shows with simple animations like flying text and slide transitions. At best such animations add visual interest; at worst, they are distracting and irritating. Effective animation supports the instruction. Be sure the animations you use draw the learner's attention to important points rather than to whatever item happens to be moving, and don't overlook the value of changing colors and highlighting in focusing the learner's attention.

Animation Basics

Adding animation begins with selecting the object or text you wish to animate, then clicking "Slide Show—Custom Animation." Figures 6.1 through 6.8 show the basics of animating objects, in this case, a "cross" AutoShape. Differences between PowerPoint 2007 and earlier versions will be noted. The newer versions of PowerPoint offer an array of animations, categorized as "basic," such as appearing, "subtle," such as fading, and "exciting," such as bouncing.

Figure 6.1. Select Object and Choose "Slide Show—Custom Animation"

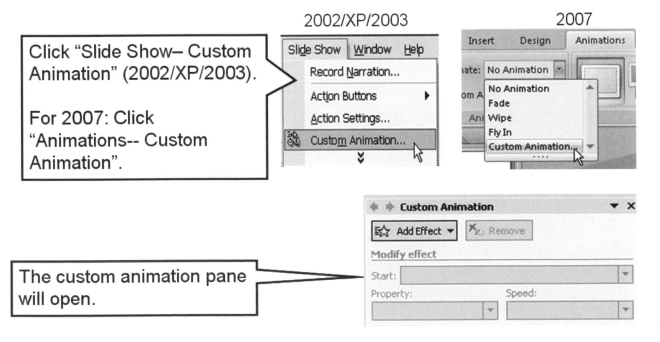

Figure 6.2. Choose Entrance, Emphasis, and Exit Effects

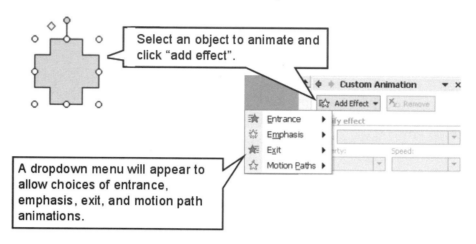

Select an object to animate and click "add effect".

A dropdown menu will appear to allow choices of entrance, emphasis, exit, and motion path animations.

Figure 6.3. Animation Effects Are Numbered and Color Coded

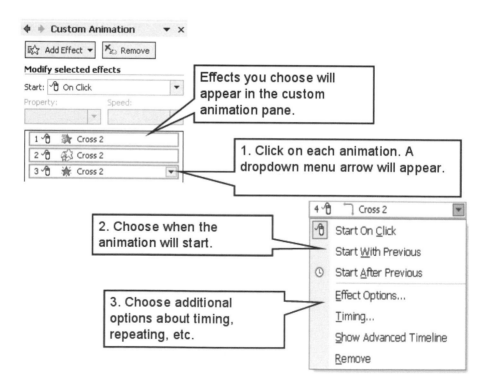

Effects you choose will appear in the custom animation pane.

1. Click on each animation. A dropdown menu arrow will appear.

2. Choose when the animation will start.

3. Choose additional options about timing, repeating, etc.

Figure 6.4. Array of Entrance Effects Available

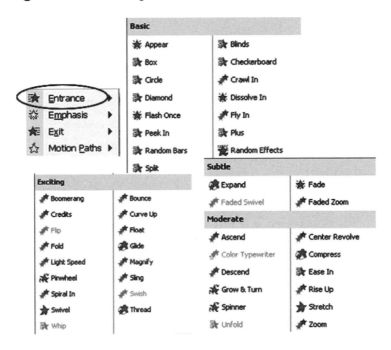

Figure 6.5. Array of Emphasis Effects Available

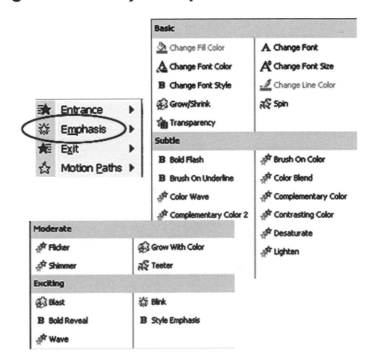

Figure 6.6. Array of Exit Effects Available

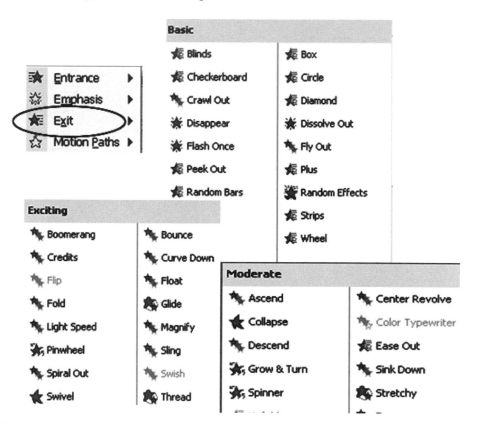

Figure 6.7. Array of Preset Motion Paths; Custom Paths Can Also Be Drawn

Figure 6.8. Set Timings for Animations

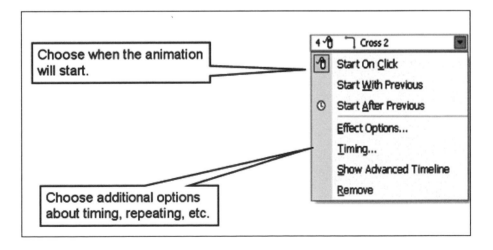

About the animation tutorials on the CD: If you open these in slide show mode (View—Slide Show), you can see the animations work. Opening them as PowerPoint files—as if you were going to edit them—will give you access to the custom animation panel. Click "Slide Show—Custom Animation." The custom animation panel will open and you can see how items on the slide were animated. Figure 6.9, for instance, is an example of an animated chart provided on the CD. The animation shows the diagonal bar on the chart climbing to indicate increase. Opening the custom animation panel shows that this animation was created by setting the bar to "Wipe" "From Bottom" at "Medium" speed. (*A trick:* any time you have access to an original PowerPoint slide containing animation—not just the ones on this book's CD—you can open the custom animation panel to see how the animation was done.)

Figure 6.9. Look at the Custom Animation Panel to See How Animations Were Created

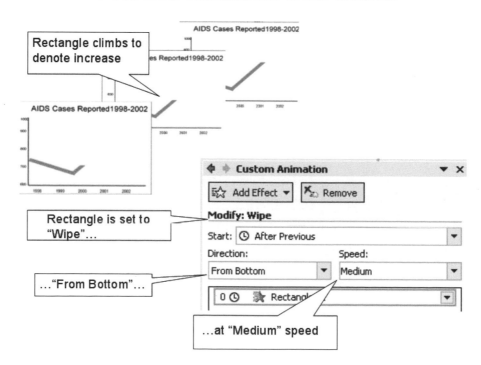

Animations That Teach

Some examples of animations that teach appear throughout the rest of this chapter. *Note:* for the purposes of illustration, this chapter shows a number of examples with transcripts of the narration added to the images. This is for the benefit of readers; the transcripts do not appear on the e-learning programs. The research of Mayer and others tells us that students learn better *when animation and narration occur together* rather than animation and on-screen text.

Process/Stages

Animation can illustrate processes, stages, or progression. In the "smoking" example shown in Figure 6.10, the name of each body part is highlighted and explanatory text is displayed as an animated line moves from the mouth down into the lungs.

 A working example of this animation is available on the CD that accompanies this book. To see it work, open the file in Slide Show mode. To see how it was created, open it as if you were going to edit it, then click on "Slide Show—Custom Animation." The animation panel will open so you can see how the animation was created.

Figure 6.10. Animated Line Shows Smoke's Path

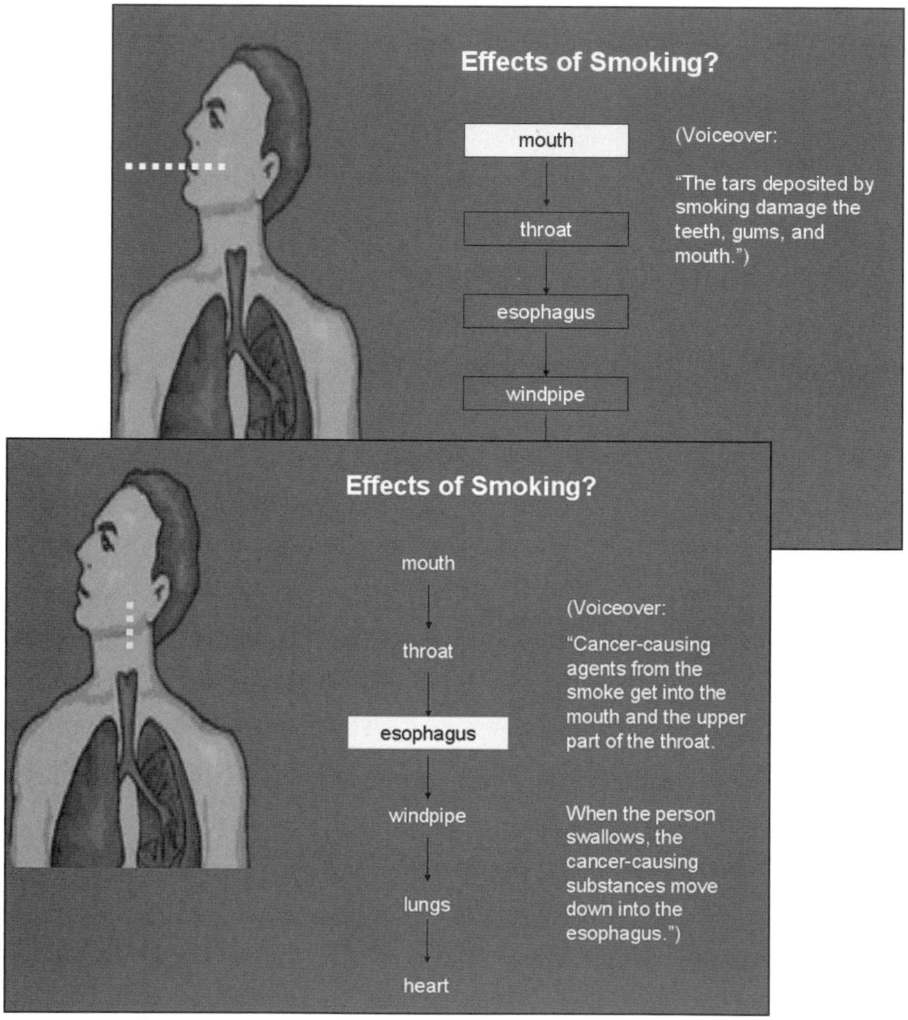

Demonstration

Animation can provide instruction in how things work. The screens shown in Figure 6.11 illustrate the concept of buoyancy in a submarine. The animation shows that as the submarine submerges the air chambers fill with water, weighing the submarine down.

Figure 6.11. Submarine Submerges as Air Chambers Fill with Water

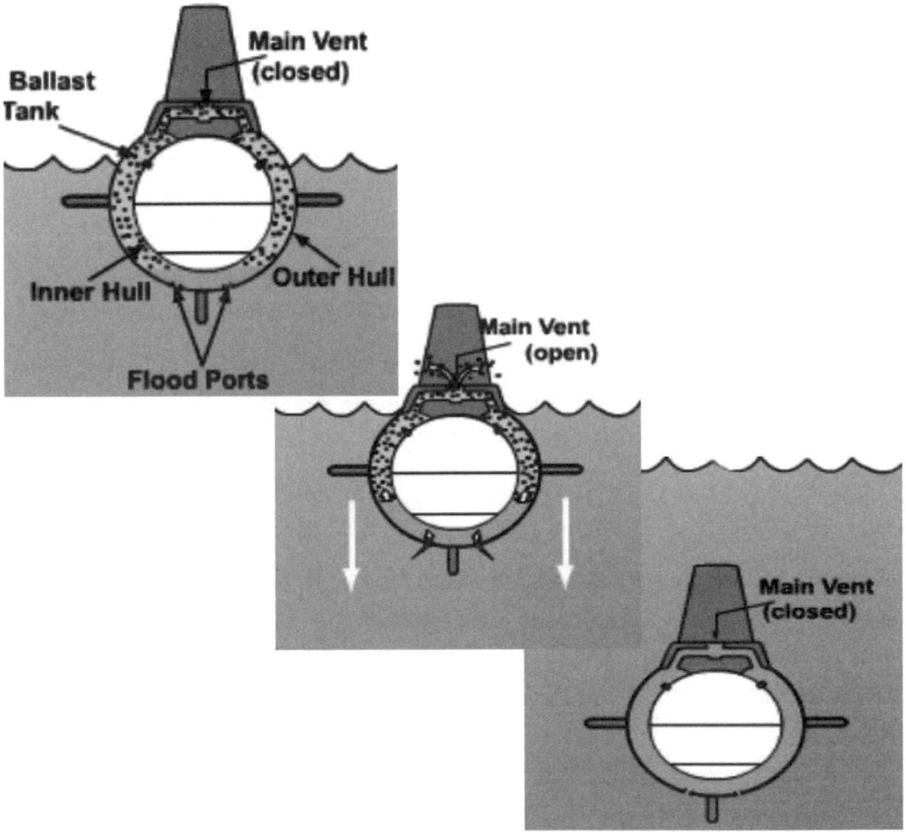

Source: Submarine buoyancy concept and original images from www.onr.navy. mil/Focus/blowballast/sub/work3.htm

In another example of demonstration, Figure 6.12 shows animation that illustrates how a simple pump works. As the pump handle moves down, pressure on the air inside forces the valve open and the air is pushed out.

Figure 6.12. Animation Illustrates Working Pump

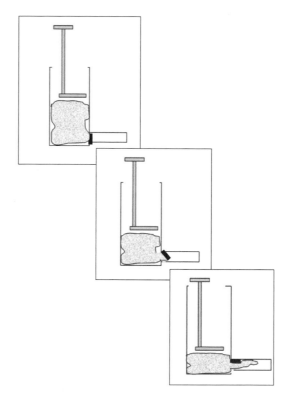

Realistic Movement

Flying, spinning text does not add to the learner's understanding. Use motion animations to illustrate motion well. Figures 6.13 and 6.14 both use "spin" animation to show the workings of things that spin or turn. The forklift image was created by combining the spin animation with a motion path to indicate forward motion. See pages 160 to 164 for more information on motion paths and combining animations.

Figure 6.13. Gear Spin Animation

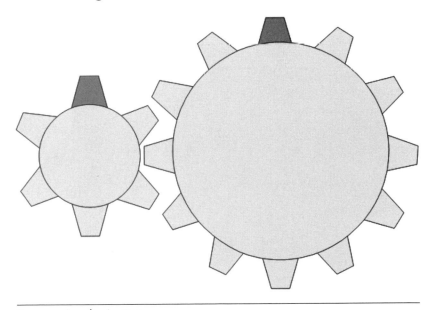

Source: Acadia Institute

Figure 6.14. Spin Animation Used to Illustrate Turn

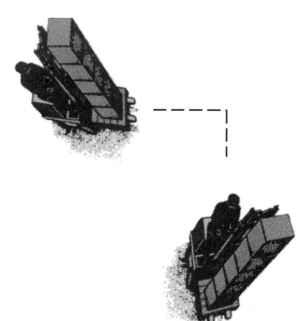

Order/Sequence

The introduction of motion path animations moved PowerPoint into real competition with higher-level animation programs. Figure 6.15 shows an example of a tutorial that uses motion path animations to teach sequencing in bagging groceries. Items appear to drop into the bag.

Figure 6.15. Motion Path Animation Allows Learner to See Order

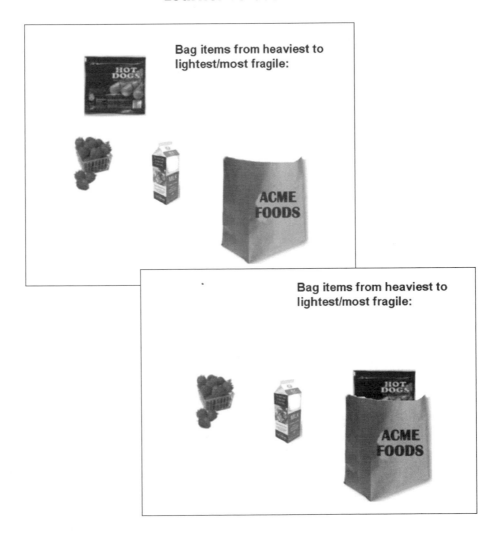

Figure 6.16 shows the motion paths. The hot dogs go first, followed by the milk and then the strawberries. By right-clicking each item and choosing "Order—Send to Back," each item disappears behind the bag, giving the illusion of dropping inside.

Figure 6.16. Motion Paths for the "Grocery" Animation

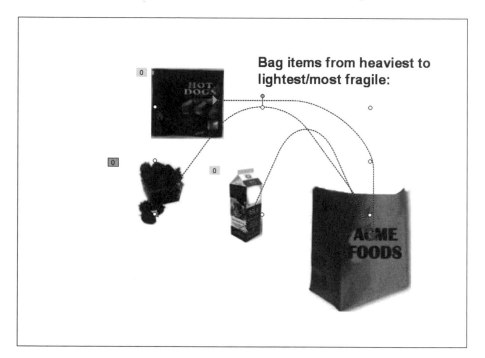

University of Toronto Professor Danton O'Day has written extensively on his experience in using PowerPoint to create animations for use in biology classes. Touting the quick development time and ease of use PowerPoint offers, O'Day frequently turns to PowerPoint for developing instructional animations. Search www.google.com for "Danton O'Day PowerPoint" for links to his articles and interviews, as well as to working examples of animations he's created.

Charts, Timelines, and Diagrams

Animate charts to show changes, trends, information over time, or to explain difficult concepts. The example in Figures 6.17 and 6.18 show before-and-after approaches to animating a chart in an online AIDS awareness program. The slide's core message is that AIDS is on the increase. Notice how the right animation can support this message.

 A working example is included on the CD.

Figure 6.17. "Before" Image from Online AIDS Program

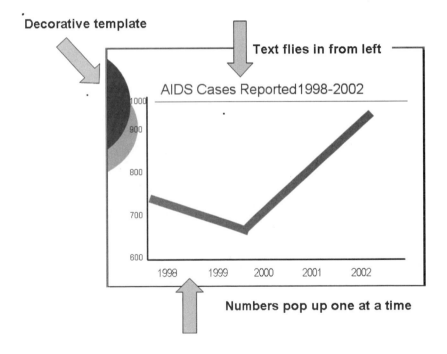

The animations used on the slide above don't emphasize the right material. Figure 6.18 shows the same slide with the template and text animations removed. The designer then emphasized the information that *matters* by using the "Wipe Up" command to animate the bar, illustrating the idea of increase.

Figure 6.18. Important Information—The Increase in Cases—Is Animated

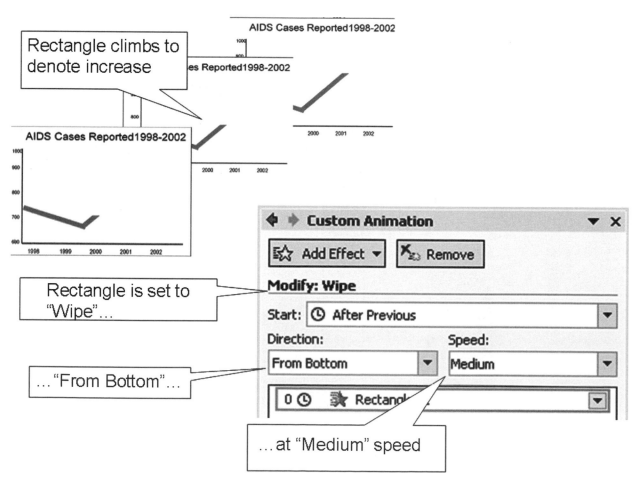

A working example of the chart shown in Figure 6.18 appears on the CD in "Chapter 6"—"charts."

Figure 6.19 shows a company's expansion history. The heavy line marker moves across the timeline at the bottom of the screen as stars appear to show new units opened in a given year.

Figure 6.19. Animated Timeline

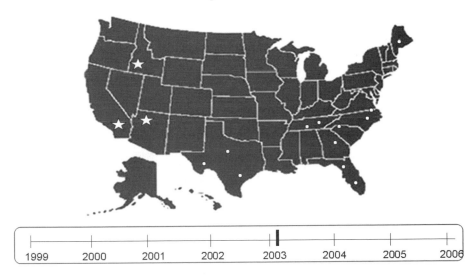

Franchise Expansion 1999-2006

A challenge can be helping learners understand that processes in the "real world" often occur in fits and starts rather than in the smoothly outlined stages that often show up in manuals and memos. Figure 6.20 shows an animated timeline of the usual reality of the employee discipline process. The animation was created by using separate lines set to animate by wiping up, down, or right.

Figure 6.20. Animated Timeline Shows the Fits and Starts in a Process

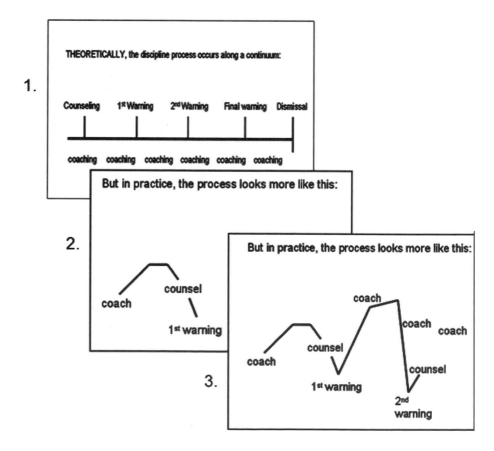

PowerPoint's animation features will allow you to animate parts of a chart; for instance, bars in a bar chart can appear in sequence or can climb, indicating growth. Pieces of a pie chart can appear in order, colors can change, etc. To animate the chart, right click on it and select an animation; choose "Effect Options" to identify elements to animate. See Figure 6.21.

Figure 6.21. Chart Elements Can Be Animated Separately

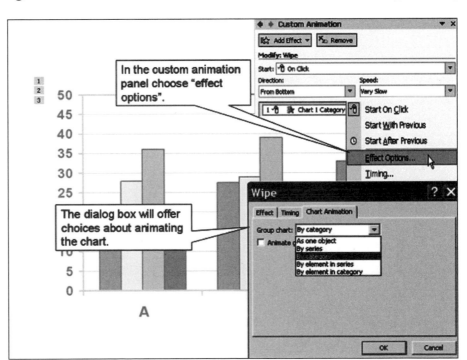

 A working example of this chart is included on the CD.

"Using visual cues—such as animation or changes in color and shape—reinforce the message that an event has occurred."

Wilson-Pauwells. Bringing it into focus: visual cues and their roles in developing attention. *Journal of Biomedical Communication, 24,* **12–16**

Similarly, elements of a diagram can be animated. This can be used to show hierarchical relationships, stages in a process, levels of management in an organization chart, etc. PowerPoint 2002/XP/2003 has a diagram gallery located on the Drawing toolbar. This feature has been greatly expanded in PowerPoint 2007 and can be accessed via the "Insert—Smart Art" command. See Figure 6.22 for options available. Figure 6.23 shows how to animate items in a diagram.

Figure 6.22. Diagramming with PowerPoint

2002/XP/2003   2007

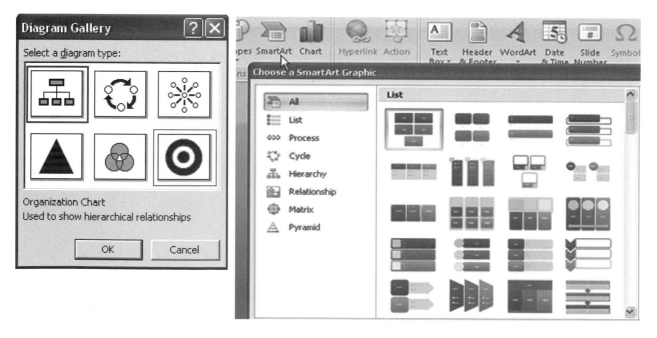

Figure 6.23. Animating a Diagram

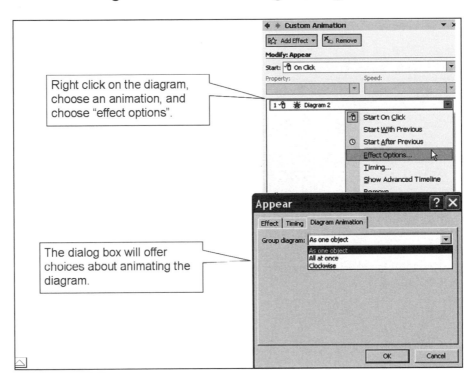

Annotating Graphics

While Mayer's research tells us to avoid substituting on-screen text for voiceover narration, animation can be used effectively to label or annotate a graphic with animated text or text boxes. Animating one item at a time (shown in Figure 6.24 by setting the text boxes to appear and disappear) minimizes the number of items on the screen, thereby reducing cognitive load, and allows the learner to see the whole image before text is introduced that might cover it.

Figure 6.24. Animation Can Be Used to Annotate Graphics

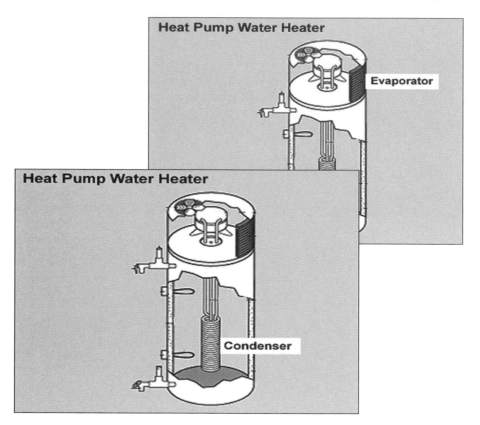

Providing Worked Examples

Research has shown that studying worked examples is often a more effective and efficient way of learning than solving conventional problems. Worked examples are also useful at reducing cognitive load and fit within Mayer's "SOI" model in helping the learner select, organize, and integrate new information (Clark & Mayer, 2002; Clark, Nguyen, & Sweller, 2006;

Mayer, 2001; van Gog, Paas, & van Merrienboer, 2004). Worked examples can be particularly effective when providing instruction for novices. Figure 6.25 provides an illustration of an animated worked example. Text is animated a section at a time to show how the problem is "worked."

Figure 6.25. Worked Example of Applying Calculation to Problem

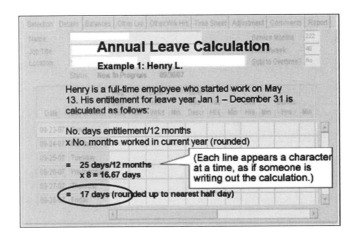

Practice makes perfect: when you see an animation you like, try to figure out how you can create a "reasonable facsimile" of it with PowerPoint. You might be surprised at what you can accomplish!

Combining Animations

Combining animations can provide effects to rival that of more expensive and harder-to-learn software programs. The forklift example in Figure 6.14 was created by combining a curved motion path with a quarter-spin animation (so the forklift will turn while simultaneously moving forward). In the animation shown in Figure 6.26 , I want the car to move toward the learner. That's easy enough to create with a motion path animation, but I also need the car to change perspective as it moves, appearing to come closer. By going to "Custom Animation—Add Effect—Emphasis—Grow/Shrink," and setting the second animation to occur "with previous," I can make the car appear to increase in size while simultaneously moving toward the learner. Figure 6.27 shows the custom animation panel for this.

 A working example of the "Car" animation is included on the CD.

Figure 6.26. Car Moves While Perspective Changes

Figure 6.27. Animation Settings for the Moving Car

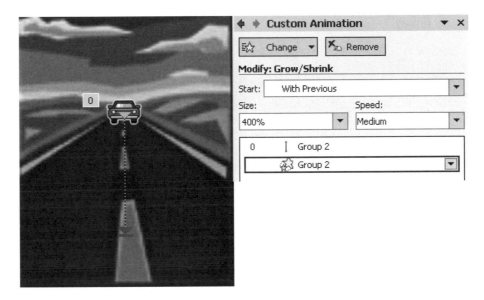

Practice

Developing skill in advanced animation techniques takes creativity, practice, patience, and, regardless of detailed instructions, some trial and error. You may also find alternate ways of achieving an effect, or find some inspiration for a future project.

Trigger Animations

Where other actions we've looked at allow you to link a slide or object to another slide, a "trigger" allows the learner to start an animation or sequence of animations on a single slide. For instance, in the "gears" example first shown in Figure 6.13, a button can be added that would enable the learner to start the animation. Figure 6.28 shows the same animation with a trigger added; Figure 6.29 shows how it was created.

 A working example of the "gears" animation is included on the CD.

**Figure 6.28. Setting the Trigger Animation
for the "Start Spin" Button**

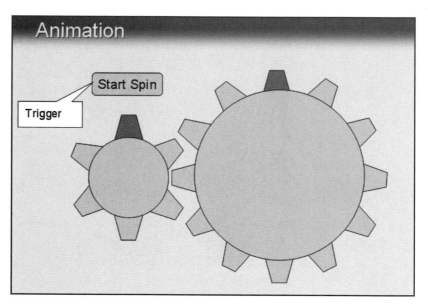

**Figure 6.29. Choose "Effect Options" to See Choices
for Setting Triggers**

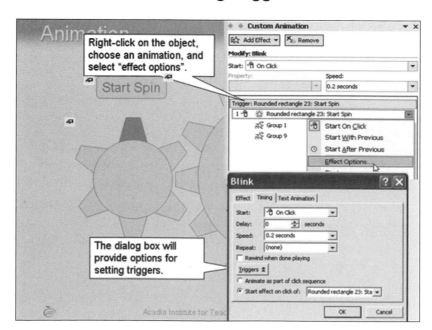

Triggers can be especially useful when you want learners to control one or more animation sequences. The "submarine" example, originally shown in Figure 6.11, is designed to begin animating as soon as the slide loads. You could set the animation to start on mouse click and create a dummy button on the screen (any click will start the animation, but the button gives the illusion of a control button). With triggers, though, you could give the learner control like this.

Figure 6.30. Triggers Allow Learners More Control

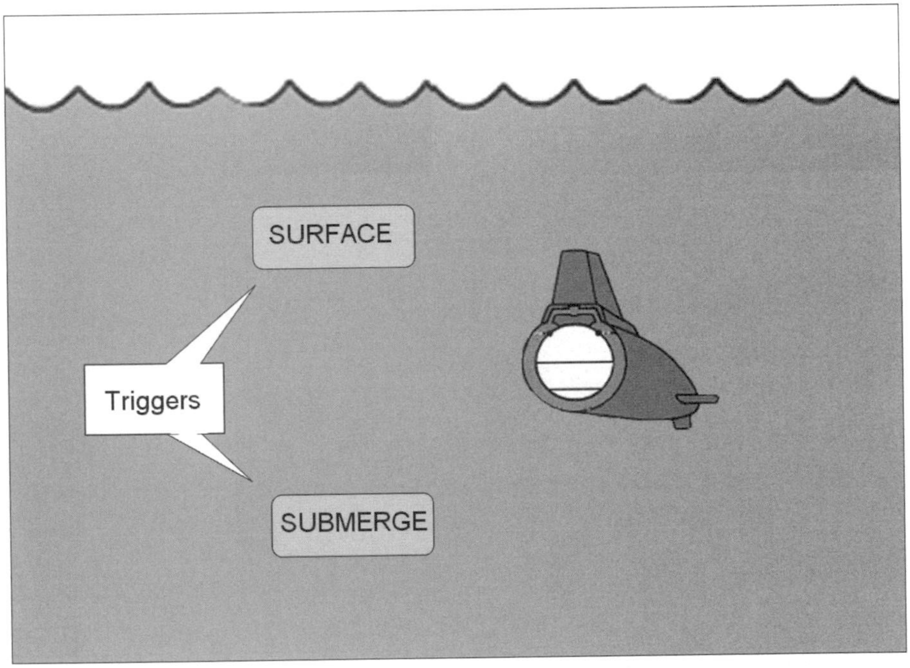

Source: www.onr.navy.mil

This "grocery" example, shown above in Figure 6.15 as an automatic animation, can be created with triggers. Learners would, upon clicking each item, start the motion path animation that moves each item to the bag, as shown in Figure 6.31. (*Note:* At this time, it is not possible to create drag-and-drop interactions in PowerPoint without learning complicated Visual Basic code. The animation shown in Figure 6.31 is a reasonable substitute for a drag-and-drop interaction.)

Figure 6.31. Triggers Can Give Learners Control Over Items

Click on items in the order they should be bagged:

Figure 6.32. Clicking the Ovals Triggers Appearance of Explanatory Text

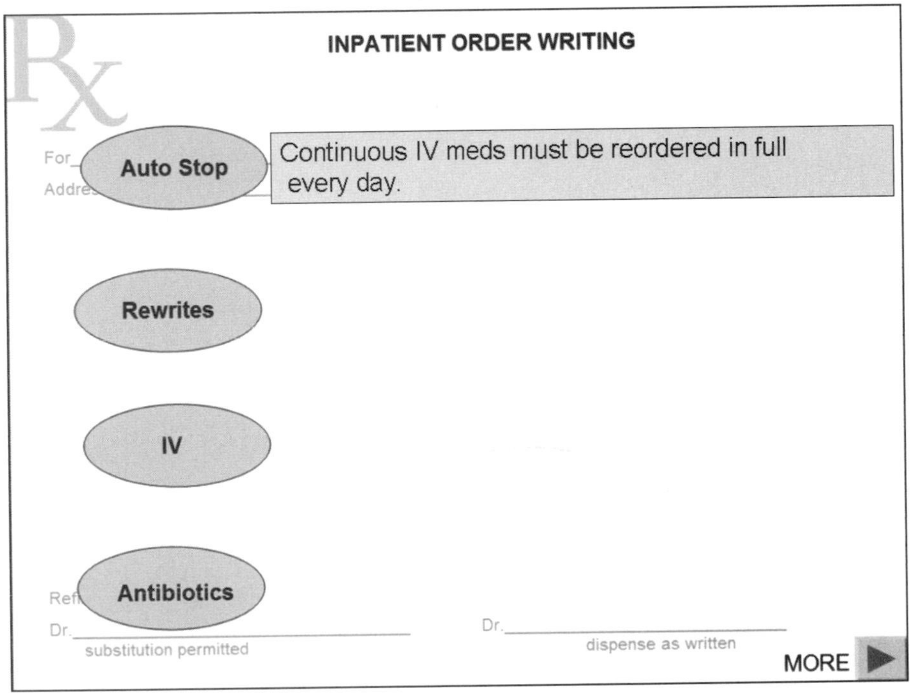

INPATIENT ORDER WRITING

Auto Stop — Continuous IV meds must be reordered in full every day.

Rewrites

IV

Antibiotics

substitution permitted   dispense as written

MORE ▶

Other uses of triggers include actions such as making quiz answers appear beside a question or provide ways of giving learners more control over content. An example is shown in Figure 6.32.

 IMPORTANT: As this book goes to press, most of the software products for converting PowerPoint to Flash—something you will likely want to use—do not support trigger animations. In order for these to work, the e-learning program would need to be uploaded to the Web as a PowerPoint file. This has been mentioned briefly elsewhere. Chapter 10 provides more information on distributing PowerPoint on the Web. Products are constantly being upgraded, however, and are usually not too far behind the most current release of PowerPoint. Check with vendors of the Flash converter products to see whether the products can handle triggers, and visit my website at www.bozarthzone.com for updates on this.

Summary

Animation, used with care, can help a designer move material from "content" to "instruction." It can help learners understand change over time, transformation from state to state, and illustrate processes. It can help learners select, organize, and integrate new learning and can reduce cognitive load. The next chapter shows ways of adding interactivity to PowerPoint-based programs to further draw in and involve the learner.

CHAPTER 7

Interactivity

t's unfortunate that so many e-learning programs take the form of screen after screen of content, serving as little more than "page turners." Clicking "next" is not interaction! A lot can be done with PowerPoint to build interactivity, from treasure hunts to interactive quizzes and even to game-show-type games. And, unlike paper-and-pencil activities, PowerPoint-based quizzes, games, and activities can be enhanced with graphics, visuals, and sound clips. It's important, though, to use interactivity thoughtfully and for the purpose of supporting instruction. This chapter covers assorted strategies for encouraging learners to interact with e-learning programs in meaningful ways: quizzes, games, simulations, and interactive case studies.

 The CD accompanying this book includes working examples and detailed instructions for creating many of the items in this chapter.

"The only appropriate exercises in an online learning course are ones that emerge directly from the objectives. Other questions and exercises might entertain learners, but because they do not directly relate to the objectives, they ultimately distract learners from the purpose at hand."

Saul Carliner, Assistant Professor of Educational Technology, Concordia University, and co-author, *Advanced Web-Based Training Strategies.*

It's All About Hyperlinking

Reminder: the crux of creating interactivity in PowerPoint lies with hyperlinking through mouse click or mouseover actions. The action takes the learner from one slide to another, or results in some other "event"—a video clip plays, an animation sequence begins, etc.—caused by the learner's actions. There are several ways to create the hyperlinks:

1. Via a text link
2. Via an action button
3. Via an object, like a shape or photo, given an action setting
4. Via a "hotspot," an invisible action button placed over part of a slide or larger image

Examples of these are shown in Figures 7.1 through 7.6.

Figure 7.1 shows an interaction created with action buttons that link to corresponding feedback slides. There are five slides associated with this interaction: the question slide, the slides corresponding to the three answers, and the "next" slide to which learners are sent upon completing the interaction.

Figure 7.1. Creating Hyperlinks with Action Buttons

What do you say next?

1 "I'm sorry you were inconvenienced." Tell me what happened so I can help you."

2 "You're the third caller this morning. We have several drivers out sick and it's causing a lot of delays."

Click on the letter beside your choice.

3 "Delivery times are only estimates. I'm sure the driver will be there soon. Please call back if he's not there by noon."

See the CD for a narrated explanation of creating this interaction.

Hyperlinks can take many forms. While the slide shown in Figure 7.1 uses action buttons, you can also use letters (text), as shown in Figure 7.3, or objects such as boxes, as shown in Figure 7.4.

Figure 7.2. Text Hyperlinks to Corresponding Slide

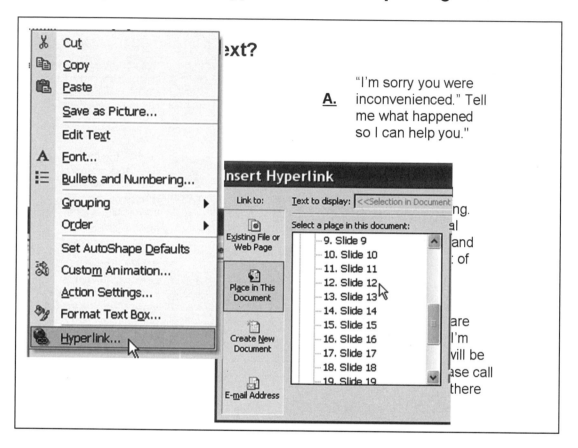

For setting hyperlinks from text or objects, first select the object, then right-click to access a drop-down menu. Choose "Hyperlink." (You can also do this via the toolbar by clicking "Insert—Hyperlink."). Then choose the corresponding slide. This is shown in Figure 7.2.

Figure 7.3. PowerPoint Action Buttons Hyperlink to Corresponding Slides

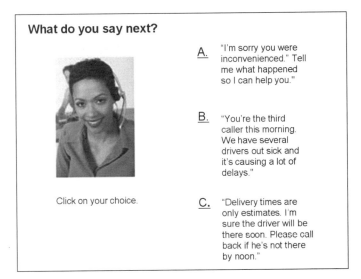

Figure 7.4. Objects (Boxes) Hyperlink to Corresponding Slides

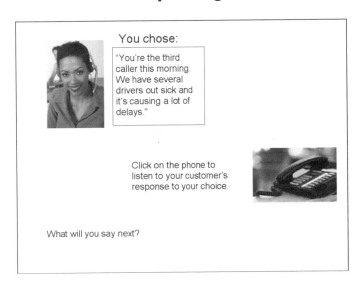

Figure 7.5 shows the use of an invisible hotspot. Figure 7.6 shows how to create it.

Figure 7.5. Invisible Hotspots Link to Corresponding Slides

Click the file cabinet to review background information, or click the door to let the client enter.

Figure 7.6. Creating a Hotspot

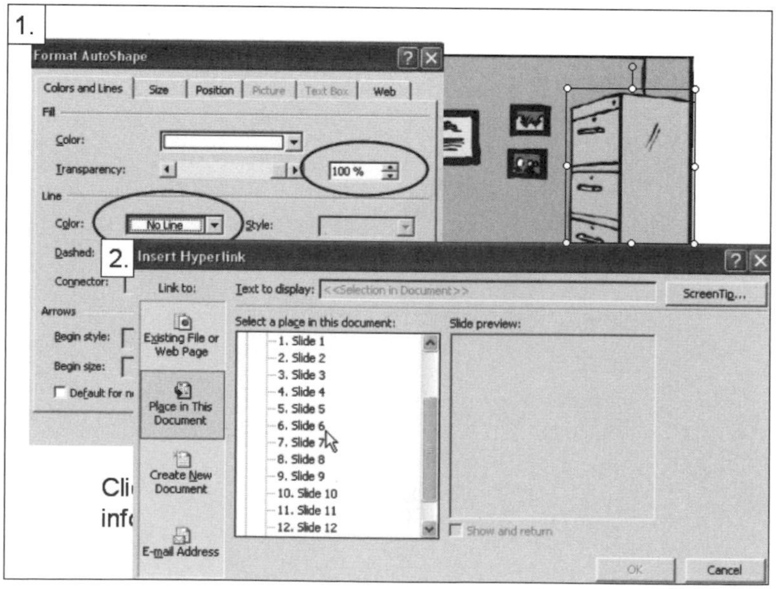

Hotspots in an image like the one in Figure 7.6 can be created by drawing an AutoShape over the object (in this case, a rectangle over the file cabinet), then creating a link as with the examples in the figures. After the link is created, right-click and format the AutoShape (the rectangle) to 100 percent transparency and "no line."

Other actions can be assigned to objects. Figure 7.7 shows an example of an object set to play an audio clip.

Figure 7.7. Object (Phone) Links to Voice Clip

Click on the phone to listen to your customer's response.

Lesson Learned

When using invisible hotspots or buttons, be sure the invisible object is on top, or PowerPoint won't "see" it. Select the button or object, then right-click and choose "Order—Bring to Front" to ensure it's positioned on top of any other objects.

Levels of Feedback

The examples in the figures above show simple interactions in which the learner chooses an answer and is taken to slides basically saying "right" or "wrong." Additional levels of feedback can be created through using additional slides. For instance, the first time the learner chooses the wrong answer the slide might ask him or her to "try again," pose the question once more, and again direct the learner to a second set of answer slides. If the learner again makes an incorrect choice, the corresponding slide might provide a hint, such as "That's still not right. Do you recall the limitations of the 'H' series printers?" and again pose the question. At the third incorrect choice, the learner might be advised to review material and return later. In this instance there would be no "next" slide; the program would end there.

 See the CD for a narrated explanation of creating quizzes with several levels of feedback.

Quizzes and Games

Basic Types of Quizzes

The visual nature of PowerPoint lets the creative designer go from plain-vanilla paper-style quizzes to more meaningful learning activities, allowing learners to more closely connect content with application.

Figure 7.8 is an example of before and Figure 7.9 is an example of after.

Figure 7.8. Text-Only Matching Quiz

Match the symptoms of aging to physical changes
in the elderly.

a. cochlear degradation   ___1. indigestion
b. loss of muscle mass   ___2. loss of hearing
c. decrement in lingual sensitivity   ___3. loss of balance
d. decreased esophogeal motility   ___4. loss of taste

Figure 7.9. Matching Quiz

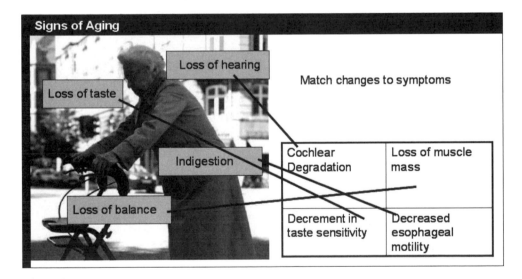

Figure 7.10a. Text-Only Multiple-Choice Quiz

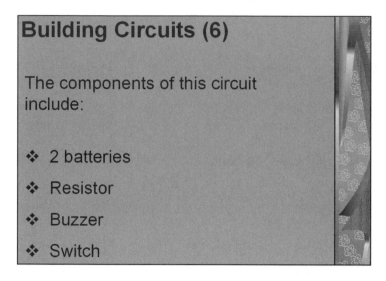

Figure 7.10b. Multiple-Choice Quiz Using Images

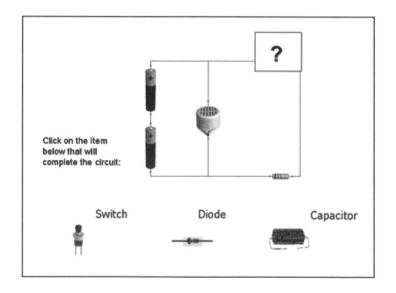

Source: Simon Drane; component images from
www.crocodile-clips.com

"Active" ≠ "Busy"

Richard Mayer (see Chapter 2) reminds us that effective instruction engages the learner's mind and encourages him or her to think. Simply being physically active—like clicking "next"—does not support transfer or retention of new learning.

It is critical that learners be provided with frequent opportunities to assess and, if necessary, correct, themselves. Familiar quiz formats, such as matching, word search, true/false, and multiple choice, are easy to create with PowerPoint. Below are photographic examples with brief information about how they were created.

Matching

Figures 7.11 and 7.12 show two different ways of setting up matching exercises: the first with connecting lines, the second with numbers.

Figure 7.11. Matching Exercise

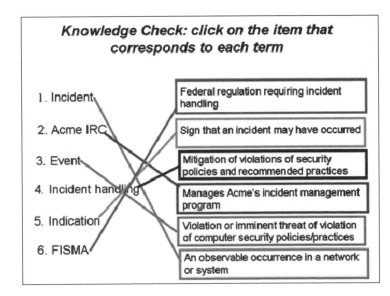

Courtesy Marirose Coulson and Donna Ebling, Booz/Allen/Hamilton

Figure 7.12. Matching Exercise

Exercise 4.1 —Security & SDLC. For each activity on the right identify the phase it occurs in from the list on the left.

Assume this is for a NEW system	
1. Initiation	_5_ Remove data as required
	_3_ Certification and accreditation
2. Development/ Acquisition	_1_ Security categorization
	_4_ Configuration management
3. Implementation	_2_ Identify operational practices
	_5_ Sanitize media
4. Operations and Maintenance	___ Integrate security requirements into design specifications
	___ Preliminary risk assessment
5. Disposal	___ Performing system backup
	___ Security testing

Booz | Allen | Hamilton

Courtesy Marirose Coulson and Donna Ebling, Booz/Allen/Hamilton

To create this, use custom animation to set numbers (or lines) to appear on click. An illustration is shown in Figure 7.13.

 A working example of these matching exercises is included on the CD accompanying this book. The interaction could also be created by inserting action buttons and setting triggers for each matching event.

Figure 7.13. Set Items to Appear on Click

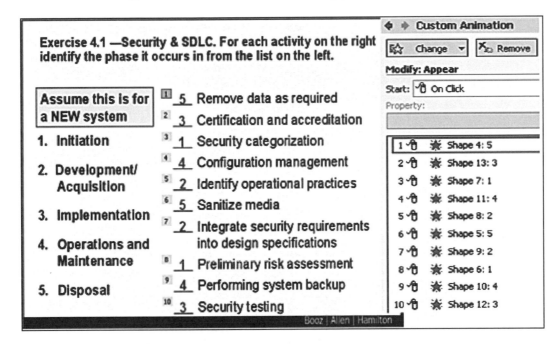

Lesson Learned

When creating slides with multiple linked textboxes and objects, take care to ensure that areas given hyperlinks don't overlap.

True/False

True/false is really just a single choice between two items, as shown in Figure 7.14. Each choice (legal or illegal) links to a corresponding answer slide. Some other substitutes for "true/false" as choices are "yes/no," "agree/disagree," and "fact/fiction."

The example on the CD, "Creating Hyperlinked Interactions," while specific to Figure 7.1, shows the same technique used in creating true/false items.

Figure 7.14. Example of True/False Quiz

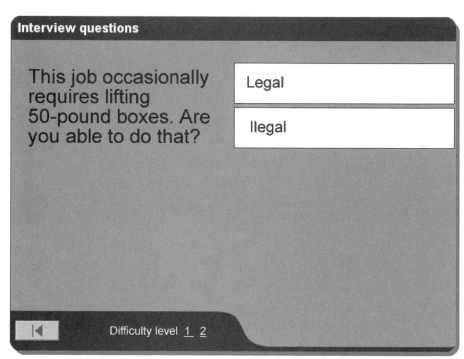

Word Search

Figure 7.15 is a word search created by Booz/Allen/Hamilton staff. Learners are asked to find terms that were covered earlier in the program. Color blocks are set to appear when learners click on a correct answer.

Figure 7.15. Word Search Puzzle

Find the terms we've covered so far. Can you define each?

R	E	S	P	O	N	S	I	B	I	L	I	T	I	E	S	A
O	S	Y	C	A	H	T	I	C	S	A	I	P	N	E	R	O
L	R	S	Y	S	T	E	M	Q	I	S	A	O	V	W	C	S
E	E	T	L	S	E	C	U	R	I	T	Y	L	R	I	R	E
S	N	E	C	D	Z	P	L	A	N	I	R	I	S	I	I	L
P	W	M	T	E	C	H	N	I	C	A	L	C	N	L	S	U
M	O	I	C	O	N	T	R	O	L	S	T	Y	N	G	K	R
S	D	D	F	I	B	S	E	C	U	R	B	O	U	S	E	E
O	P	E	R	A	T	I	O	N	A	L	C	T	L	S	X	P
M	A	N	A	G	E	M	E	N	T	C	O	N	T	R	O	L
S	T	T	E	S	J	N	S	S	E	C	C	A	L	S	N	G

Thanks to Marirose Coulson and Donna Ebling, Booz/Allen/Hamilton

In the figure, colored blocks, created by setting AutoShape rectangles to 75 percent transparency so the letters will show through, appear as learners identify words. All items are set to appear "on click." Figure 7.16 shows a completed puzzle.

 A working example of this word search is included in the Chapter 7: Quiz Templates file on the CD accompanying this book.

Figure 7.16. Completed Word Search Exercise

R	E	S	P	O	N	S	I	B	I	L	I	T	I	E	S	A
O	S	Y	C	A	H	T	I	C	S	A	I	P	N	E	R	O
L	R	S	Y	S	T	E	M	Q	I	S	A	O	V	W	C	S
E	E	T	L	S	E	C	U	R	I	T	Y	L	R	I	R	E
S	N	E	C	D	Z	P	L	A	N	I	R	I	S	I	I	L
P	W	M	T	E	C	H	N	I	C	A	L	C	N	L	S	U
M	O	I	C	O	N	T	R	O	L	S	T	Y	N	G	K	R
S	D	D	F	I	B	S	E	C	U	R	B	O	U	S	E	E
O	P	E	R	A	T	I	O	N	A	L	C	T	L	S	X	P
M	A	N	A	G	E	M	E	N	T	C	O	N	T	R	O	L
S	T	T	E	S	J	N	S	S	E	C	C	A	L	S	N	G

Multiple-Choice and Game-Show

Although most people probably have never noticed, television game shows often take the form of multiple-choice quizzes. Using a game-show format provides learners with what e-learning expert William Horton calls "a seductive test." Game-show formats are familiar to learners so there is usually little time needed for understanding rules. Try to be creative; don't just think of quizzes as testing recall only. With some creativity, you can formulate questions that require application and evaluation of content. Some examples are shown in Figures 7.17, 7.18, and 7.19.

The example on the CD "Creating Hyperlinked Interactions," while specific to Figure 7.1, shows the same technique used in creating multiple-choice items.

Figure 7.17. Multiple-Choice Quiz

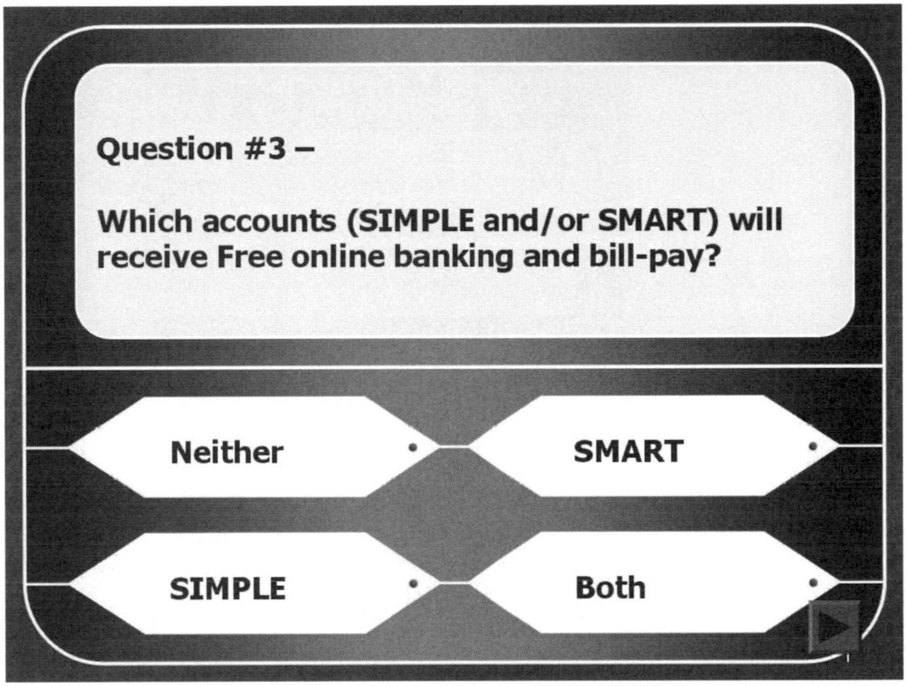

Question #3 –

Which accounts (SIMPLE and/or SMART) will receive Free online banking and bill-pay?

Neither   SMART

SIMPLE   Both

Thanks to Kathy Keller

Figures 7.18 and 7.19 show a game-type variation on the multiple-choice quiz, this one regarding diversity issues from Kwango.com. Learners are presented with an example of a problem situation and asked to choose the type of discrimination. Each character is covered with an invisible action button; on mouseover, more information appears about the character's opinion. Learners then click the character to select their choice of answer.

Figure 7.18. Diversity Challenge Question and One Character's Opinion

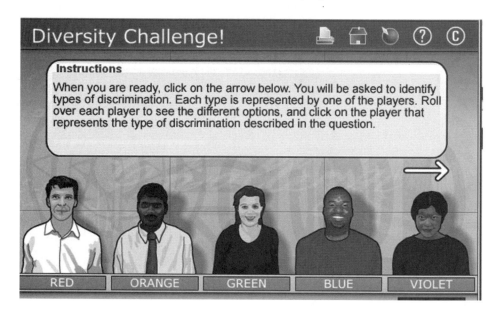

Figure 7.19. Another Character's Opinion

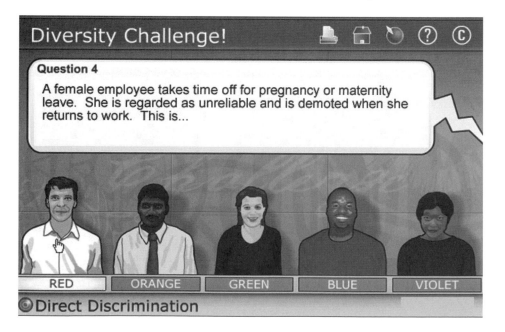

Basic Types of Games

Jeopardy-Type Games

Jeopardy-type games are an excellent way to review material or deliver a good deal of new information in a way perhaps more interesting than straight presentation of content. Figure 7.20 shows a Jeopardy-type game used in an online program on troubleshooting skills for heat and air conditioning repair technicians. Each button on the main board links to an answer slide, which in turn links to the question slide, which has a link for returning back to the main board. (Remember, in Jeopardy the learner is presented with the answer first and then has to ask the question.)

Figure 7.20. Jeopardy-Type Game

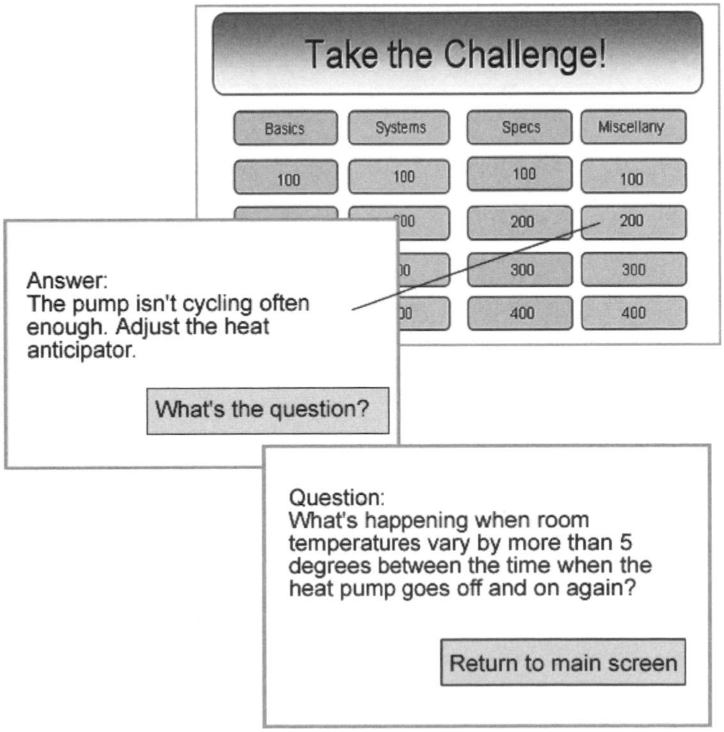

The CD includes a template for a Jeopardy-type game called "Challenge Board."

Pyramid Games

Similar to Jeopardy, the pyramid (shown in Figure 7.21) offers learners categories, which in turn lead to questions. This example is from a program on sales techniques.

Figure 7.21. Sample "Pyramid" Game

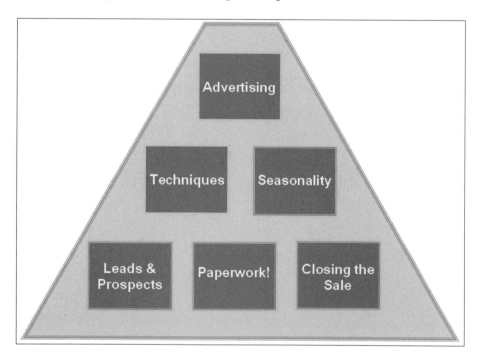

The CD includes a template for a Pyramid game.

Hollywood Squares Games

This is another variation on the multiple-choice approach, with characters asking questions to which the learner is asked to respond. Variations of this could include audio clips of the characters asking questions or photos of real company "characters" (HR Director, Benefits Rep, Shop Foreman, etc.) instead of clip-art images.

Figure 7.22. Sample Squares Game Board

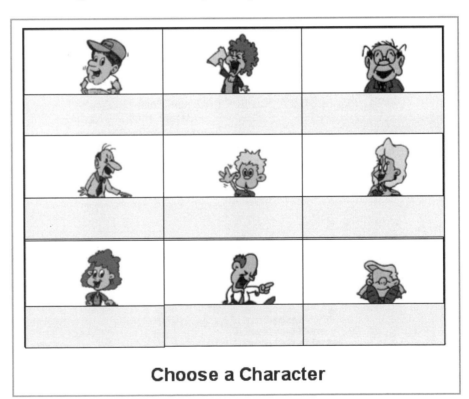

Choose a Character

Figure 7.23. Sample Squares Question

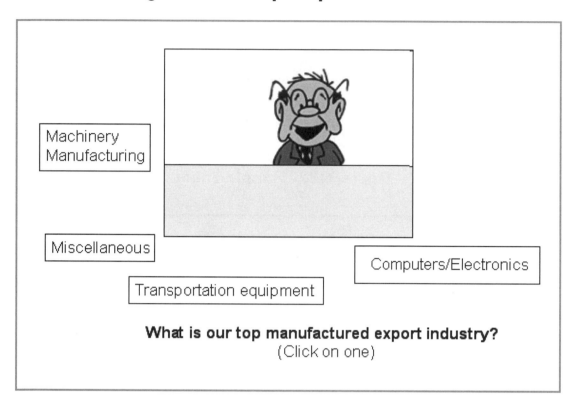

What is our top manufactured export industry?
(Click on one)

"Millionaire" Games

Figures 7.24 and 7.25 show a multiple-choice quiz designed to resemble the "Who Wants to Be a Millionaire?" game. As with the TV version of the game, options exist for choosing hints and reducing the number of choices by selecting "50/50."

In Figure 7.24, the 50/50 option hyperlinks to a slide with two choices removed, shown in Figure 7.25.

Figure 7.24. "Millionaire"-Type Game with Hints

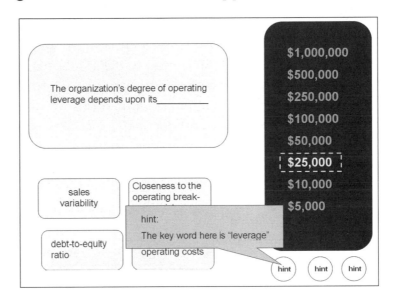

Figure 7.25. "50/50" Option Takes Away Half the Choices

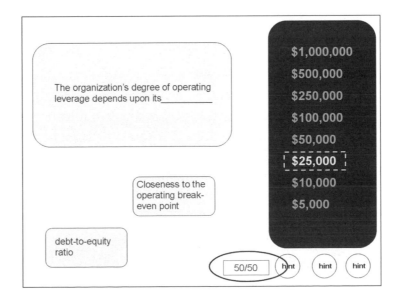

The CD includes a template for a "millionaire"-type game.

(*Note:* You probably know that there are often more ways than one to achieve a particular effect in PowerPoint. The examples for adding the hints and 50/50 option to the "Millionaire" game shown in the figures use hyperlinks to additional slides. They could also be created with trigger effects in which animations would take place on one slide rather than linking to others. The choice may depend on your plans for distributing the program to your learners. At this time, trigger animations do not work in most PowerPoint-to-Flash converter products. Personally, for an activity like this, I find it easier to create multiple hyperlinked slides than to work with a sequence of animations on one slide.)

Lesson Learned

When using quizzes, be sure to give learners access to the correct answers! For instance, use feedback slides ("Sorry, the correct answer is B.") or use hyperlinks to direct learners back to reference material.

Timed Quizzes

There are several ways to add an element of timing to PowerPoint-based quizzes. The easiest: set slides to advance after a given period of time, as shown in Figure 7.26. You can also add a running timer, clicking off seconds or other increments, by creating one slide per time frame (one per second, per fifteen seconds, etc.). Both of these would lend themselves nicely to a virtual flash-card activity. It's also possible to add a running-clock-type timer to the screen. An example of this is shown in Figure 7.26.

Figure 7.26. Setting Up Timed Quiz: Slide Advances After Ten Seconds

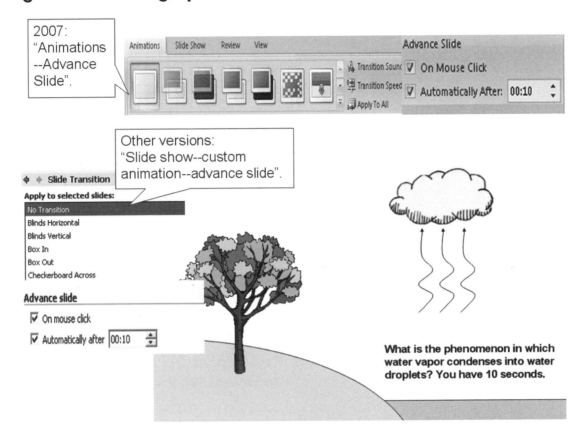

Timed Photo Reveal Quizzes

Figures 7.27 and 7.28 show screens from a visual recall quiz for machine field repair staff. Slides are set to advance every five seconds, and point values decrease as additional information is revealed.

Figure 7.27. Photo Reveal Activity—First Screen

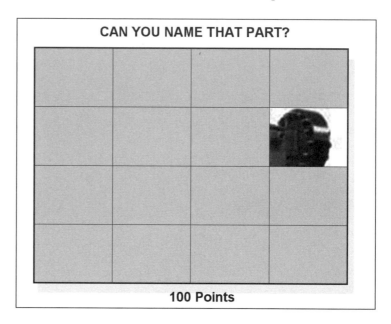

Figure 7.28. Point Value Decreases as More of the Image Is Revealed

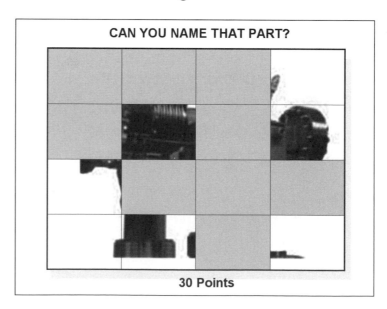

Running Timer

Quizzes can be set up so that the learner sees a countdown in time increments. This is done by creating a separate slide for each time frame (in the case of Figure 7.29, one per second), then slides are set to advance in accordance with that time frame. (**Note:** This can become very cumbersome. While you can copy and paste the question text from slide to slide, you will still have to go in and manually enter the time on each slide—and counting down a minute by seconds means editing *sixty* slides. If you really want to do this, try searching www.google.com for "PowerPoint timer." You will find some add-ins and templates you can download and edit.)

Figure 7.29. Timer Changes with One Slide Per Second

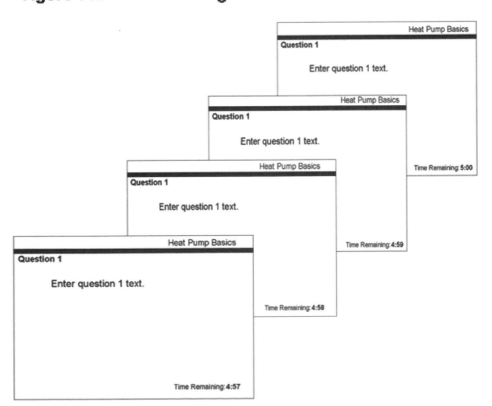

Another way of creating a running timer is by inserting a small clock or counter on the slide. Figure 7.30 shows a timer created by animating pieces of a pie chart to appear every ten seconds. The slide then advances at the sixty-second mark.

Figure 7.30. Clock-Type Timer Used in a Quiz

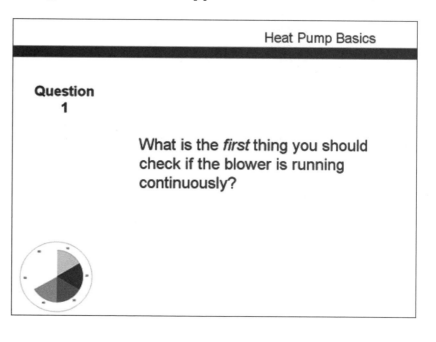

Board Games

The board game format is also an option, as shown in Figure 7.31, the home screen from "Bacteriopoly." Players begin with 100,000 bacteria; the object is to reduce this as much as possible. While this was originally designed as a classroom team game for use in schools, I recently repurposed it for use in a "lab safety" refresher program for adult learners. The squares on the board hyperlink to corresponding slides. The original game is available in an editable form at http://ferl.becta.org.uk/display. cfm?resID=11804 (although accessing it would probably be easier by just going to www.google.com and typing "bacteriopoly" into the search box).

Figure 7.31. "Bacteriopoly" Game Board

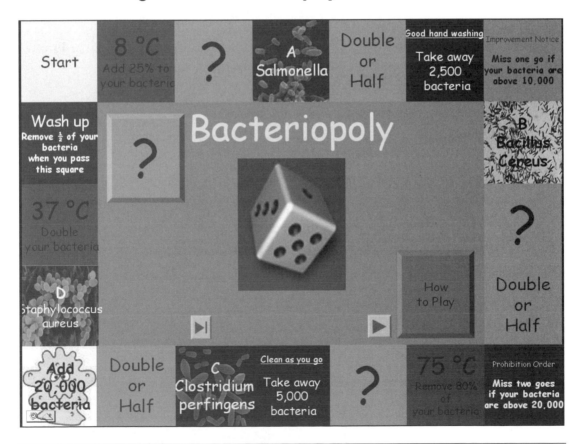

Thanks to designers Martyn Hulme and Jon Kent

Linking to External Games and Quizzes

Want more? It is an easy matter to insert a hyperlink from your Power-Point program to an external quiz or game. The lowest-level example would be linking to a Word- or Excel-based quiz. For higher-level interactions, inexpensive (ranging from free to under $100/year for a subscription) game and quiz engines can simplify the creation process and can offer some activities difficult or impossible to create with PowerPoint, such as fill-in-the-blank quizzes. Figure 7.32 shows a PowerPoint screen with a hyperlink to a quiz created with a commercial Flash game template. This quiz is from Quia, a company that offers many easy-to-use game and quiz templates *and* hosts them on their own servers. You create the item, then Quia stores it and provides you with a link to it. See also Figure 7.33, a link to an online game.

Figure 7.32. PowerPoint Linking to External Quiz

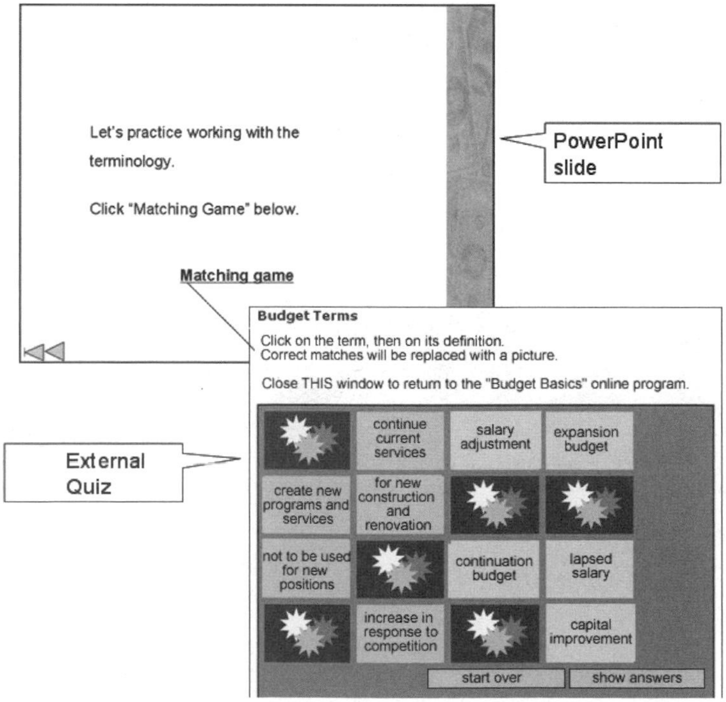

Thanks to Quia (www.quia.com)

Figure 7.33. Insert a Hyperlink from the PowerPoint Slide to the Online Game

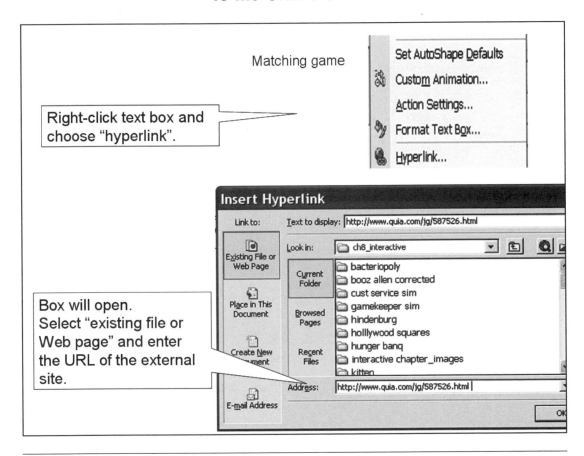

Thanks to Quia (www.quia.com)

 Need to track test scores? You can link from your PowerPoint slide to externally hosted quiz or online survey engines (search www.google.com for "quiz engines").

The example shown in Figure 7.34, created in minutes with an online template from Quia, shows an example of a link to an online test, along with one of the accompanying score reports available (Figure 7.35). Figure 7.36 is the "trouble spots" report, which points out any learners who are having trouble or indicates questions that may be problematic.

Figure 7.34. PowerPoint e-Learning Program
Links to Online Quiz

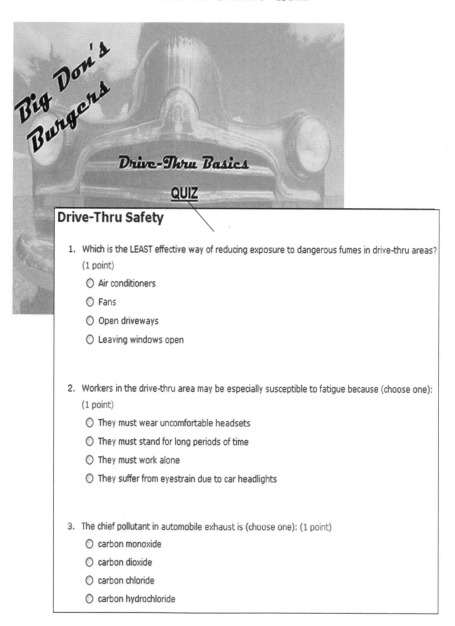

Thanks to Quia (www.quia.com)

Figure 7.35. Example of Feedback
Provided to Learner

Drive-Thru Safety

Thank you. Your responses have been computer graded. Here are your results.

Score Summary		points earned	points possible
(Click on question number to jump to question.)			
Question 1	correct	1	1
Question 2	incorrect	0	1
Question 3	correct	1	1
Question 4	correct	1	1
	Score: (75%)	3	4

1. Which is the LEAST effective way of reducing exposure to dangerous fumes in drive-thru areas?

   - Air conditioners
   - Fans
   - Open driveways
   - Leaving windows open (correct answer, your response)

   Points earned: 1 out of 1

2. Workers in the drive-thru area may be especially susceptible to fatigue because (choose one):

   - They must wear uncomfortable headsets
   - They must stand for long periods of time (your response)
   - They must work alone
   - They suffer from eyestrain due to car headlights (correct answer)

   Points earned: 0 out of 1

3. The chief pollutant in automobile exhaust is (choose one):

Thanks to www.quia.com

Figure 7.36. "Trouble Spots" Report, One of Several Reports Available

Trouble Spots Report

Activity: Drive-Thru Safety

QUIA

Overall Summary

Low Score	High Score	Mean	Median	# of Students
2 (50.0%)	3 (75.0%)	2.75 (69.0%)	3 (75.0%)	4

Students who scored zero or who started but did not submit answers

None

Students who scored 70% or less

Student Name	Points (out of 4)	Percentage
Diamonds, Carol	2	50%

Questions answered correctly 70% of the time or less

Question	Average Score	Number of Times Received
1. Workers in the drive-thru area may be especially susceptible to fatigue because (choose one):	0%	3
2. Workers in the drive-thru area may be especially susceptible to fagtigue because (choose one):	0%	1
3. Which is the LEAST effective way of reducing exposure to dangerous fumes in drive-thru areas?	67%	3

Thanks to Quia (www.quia.com)

About Quia

For those on tight budgets—and even those who are not—Quia (www.quia.com) is an excellent all-around quizzing and tracking tool. A corporate subscription is only $99 per year and offers access to Flash game templates, templates for several different types of

(continued)

quizzes, surveys, score reports, feedback to learners, and even class web page hosting. It is hosted on Quia's servers, so no downloads are required, and—this is important—you can deploy activities to *unlimited* users. While it was developed for use by school teachers, I know a number of private organizations and government agencies using Quia to support workplace training efforts.

Simulations

Simulations ask the learner to perform a skill in some sort of context. The example of bagging groceries using trigger animations first shown in Chapter 6 (and repeated in Figure 7.37) provides learners with a simulated task.

Figure 7.37. One Type of Simulation Provides Practice with a Task

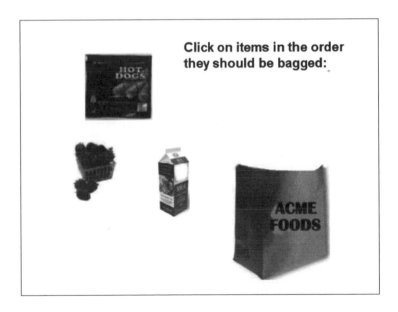

A more common type of simulation involves branching decision making as learners move through a series of problems. These types of interactions can be quite powerful, as learners can see the consequences of their actions. Creating good simulations is a matter of choosing realistic situations and sketching the "branching" that the simulation will require. As with creating quizzes, it's a matter of laying out a series of "if-then" statements, followed by "and then," "and *then.*" The simulation will involve branching decision making; you may have seen this represented as a decision tree. Figure 7.38 shows the layout of a simple simulation. Boxes represent separate slides.

Figure 7.38. Decision Tree for a Simple Simulation

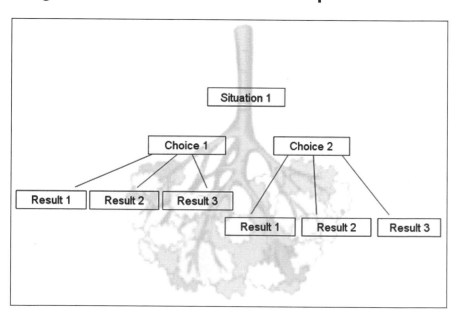

Simulations are instructionally powerful, as learners experience the consequences of their own actions and decisions. While they can become quite elaborate and intricate, their success depends on careful planning—in the laying out of the decisions and results—more than on technical skill.

Figures 7.39 and 7.40 show a sample from a PowerPoint-based customer service simulation. The learner chooses a role, is presented with a problem situation, then receives feedback.

Figure 7.39. Choice of Role

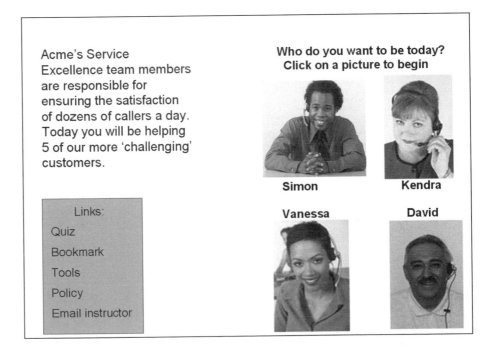

Acme's Service Excellence team members are responsible for ensuring the satisfaction of dozens of callers a day. Today you will be helping 5 of our more 'challenging' customers.

Links:

Quiz

Bookmark

Tools

Policy

Email instructor

Who do you want to be today?
Click on a picture to begin

Simon   Kendra

Vanessa   David

Figure 7.40. Presentation of Problem

Click on the phone to hear
what the caller has to say.

This customer service simulation is especially strong due to the addition
of "customer" voice clips (see Chapter 10 for instructions on adding
voice clips). Figure 7.41 shows another screen from the customer service
simulation. The learner has chosen a reply that only escalates the situation. Clicking the telephone plays an audio clip of an angry voice saying, "Every time I call I get more excuses from you people. If I'm the
third caller, then why isn't someone already working on this?! I am
SICK of all the problems with deliveries!" Again, a good simulation lets
learners experience the consequences of their actions.

Figure 7.41. Learner Presented with Choices and Result of Decision

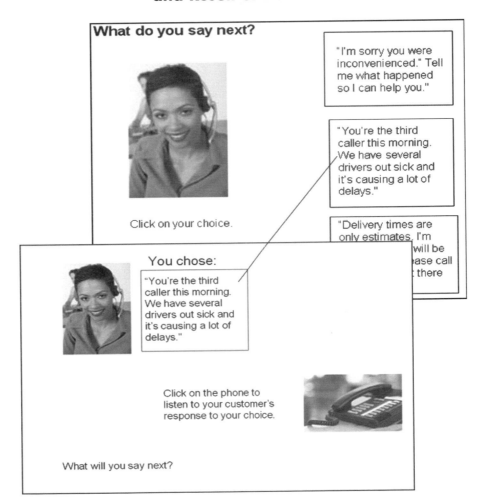

Figure 7.42 shows another screen from the same simulation, this one asking the learner to respond to an email complaint.

Figure 7.42. Simulation Showing Email Interaction

EMAIL

To: CustServ@abc.com
From: FrankL@symp.net
Subject: NO DELIVERY!!

I am FED UP with your delivery department's inability to ever keep any promises. As usual, the shipment arrived 2 weeks late. You say the fifteenth, but you mean the first. WHY don't you just say the first in the first place!

Click on the best response:

TO: FrankL@symp.net
From: Vanessa@abc.com
Subject: NO DELIVERY!!

I can see that you're upset about this. Delivery times are only estimates. I will forward your comments to the shipping department so they will be more careful next time.

TO: FrankL@symp.net
From: Vanessa@abc.com
Subject: No delivery

Mr Lyons,
I regret that you've been inconvenienced and I want to help. Let me make sure I understand: you were promised delivery on the 15th and you did not receive the product until the first of the following month. Is that correct?"

Figure 7.43 is the decision tree from another simulation, "Hindenburg's Dilemma," for use in online leadership training. Hindenburg's choice of reactions to the new constitution leads to still more decisions or undesirable consequences.

Figure 7.43. "Hindenburg's Dilemma" Provides Choices and Consequences

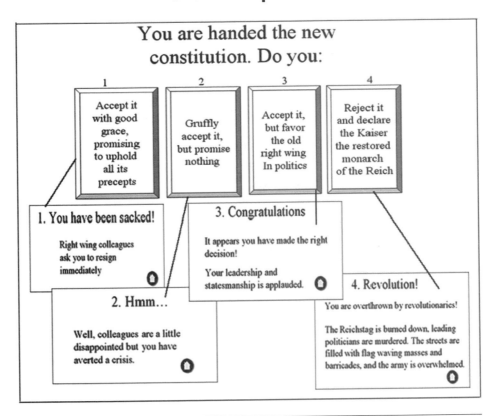

"Hindenburg's Dilemma" is used with permission of creator Rob Johnson; you can see the full program at http://ferl.becta.org.uk/display.cfm?resID=5023

Figures 7.44 shows a program created by the Royal Veterinary College. It is from the "Emergency Case Simulator," in which veterinary students are presented with a case and must choose from possible actions/treatments set as hotspots across the bottom of the screen. This simulation is especially noteworthy for providing realistic practice with a critical task, minimizing the costs—both monetary and other—associated with the topic, and confronting learners with the ultimate consequence: death of the pet. The program can be accessed at www.rvc.ac.uk/Review/Cases/Index.htm.

Figure 7.44. Icons Hyperlink to Choice of Actions

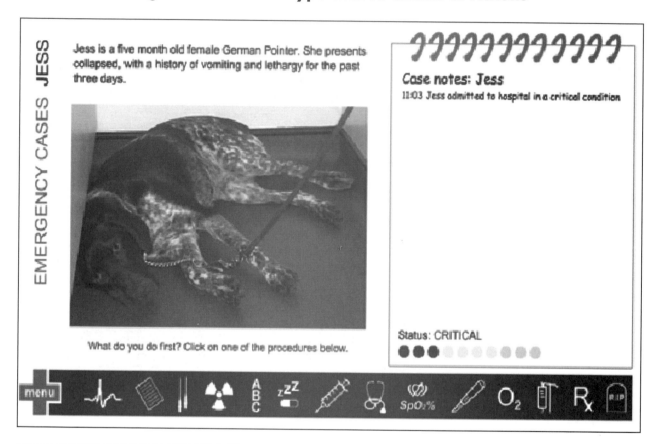

Source: Royal Veterinary College

Another online course from the Royal Veterinary College, "Gamekeeper's Conundrum" is shown in Figure 7.45. Part of a series called "Pitfalls in Practice," this is an ethics program developed in response to negligence claims filed against veterinarians in their first year in practice. Each photo links to a text slide of "advice" from the person chosen. Note the use of simple photos with AutoShape callouts and text at the bottom of the screen. It's available online at www.rvc.ac.uk/Review/Pitfalls/pitfalls.htm.

Figure 7.45. Screen from "Gamekeeper's Conundrum" Simulation

Source: Royal Veterinary College

Case Studies/Stories

Cliff Atkinson, author of *Beyond Bullet Points,* speaks of the importance of developing a strong story. Use of characters, plot, and a good storyline can provide compelling learning: think of good storytellers you know. Screens from Eduweb's online program, "A. Pintura: Art Detective" uses the theme of a *noir* movie mystery to take learners through a tour of art history. The scenario uses the characters of A. Pintura, Art Detective and the distraught client Miss Featherduster to build a story around the mystery of a painting found in an attic. The designer uses this as a clever launching point for taking learners through an overview of art history and comparison of several painters. Figures 7.46 through 7.56 have been adapted from the original for purposes of printing clearly here. The program can be accessed at www.eduweb.com/pintura.

To ensure that my point here is not lost: there are a thousand ways to present information on art history that are *not* interesting or engaging. This designer found a way to make it quite compelling.

Again: It's about design, not software.

Figure 7.46. Title Screen

Used with permission of Eduweb

Figure 7.47. Setting and Introduction of "A. Pintura, Art Detective"

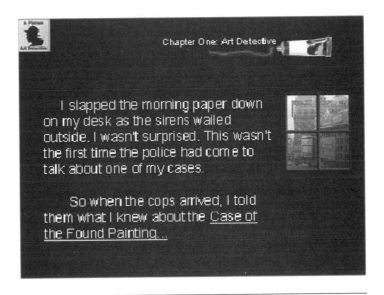

Used with permission of Eduweb

Figure 7.48. Introduction of "Miss Featherduster" Character

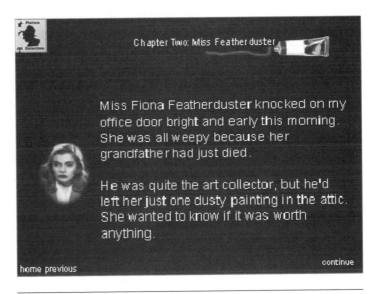

Used with permission of Eduweb

Figure 7.49. Learner Chooses Next Action

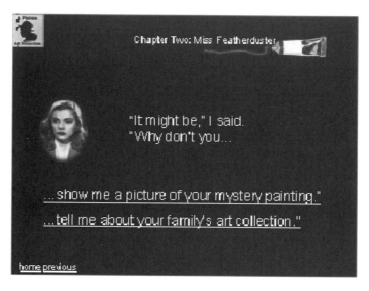

Used with permission of Eduweb

Figure 7.50. Initial Look at the Found Painting

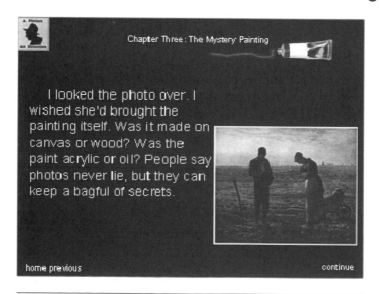

Used with permission of Eduweb

Figure 7.51. Learner Chooses Artist to Study

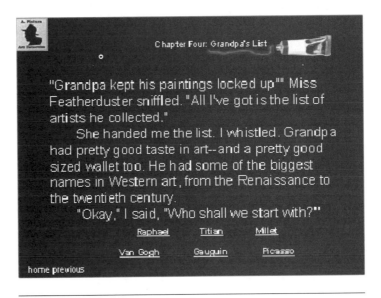

Used with permission of Eduweb

Figure 7.52. Learner Has Chosen Raphael

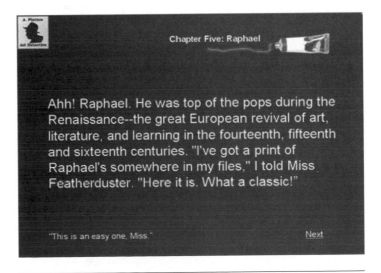

Used with permission of Eduweb

Figure 7.53. Comparison of Found Painting to a Raphael

Used with permission of Eduweb

Figure 7.54. Close-Up of Raphael with Comment on Perspective

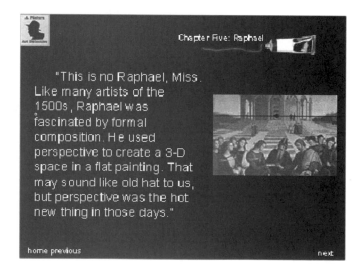

Used with permission of Eduweb

Figure 7.55. Further Explanation

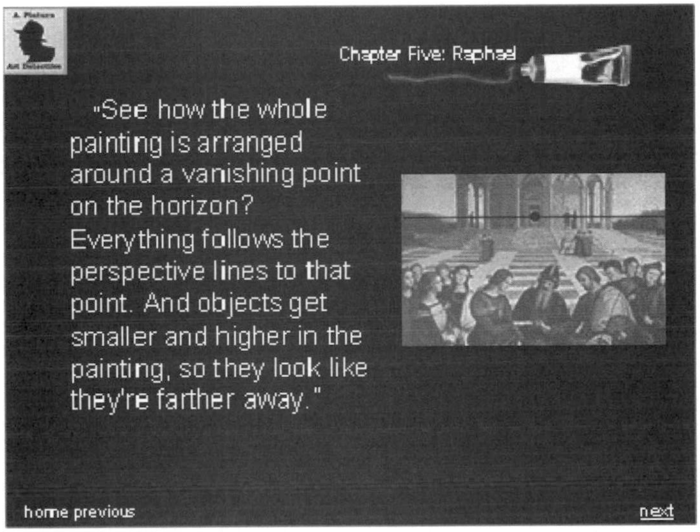

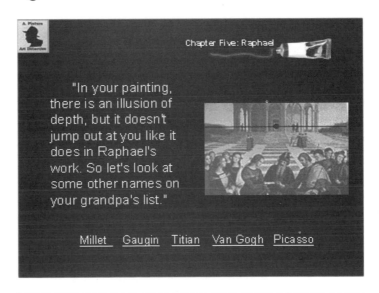

Used with permission of Eduweb

Figure 7.56. Learner Makes Another Choice

Used with permission of Eduweb

Figures 7.57 and 7.58 show screens from another interactive online experience, the "Hunger Banquet" case studies.

The program is available in full at www.hungerbanquet.org. Learners are offered a choice of characters, provided with scenarios from the characters' daily reality, and then asked to make choices about actions to take. This program is created entirely with photographs, simple images, and hyperlinks. As with the "A. Pintura: Art Detective" program, the designers of Hunger Banquet found a way to make dry factual and statistical information engaging and compelling.

Figure 7.57. One Case from www.hungerbanquet.org

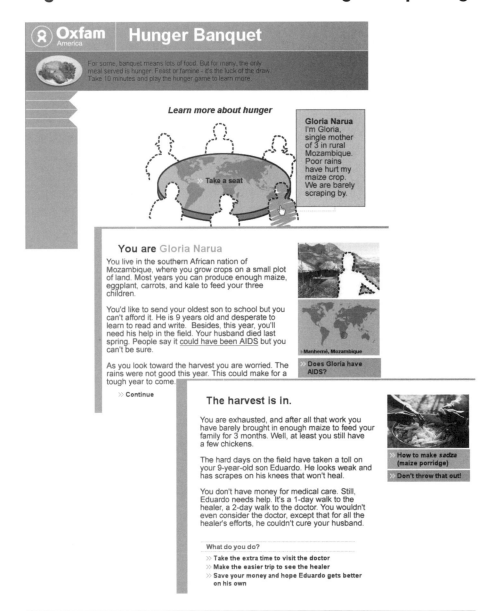

Used with permission of OxFam

Figure 7.58. Continuation of the Case

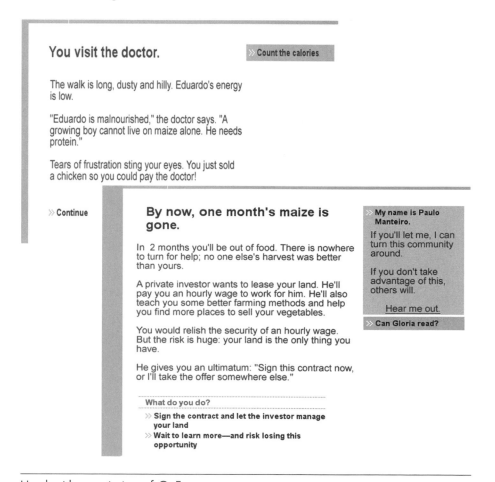

Used with permission of OxFam

Mazes

One last interesting interaction is the maze, created by assigning mouseover action settings to images on a slide. Mazes can be used for problem solving, decision making, or teaching sequence and process. The one shown below, ideally suited to mouse training for new computer users or tasks involving similar motion, is reminiscent of the battery-operated child's game of "Operation," in which touching tweezers to metal parts of the "body" causes a buzzer to sound. The example shown in Figures 7.61 and 7.62 was created by assigning the "collapse" animation to each girder; if touched by the cursor, the pile falls. (*Note:* This example is intended to illustrate another of the many possibilities PowerPoint offers to a creative designer. No malice is intended toward kittens!)

Figure 7.59. Girders Collapse If Learner Touches with Cursor

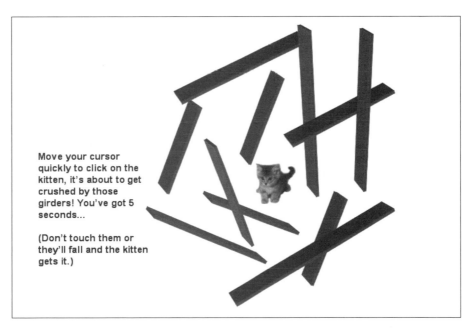

Figure 7.60. Girders Are Set to Collapse on Mouseover

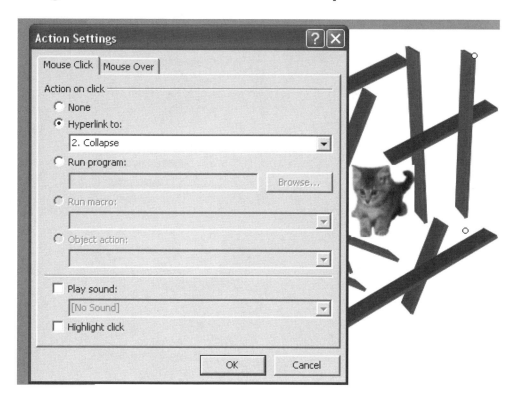

From online PowerPoint manual available at www.agsci.utas.edu.au/ppmultimedia/.
Authored by Nicholas D'Alessandro, Simon James, Anna McEldowney, and Ruth
Osborne, University of Tasmania. Copyright: Commonwealth of Australia. Copyright
Regulations 1969. This material has been reproduced and communicated to you by
or on behalf of the University of Tasmania pursuant to Part VB of the Copyright Act
1968 (the Act). The material in this communication may be subject to copyright under
the Act. Any further reproduction or communication of this material by you may be the
subject of copyright protection under the Act.

Treasure Hunts

Training on tasks involving research—using the company intranet, procedures manuals, or other guidelines—can be enhanced through a "treasure hunt" or "scavenger hunt" activity. Learners are assigned problems that require them to use these resources. The example in Figures 7.61 was created by a pharmaceutical company: callers interested in purchasing prescription drugs online knew more about the process than the employees manning the company's hotline. The activity shown in Figure 7.61, a single PowerPoint screen with hyperlinks, helped familiarize staff with the same information being accessed.

Figure 7.61. Treasure Hunt

Treasure Hunt   **Topic: Internet Sales of Prescription Drugs**

Clue # 1	Clue # 2
Go to our page: FAQs about purchasing prescription drugs online What are the three most important things to Keep in mind when counseling callers on this issue? Where else can callers find information on Purchasing prescription drugs online?	Click here to go to the US Department of Commerce What are the rules for importing prescription Drugs from outside the U.S.? What is the ONE thing we must ALWAYS caution consumers about?

Source: Bozarth, J. (2005). *e-Learning Solutions on a Shoestring: Help for the Chronically Underfunded Trainer*

About Visual Basic for Applications (VBA)

Visual Basic for Applications is a rich programming language used by PowerPoint. With it you can create macros, which are auto-run commands for repetitive tasks. (The rolling die used in the "Bacterio-poly" game shown earlier uses macros; one handles the rolling die. You can see the program in full at (http://ferl.becta.org.uk/display.cfm?resID=11804). Learner machines need to have macros enabled in order to run programs that use them. VBA also allows for creation of "mini-applications." While I recommend using an external product for managing test scores, you can, with VBA, set up a self-scoring quiz entirely within PowerPoint. VBA is, however, quite challenging to learn—especially for those with no other experience with programming languages or working with code—and is beyond the realm of what most typical PowerPoint users would ever be interested in using. For the trouble it would take to develop skill at the coding required for VBA, particularly with the goal of distributing programs as e-learning products, you could buy and learn another more robust product.

If VBA really interests you, I recommend David Marcovitz's 2004 book *Powerful PowerPoint for Educators: Using Visual Basic for Applications to Make PowerPoint Interactive.* While it focuses largely on VBA for classroom use, it is really the only book, at this time, specifically aimed at using VBA for educational applications. The book's companion website is a good resource and offers a number of examples of the types of interactions you can create with VBA: www.loyola.edu/edudept/PowerfulPowerPoint/.

If you're curious about this, the next few figures show how to access the VBA editor. See Figure 7.62 for opening VBA in 2002/XP/2003 and Figure 7.63 for opening it in PowerPoint 2007. (Note that 2007 will additionally require you to open the "Developer" tab.) The VBA editor will then open a new window, shown in Figure 7.64, for working with VBA.

Figure 7.62. Click "Toolbars—Visual Basic" to Open the VBA Editor

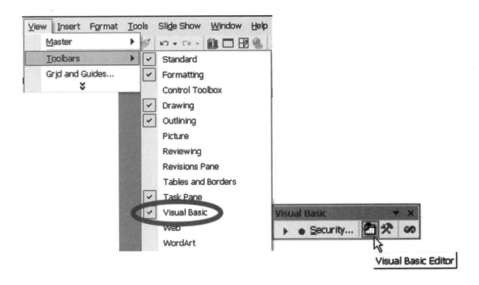

Figure 7.63. Accessing VBA in PowerPoint 2007

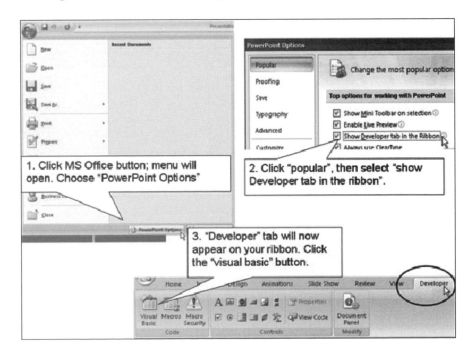

Figure 7.64. The VBA Window

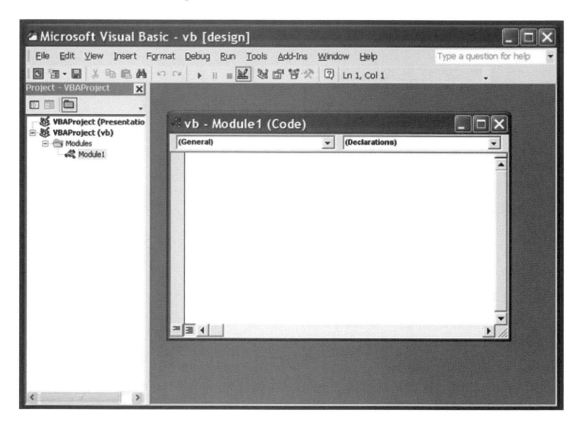

Summary

One of the best, yet most underutilized, capabilities of PowerPoint is that of hyperlinking/action settings. From creating interesting quizzes that offer realistic practice to making content more interesting through the use of games, to providing simulations supplemented with audio and even video clips, PowerPoint offers the creative designer wonderful tools for creating interactivity. There is far more than just clicking "next."

So far we've discussed using PowerPoint to create asynchronous stand-alone programs. Chapter 8 offers some suggestions for blending your PowerPoint-based e-learning courses with other experiences and provides information about a low-cost tool that will let you add animated talking characters to your programs.

Add-Ons, Blending, Performance Support, and Job Aids

t's easy to extend your PowerPoint-based e-learning program. This chapter explores add-in tools, design tricks, job aids, and other ways of making your program more robust and providing additional support for your learners.

Other Documents

A common problem with PowerPoint-based shows is that the designers try to use PowerPoint to display documents that just don't fit the Power-Point screen. Use the "Insert—Hyperlink" command (Figure 8.1) to link to other files such as Word or Excel documents or to larger files such as manuals and troubleshooting guides. This will give the learners some control, as well as allow the documents to be viewed as they were really intended. Links can also be used to give learners access to printable training handouts.

Figure 8.1. Hyperlink to Other Documents

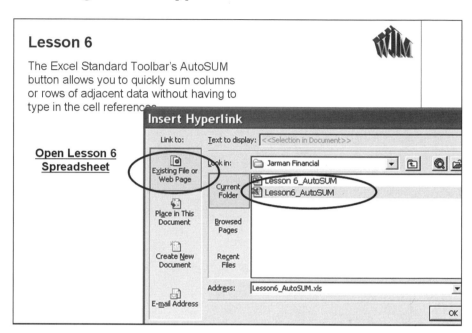

Site Samplers

A struggle in designing any training, online or otherwise, is paring the content down to the critical "must know" and culling out the "nice to know." Distilling a program to its essential elements is crucial to the success of an e-learning program, but the ruthless editing demanded results in difficult choices. Site samplers, aka "hotlists" provide a free, easy-to-build mechanism for giving learners access to the nice-to-know content. They also provide a good way for learners who want to know more to access additional information. Site samplers can easily be created by adding hyperlinks to slides. Figure 8.2 shows a site sampler placed at the end of an online program on project management.

Figure 8.2. Example of a Site Sampler

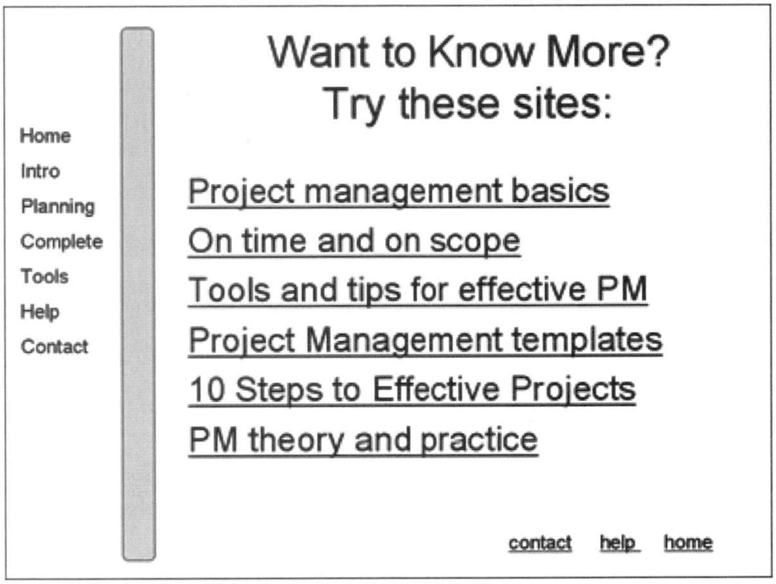

Home
Intro
Planning
Complete
Tools
Help
Contact

Want to Know More?
Try these sites:

Project management basics
On time and on scope
Tools and tips for effective PM
Project Management templates
10 Steps to Effective Projects
PM theory and practice

contact   help   home

Add-On Software

Animated Characters: Vox Proxy

A product called Vox Proxy, from Right Seat Software (www.voxproxy. com), offers a gallery of animated, talking characters or "avatars" that can be placed into your PowerPoint shows. An example is shown in Figure 8.3 and the selection is shown in Figure 8.4.

Figure 8.3. Online Character Used in Employee Timekeeping Tutorial

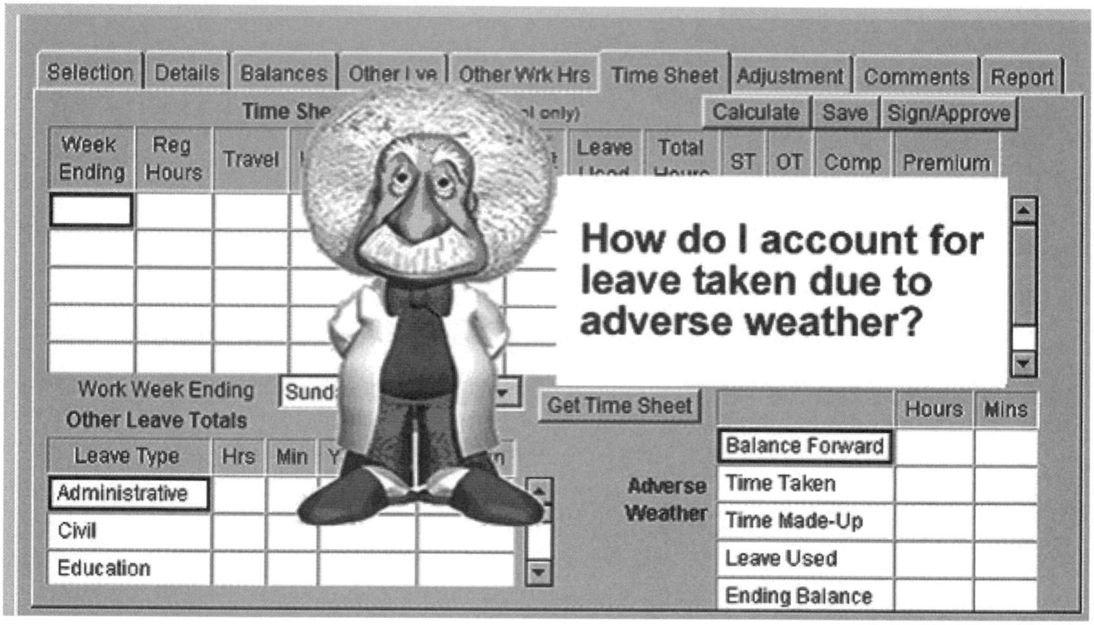

Source: J. Bozarth, *e-Learning Solutions on a Shoestring*. Vox Proxy Scientist Character courtesy Right Seat Software.

Working samples of using Vox Proxy are included on the CD accompanying this book. Some ideas here include offering a character as a guide on a virtual tour of your organization's campus for new hires, a wizard to help decipher the automated timekeeping system, or a host for a new game show on sales techniques. They can also serve as the difficult customer in a simulation or play the role of the skeptical learner, posing questions that learners in a traditional face-to-face training situation might ask. Characters are inserted much like clip art, then drop-down menus allow for easy animation (for instance, you just click on "confused" to get a puzzled facial expression or "wave right arm" for that motion). The characters then speak aloud whatever text you have typed into simple text boxes.

Figure 8.4. Characters Included with Vox Proxy

Source: Vox Proxy

Use of such characters can humanize the online learning experience, and the sense of having a "partner" can reduce the sense of isolation that some people feel in the asynchronous training environment. They can also make challenging information less threatening. Instructional designer Patti Shank, co-author of *Making Sense of Online Learning*, advocates for the use of avatars since, as she says, "People are more affected by social interaction than words."

Vox Proxy is a software download that includes more than twenty-five different characters with dozens of easy-to-add animations available for each. The characters additionally have the advantage of coming in different shapes, genders, and ethnicities, allowing you to provide a character that best reflects the particulars of your target audience. Still more characters are available at extra cost, and the company can arrange for the creation of custom characters if you like. Movements and facial expressions are added from simple drop-down menus (see Figures 8.5 and 8.6). The designer then types in the speech he or she wants the character to say.

Figure 8.5. Facial Expressions and Animations Are Added from Drop-Down Menus

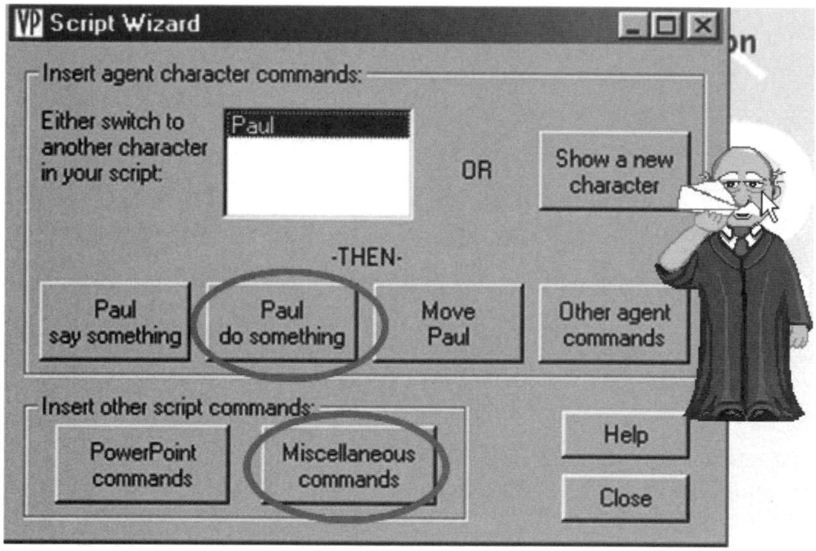

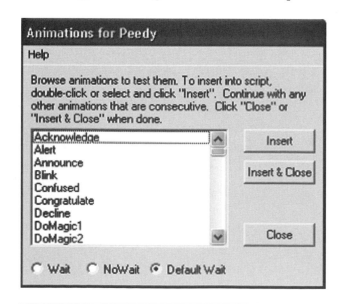

Source: Vox Proxy

Figure 8.6. One-Click Commands Make Programming Characters Easy

Source: Vox Proxy

Vox Proxy now also supports the AT&T "Natural Voices®" text-to-speech engines, which provide voices that sound less synthetic and "computerized" than such voices have been in the past. Qualities of the voices such as speed, pitch, and tone can be altered, the characters can speak in different languages, and both American and British English voices are available. As this book goes to press, the standard edition of Vox Proxy is available for US $199; a free trial period is also available.

There are several options for distributing programs with Vox Proxy characters to your learners. Uploading programs as PowerPoint shows will require that learners have the free Vox Proxy Player installed. Or you can capture the program with a screen recorder, such as Camtasia (about $300 from www.techsmith.com) and save it as a video file.

 The Vox Proxy demo on the CD was captured with Camtasia.

Camtasia and SnagIt

While I am hesitant to make endorsements, there are several other add-on products that really will make life easier for the designer or trainer seeking to create e-learning with PowerPoint. They are also products for which, at the time this book goes to press, there really is no competition. In addition to Vox Proxy, discussed above, are the excellent, easy-to-use "capture" tools, SnagIt and Camtasia, both from www.techsmith.com. SnagIt is intended primarily as a screen capture tool, from which you can take a shot of your entire desktop or an item on it. Virtually every image in this book, and the images used to create them (for instance, pieces of art placed on a sample PowerPoint slide) was created by capturing it with SnagIt. A one-click command brings up a small crosshair tool, which you can click and drag to select the area you wish to capture. SnagIt provides tools for editing captured images such as cropping, adding borders and text, recoloring portions of the shot, highlighting areas, etc. Figure 8.7 shows a capture of the image from Figure 8.5 (reduced for the illustration here).

Figure 8.7. SnagIt Offers Options for Editing Screen Captures

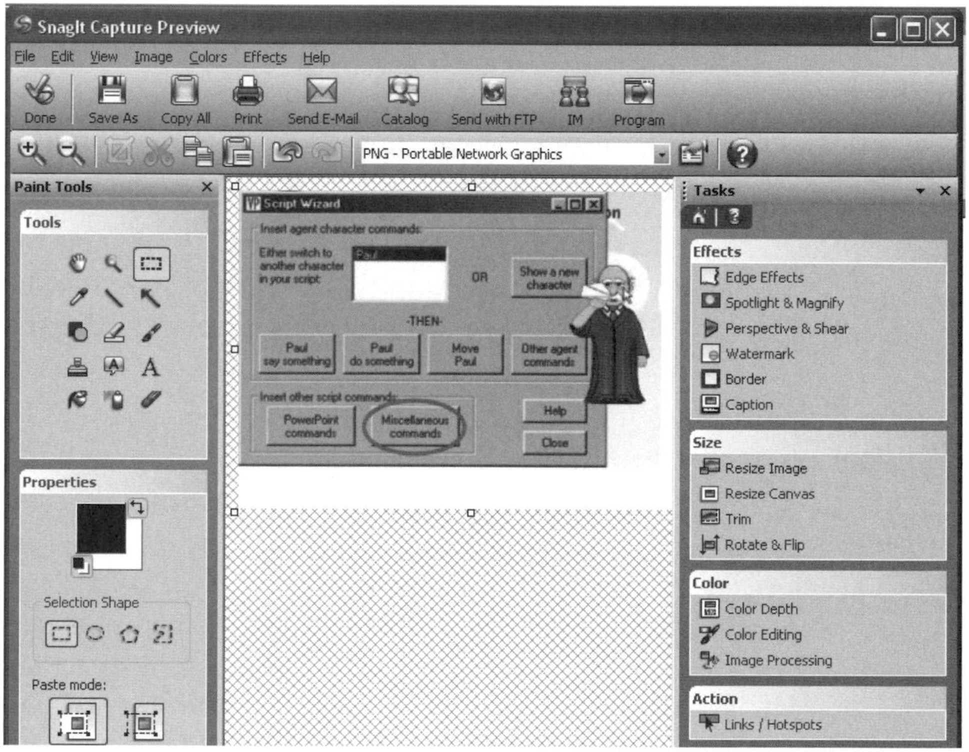

Source: www.techsmith.com

The SnagIt tools appear across the top and down the sides of the captured image. At the time this book goes to press, SnagIt sells for US $35. SnagIt additionally allows for recording of desktop animations, such as a simple narrated tutorial, although there are limitations on length of these captures and there are no editing capabilities. The tutorial for inserting movies in Chapter 9 uses a clip of an Excel tutorial captured with SnagIt.

For more extensive screen recording, TechSmith offers the Camtasia Studio. This allows for longer recordings and extensive editing capabilities. The Vox Proxy demo included on the CD was created with Camtasia.

The Template Issue

On one hand, I am not a fan of what tend to be known as "templates." They're beautiful, but most were developed as backgrounds for classroom or conference room presentations, not e-learning purposes. Figure 8.8 shows the problems that can come with presentation templates for e-learning: sidebars and other elements can eat up screen real estate and offer only decorative images, doing nothing to add to the instruction.

On the other hand, as discussed in Chapter 3, it's important to create a consistent look and feel for your program. Creating your own GUI is essentially designing your own "template" and, generally, your program will be enhanced by doing it yourself rather than by trying to fit your program into someone else's presentation template. For inspiration, though, do take a look at the thousands—really, thousands—of free PowerPoint templates available on the Web. Search www.google.com for "free PowerPoint templates" and their close relation, "PowerPoint backgrounds." Two good sources of these are Geetesh Bajaj's www.indezine.com site and the Microsoft site www.brainybetty.com.

Figure 8.8. Template Elements Take Up Nearly Half the Slide Space

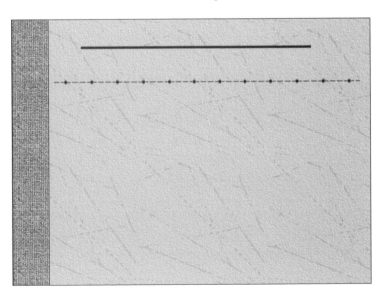

MS Producer

A free add-on available from Microsoft to those with a licensed copy of PowerPoint, Producer allows for easy synchronization of PowerPoint slide shows with other media elements. Although it has good capabilities and was widely touted as a way of developing "media-rich" presentations, in reality it has more often been used to deploy lengthy presentations of talking-head video clips accompanied by verbatim written transcripts. While there were no technical problems with the tool, it has not been widely embraced, and is just going away. It is not available for Power-Point 2007.

Other Add-Ons

A search of www.google.com for "PowerPoint add-ons" will give you an idea of the array of products available. Apart from sites offering templates, there are many resources for timers, video clips, music clips, and sound effects. You'll also find designers able to help you bring complicated ideas to life and, perhaps more than anything else, will find new ideas and approaches.

"Blending"

While "e-learning" is often used synonymously with "asynchronous" or "standalone," it can also be used in conjunction with other methods—particularly on the job and in the virtual or traditional classroom—for a more robust instructional experience. The virtual classroom provides an excellent bridge between the standalone and traditional classroom worlds; products such as WebEx (www.webex.com) and Elluminate (www.elluminate.com) provide extensive functionality for learners to participate via verbal discussion, written chat, whiteboarding, group activities, and even in private group breakout rooms. If you have not yet had experience with interactive synchronous training (this is distinct from "webinars," in which participants just listen to an online presenter), Jennifer Hofmann of Insync Training offers free weekly orientation sessions. Visit her at www.insynctraining.com.

While I would argue that there is nothing that happens in a classroom that cannot be replicated online, particularly in the age of robust virtual classroom products, many instructors and learners still want some "face time" for skill practice, role play, and group discussion activities. Should you want to blend your PowerPoint-based e-learning programs with traditional classroom activities, take a look at the best qualities of both approaches. Use the "live" classroom for social tasks that are difficult (but, again, not impossible) to re-create online.

"Blending" means more than just classroom activities, however. Pre- and post-reading assignments can supplement the e-learning program and sometimes make more sense than trying to adapt the material to screens of content. (As noted earlier: If your e-learning program can be printed out as a Word document, then it should be.) Additional opportunities for "blending" your e-learning programs include add-on collaborative experiences through the use of wikis, blogs, and discussion boards. Email also provides opportunities for learner interaction via team assignments and relay games.

Performance Support, Job Aids, and the Nice to Know

An increasingly important distinction for trainers and instructional designers is clarifying the difference between the learner having to *memorize* information versus having to *find* it. A great deal of training time (and money) is spent on providing learners with information they don't need to commit to memory. Performance of one-time procedures, rarely used skills, and multi-step processes can often be enhanced and eased by the use of job aids. This chapter offers some ideas for providing aids outside of a "training" situation.

There are also some challenges in dealing with "nice-to-know" rather than "must-know" information. This is often lost through the culling and distilling process necessary in creating on-target e-learning programs. This chapter also includes some ideas for PowerPoint-based reference and "background" tools.

> "You can memorize your way out of a labyrinth if it is simple enough and you have the time and urge to escape . . . but the learning is of no use for the next time when the exit will be differently placed."
>
> **David Hawkins**

One-Time Tasks

Figure 8.9 shows an example of a screen from a new hire orientation program. Learners are provided with blank forms as animated help notes pop up to walk them through instructions of filling out each one.

Figure 8.9. Animated Help Notes Walk Learners Through Filling Out Form

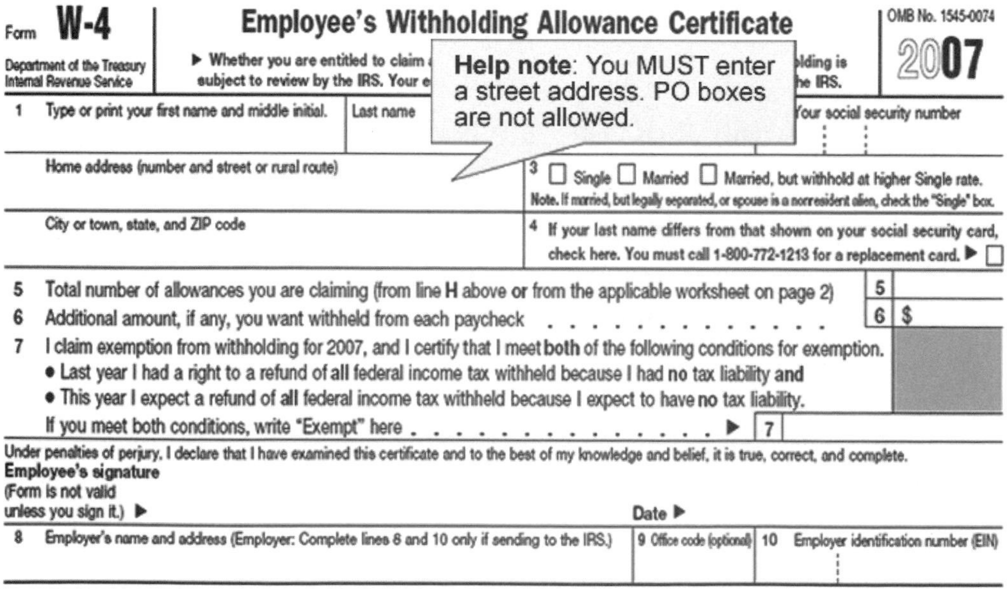

Form **W-4**
Department of the Treasury
Internal Revenue Service

Employee's Withholding Allowance Certificate

▶ Whether you are entitled to claim … subject to review by the IRS. Your e… …lding is …he IRS.

OMB No. 1545-0074
2007

Help note: You MUST enter a street address. PO boxes are not allowed.

1 Type or print your first name and middle initial. | Last name | Your social security number

Home address (number and street or rural route)

3 ☐ Single ☐ Married ☐ Married, but withhold at higher Single rate.
Note. If married, but legally separated, or spouse is a nonresident alien, check the "Single" box.

City or town, state, and ZIP code

4 If your last name differs from that shown on your social security card, check here. You must call 1-800-772-1213 for a replacement card. ▶ ☐

5 Total number of allowances you are claiming (from line **H** above **or** from the applicable worksheet on page 2) 5
6 Additional amount, if any, you want withheld from each paycheck . . . . 6 $
7 I claim exemption from withholding for 2007, and I certify that I meet **both** of the following conditions for exemption.
• Last year I had a right to a refund of **all** federal income tax withheld because I had **no** tax liability **and**
• This year I expect a refund of **all** federal income tax withheld because I expect to have **no** tax liability.
If you meet both conditions, write "Exempt" here . . . . ▶ 7

Under penalties of perjury, I declare that I have examined this certificate and to the best of my knowledge and belief, it is true, correct, and complete.
Employee's signature
(Form is not valid unless you sign it.) ▶
Date ▶

8 Employer's name and address (Employer: Complete lines 8 and 10 only if sending to the IRS.) | 9 Office code (optional) | 10 Employer identification number (EIN)

Sometime Tasks/Reference

Figure 8.10 shows an interactive table of the elements. This offers a quick overview of the chart, with user options for delving more deeply. Each item is covered with a separate transparent rectangle set to hyperlink to the corresponding explanatory slide. The explanatory slides, in turn, provide hyperlinks to external websites offering still more detail. The full program can be accessed at http://www.internet4classrooms. com/periodic_table.ppt.

Figure 8.10. Interactive Periodic Table of the Elements

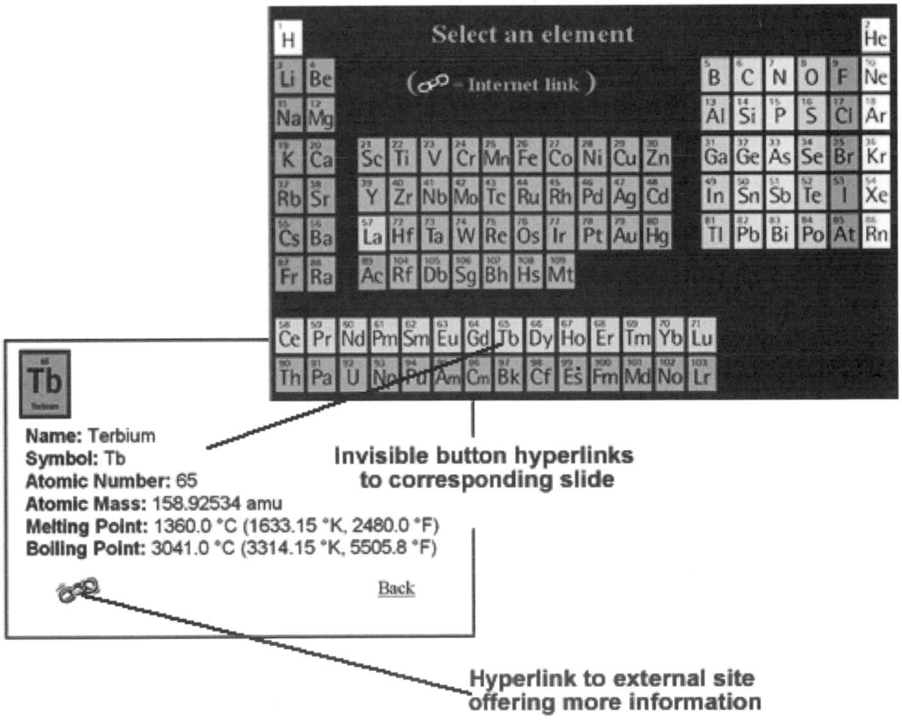

Thanks to Bill Byles

In developing job aids, consider: Where is there a great deal of rework? Where do the most questions arise, or the most mistakes occur? What's the "Hey, Joe" factor: Why do people stick their heads out into the hallway and call out "Hey, Joe! Can you show me how to. . ." "Can you tell me again about. . .?" "I don't remember how this. . . "? If you're transforming an existing classroom course to an online format, what information would work better as support tool than "presentation"? And what information is nice to know, but not critical to performance, and might better reside outside of training?

Figure 8.11 shows a screen from animated, narrated tutorials provided to employees when the company's new phone system was installed. It gives phone users access to quick help for operations they may perform only occasionally. Figures 8.12 through 8.15 show other tutorials for employees in a new hire program.

Figure 8.11. Telephone Tutorial

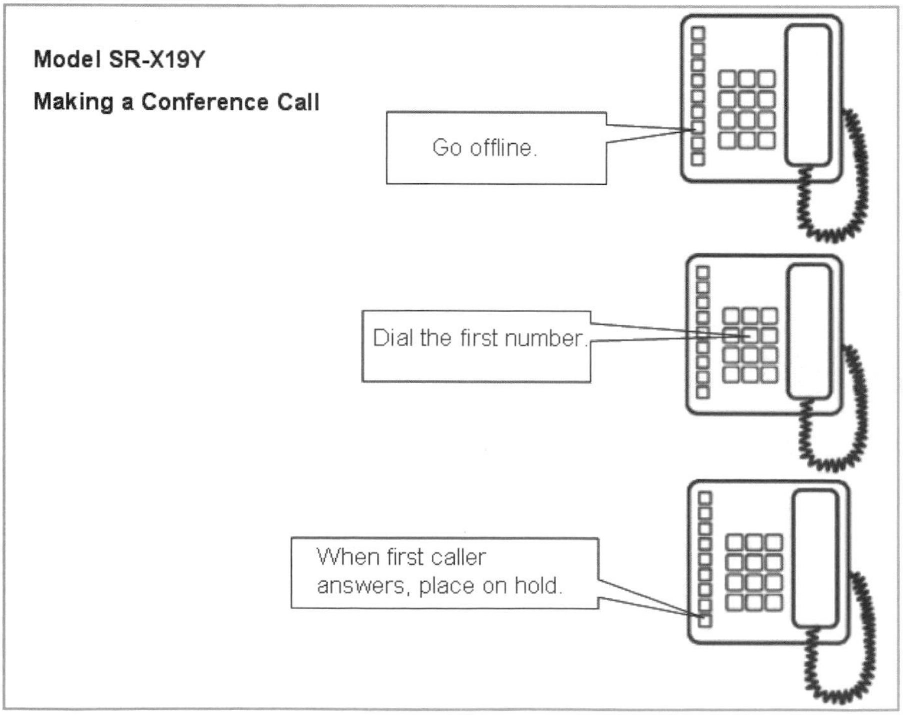

Model SR-X19Y

Making a Conference Call

Go offline.

Dial the first number.

When first caller answers, place on hold.

Figure 8.12. Interactive Map

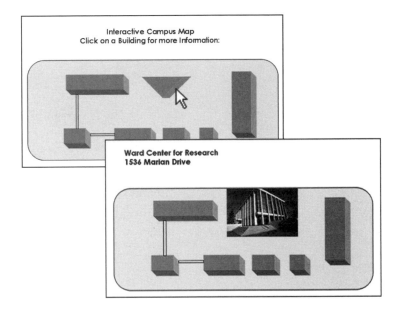

Figure 8.13. Company History

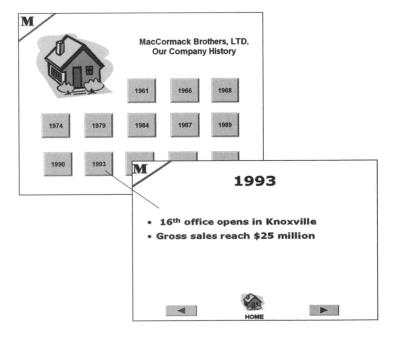

Figure 8.14. Organization Chart

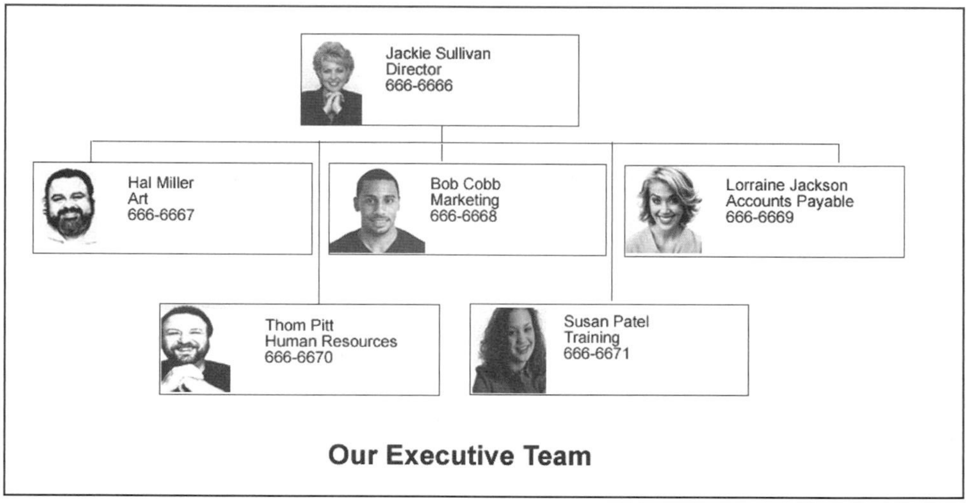

Jackie Sullivan
Director
666-6666

Hal Miller
Art
666-6667

Bob Cobb
Marketing
666-6668

Lorraine Jackson
Accounts Payable
666-6669

Thom Pitt
Human Resources
666-6670

Susan Patel
Training
666-6671

Our Executive Team

Figure 8.15. From PowerPoint-Based New Hire Orientation Program

Prompters of Process

PowerPoint's drawing tools can make it easy to create diagrams of processes. The template in Figure 8.16 could be used as either an online product or as a printable document.

Figure 8.16. Process Map Created with PowerPoint Art Tools

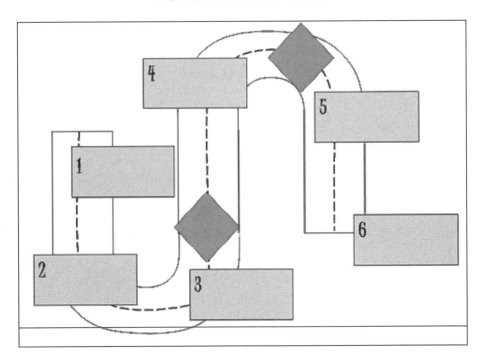

One challenge with job aids is making sure they're accessible: learners have to be able to find them. Figure 8.17 shows a desktop setup for a new hire's first day. The "Help" section contains quick tutorials on using office equipment, an interactive company map, and links to policies, forms, and other documents.

Figure 8.17. New Hire's First Day

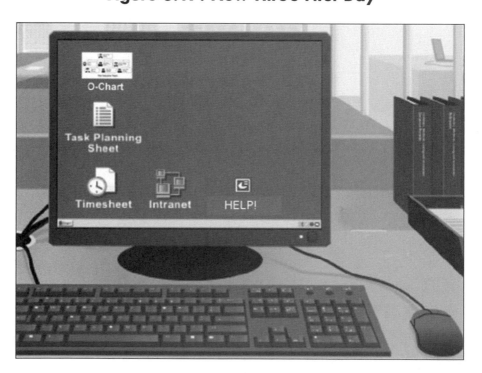

Summary

The idea of creating e-learning with PowerPoint isn't necessarily confined to PowerPoint slides. Linking to external sites and documents, blending the e-learning course with live classroom events, and involving learners in online collaborative activities can all shore up the effectiveness and extend the reach of your e-learning program. Good job aids can help link training—e-learning, classroom, or otherwise—back to on-the-job performance. The thoughtful use of an animated character can add appeal and a "human" touch as well.

The next chapter brings us to the final stage in e-learning program development: adding narration and multimedia elements.

Adding Narration and Multimedia

The last step in development of your e-learning program is adding narration and sound effects. Waiting until other development is completed will save time and effort, and perhaps money, as narration will only have to be recorded once. This chapter covers ways of adding narration and other multimedia, such as sound effects, video, and Flash objects, to your PowerPoint-based e-learning program.

 See the CD for tutorials on adding narration, sounds, and video.

Adding Narration

By far the bulk of the "What do you think?" calls I receive are on the issue of narrating PowerPoint. Most often the calls come because some-one has discovered a software product that he or she believes will "let" him or her add narration. This capability is already built in to Power-Point, and is a simple three-click ("Slide Show—Record Narration—ok") proposition. I am providing some detailed directions here, as the prospect of adding narration seems so daunting for many PowerPoint users. (And I can't help but wonder whether the salespeople for some of these other products are making narration sound complicated and tricky.) Recording narration really is a very user-friendly process and is certainly easier than having to install and learn to use an external product.

> **Remember** Mayer's findings on the split attention principle: Learning is enhanced when audio is not just a word-for-word repeat of onscreen text. This causes cognitive overload, as the audio and written material compete with each other for the learner's attention.

Microphones

While many computers now come with built-in microphones ("mics"), they tend to be of low audio quality and cannot be positioned. External computer mics can be purchased at computer supply and electronics stores and range in price from US $5 to hundreds of dollars. While I have an assortment of mics, several of them quite expensive, I get the best results from a $20 tabletop version I picked up at an office-supply store.

Narrator

Voice quality matters to program credibility and the learner's willingness to listen. If you are working with learners in different parts of the world, be sure to use the voices that learners will find most relevant to their day-to-day work settings. Your audience's needs are important here, even if it means recording English narration separately with British, Australian, and American voices. Also, it's worth the effort to find a narrator with a clear, pleasing voice. Check the phone book for local acting or broadcasting schools or talent agencies. I am fortunate to have a co-worker, a former radio station disc jockey, who happily lends us his "golden tones" from time to time. Provide your narrator with a legible script, and try to reduce the number of pages you ask him or her to handle at one time, as mics will pick up the rattling of pages.

Lesson Learned

Before bringing in the narrator, read the text aloud yourself. You will likely be surprised at how wordy your script sounds and how long the script takes to read. Go back and edit—ruthlessly—before recording.

Location

While you can spend plenty of money on building or renting a sound-proof recording room, in truth you can probably get by with any space in which you can reduce echoes and outside noise. A small closet or storage room with walls lined with carpet remnants will do just fine, and failing that, a closet filled with clothes can make a passable "studio." Be sure to close windows and remove anything that creates ambient noise, such as printers, and cut off air conditioning units. You may also need to place the computer itself outside of the recording space so the mic doesn't pick up the sound of the computer fan running. If you're using a makeshift studio, like a home closet, be sure to provide your narrator with a lamp.

"The *personalization effect* is that students learn more deeply from a multimedia explanation when the words are presented in conversational style rather than formal style."

Richard Mayer, *The Promise of Multimedia Learning*

Recording Voice: Step by Step

You can, if you want, record one long continuous voice file. You'll likely find, though, that it creates a single enormous file that will be difficult to edit. PowerPoint will let you add narration to each slide, then let you save these audio clips as separate files associated with the corresponding slide.

 As I mentioned earlier in this chapter, there is a "narration" tutorial on the CD accompanying this book, but as this seems to be a task of particular interest, I am also providing step-by-step instructions here, shown in Figures 9.1 through 9.5.

Note: If you are starting on a slide subsequent to the first one, you'll be presented with the choice seen in Figure 9.5.

Figure 9.1. Click "Slide Show—Record Narration"

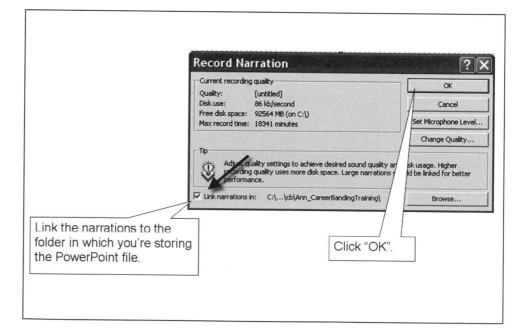

Figure 9.2. Set the Microphone Level

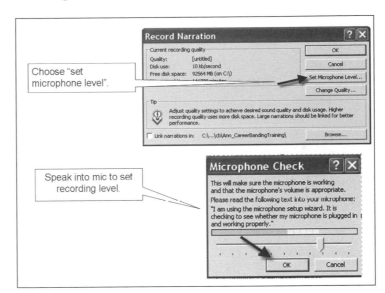

Figure 9.3. Set the Recording Quality

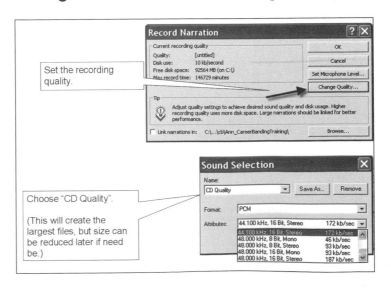

Figure 9.4. Link Narrations in Folder

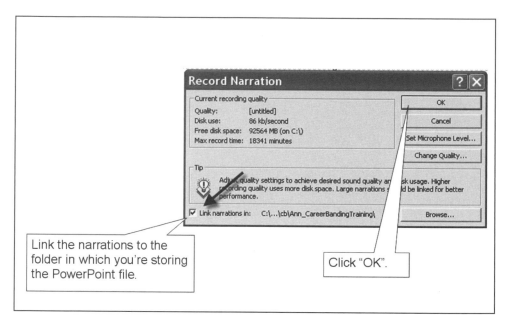

Link the narrations to the folder in which you're storing the PowerPoint file.

Click "OK".

Figure 9.5. Choice of Starting Place May Appear

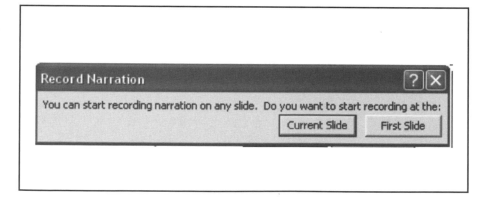

The program you're narrating will now open as a slide show. Simply begin speaking, using the arrow keys to advance from slide to slide. Your narration will be saved as separate files associated with each slide. Use the "Esc" key to end recording. *Note:* You must advance to the next screen in order for audio to be saved on the current screen. So even if you are finished recording, always advance one more screen before exiting the program.

Editing Sound

You may not know that your computer came with a sound editing tool, Microsoft (MS) Sound Recorder. (Click "Start—Programs—Accessories—Entertainment—Sound Recorder.") While you can record all your narration with this product, you'll then have to go back and match clips to slides. It will be less cumbersome to record directly into PowerPoint, then use MS Sound Recorder to edit any clips that need additional tweaking. You may, for instance, need to cut out the sound of the narrator clearing her throat at the beginning of a clip or add a pause at the end of a clip. There are a number of commercial software programs available for more sophisticated editing tasks, but you may find that MS Sound Recorder is all you need. Figures 9.6 through 9.8 show an example of editing a sound file; in this case, the designer wishes to edit out a long pause before the narrator begins speaking.

 A tutorial for editing this clip is included on the CD.

Figure 9.6. Open Sound Recorder, Then Browse for Audio File

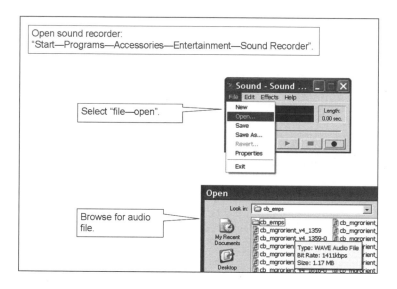

Figure 9.7. "Edit" Allows You to Eliminate Parts of a Clip

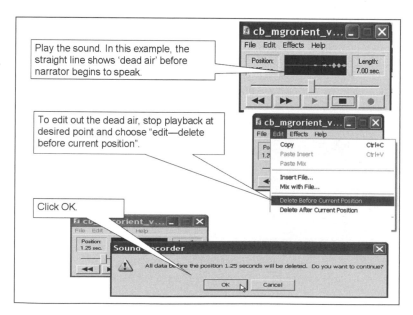

Figure 9.8. Save Edited File

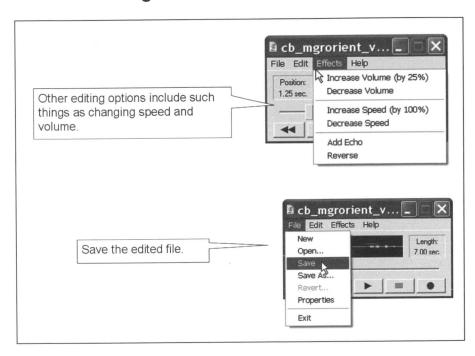

Other editing options include such things as changing speed and volume.

Save the edited file.

Adding Sound Effects and Music

Slide 9.9 (from the "challenging caller" simulation first shown in Chapter 7) has two sound effects. When the slide loads, learners hear a ringing phone, then are asked to click on that phone to hear comments from an angry caller. The ringing phone sound effect was downloaded from an online clip art service and saved in my files. It was inserted via the command "Insert—Movies and Sounds" and is set to play when the slide loads. The angry caller's voice was recorded in PowerPoint, then edited and saved with MS Sound Recorder. To play the voice clip, an action setting was assigned to the photo of the phone: when the learner clicks on the photo, the voice clip will play. Figures 9.9 through 9.14 provid an overview of creating the slide.

 A working example and instructions for creating this "angry example are included on the CD.

Figure 9.9. Slide Contains Two Sounds: Ringing Phone and Caller's Voice

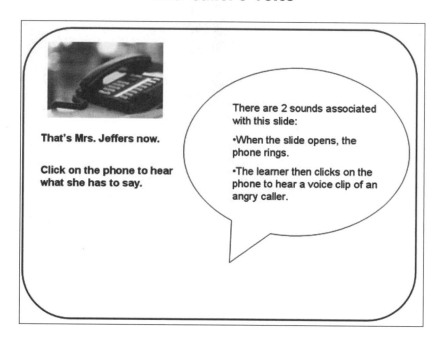

Figure 9.10. Insert Ringing Phone Sound from Clip Art Gallery

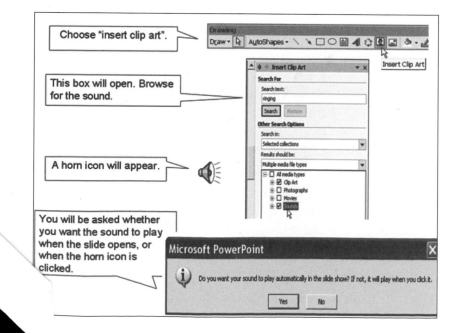

Let's look first at how to create the ringing phone. It's inserted ("Insert—Movies and Sounds") from the file where I saved it, in this case my own clip art gallery. Note that once the sound is inserted, a small horn icon will appear on the screen. This can be resized, as shown in Figure 9.11. I can also click on it and drag it to another part of the screen. If I don't want this icon to show, I usually just put a small rectangle, the same color as the screen, over it.

Note: Don't place the horn icon under a navigation button or other image on which users will click, as it may cause the sound to play again.

Figure 9.11. Horn Icon Can Be Moved and Resized

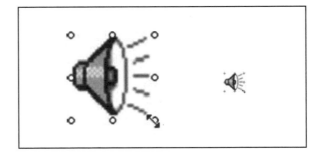

For additional playback options right-click on the horn icon and choose "Custom Animation—Effect Options," as seen in Figure 9.12.

The "Play Sound" dialog box will open. Clicking the "Timing" tab at the top of this box allows for more options, shown in Figure 9.13. In this case we've set the phone to ring three times.

Figure 9.12. More Options in Custom Animations

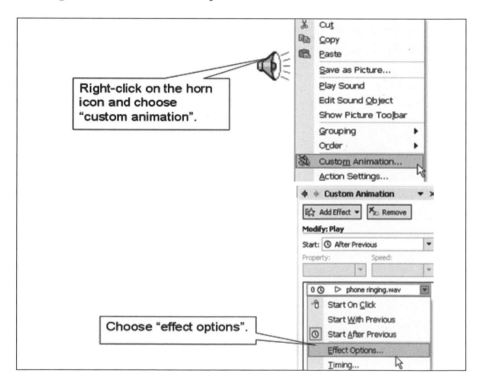

Figure 9.13. Setting Additional Sound Properties

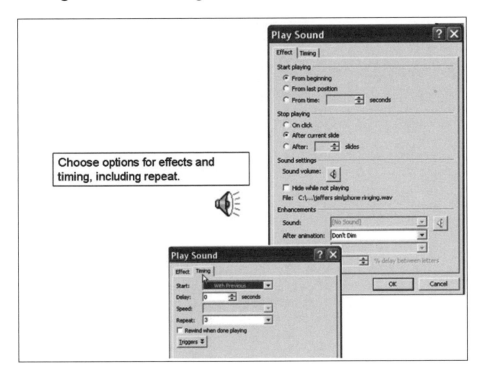

Open the slide in slide show mode to hear the sound play back as you've set it.

Now let's look at the second sound, the voice clip from the angry caller, Mrs. Jeffers, which was recorded in PowerPoint. This sound is learner-activated, so we need to select the photo of the phone and give it an action setting ("Slide Show—Action Settings"). Choose "Mouse Click" and browse for the voice clip, as shown in Figure 9.14.

Figure 9.14. Set Audio Clip to Play When Phone Is Clicked

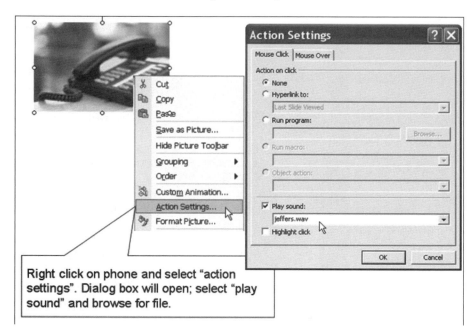

Right click on phone and select "action settings". Dialog box will open; select "play sound" and browse for file.

Open the slide in Slide Show mode. The phone will ring three times. Click on it to hear the customer's voice.

Recording Sounds—Another Option

As with the "Slide Show—Record Narration" function, PowerPoint also provides a tool for recording sound effects. You can access this via "Insert—Record Sound," but MS Sound Recorder included with Windows is a more robust tool, with editing capabilities, so you might prefer to record sound effects using Sound Recorder in the first place.

Figure 9.15 shows how to access the "record sound" tool.

Figure 9.15. Accessing the "Record Sound" Tool

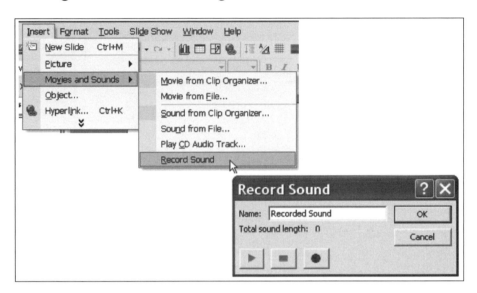

Adding Music

The process for inserting music is the same as with any other sound: "Insert—Movies and Sounds—Sound From File." The trick is in finding or converting music to the *.wav* file format, which is what PowerPoint recognizes. It is possible to find music clips, particularly short (ten seconds or so) ones, in clip art galleries. Most music comes in the *MP3* format. If you want to add music from a CD, you'll likely need to convert it from MP3.

You can find free or low-cost converter software for this: go to www. google.com and search for "convert MP3 to wav" and see what comes up on the first couple of pages. Music from Apple's iTunes requires a special converter, also available online. (See the next text box for comments about copyright!) Once you have the material in a .wav file, save it in the folder where you're storing your program materials. Then click "Insert— Movies and Sounds—Sound From File" and browse for your .wav music file. As with sound effects, you can choose when the sound will play and

Figure 9.16. Playing Music Across Multiple Slides

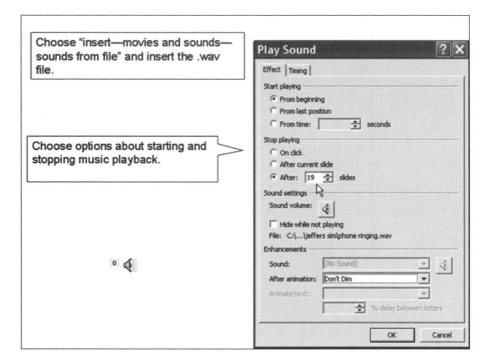

whether it will repeat. When you insert the file, a moveable, resizable horn icon will appear on the slide. To play music continuously across your program, right-click on the horn icon and choose "Custom Animation." Use the Effects Options tool to choose the number of slides across which you want the music to play, as shown in Figure 9.16.

Copyright

When using music and sounds in your program, be sure you have copyright clearance before using any audio files intended for "public performance," including e-learning as well as classroom applications. Even music and sound effects offered online as "royalty free" still come at a fee for use, just not on a per-play basis, as is the case with, for instance, songs played by radio stations. Write the copyright holder for permission to use music, or subscribe to one of the many online clip art services that also offer music files.

Adding Video

Adding video to PowerPoint is really quite easy and can be a very effective way of, for instance, adding a welcome from your CEO or commentary from a subject-matter expert, showing an overview of the workings of a piece of machinery, or incorporating video material created in another program, such as an Excel tutorial captured with Camtasia or SnagIt.

 See the CD for instructions on adding video; these use an example from an Excel tutorial.

Adding video is done in the same way as inserting any other medial element: choose "Insert—Sounds and Movies," then browse for the video clip. Digital video files come in a number of formats, such as AVI, QuickTime, and MPEG, and have file extensions like .avi, .mov, .qt, and .mpg. As with other effects, you have several options for playing the file: automatically when the slide opens; when clicked with the mouse; or by setting a timer so that it plays after a delay.

Another alternative is to set the video to play through the Windows Media Player, which will provide the learner with playback and volume controls. The process for this is shown in Figures 9.17 through 9.20, and a last option, converting the video to a Flash (.swf) file and inserting it as a Flash object, is shown in Figures 9.24 through 9.27.

However, due to the large file size associated with most video clips and the fact that some converter tools (see Chapter 10) can't handle video conversion, another **and possibly best** alternative is to insert a hyperlink to your video clip so that it isn't packaged within the PowerPoint file. You may find this gives better playback results as well as reduces file size. Test before launching and see which approach seems better for your program.

Figure 9.17. "Insert Object—Windows Media Player"

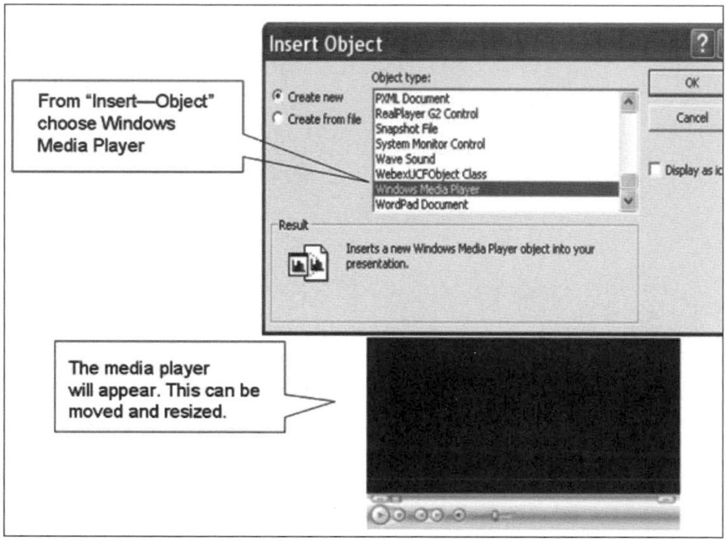

Figure 9.18. Open the Properties Panel

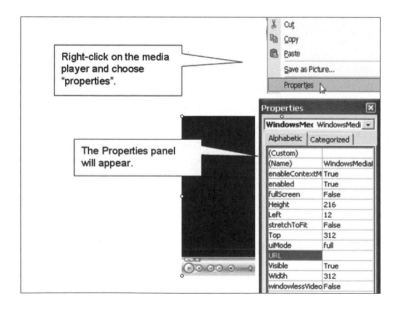

Figure 9.19. Choose "Custom" and Browse for the File

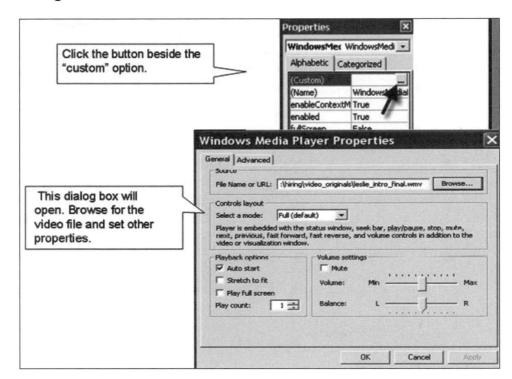

If you choose this option, the video clip will appear inside the Windows Media Player; learners can start and stop the video and adjust the volume using the player's controls. Both the player and the video clip can be resized and repositioned, as shown in Figure 9.20.

Figure 9.20. Video Clip in Context

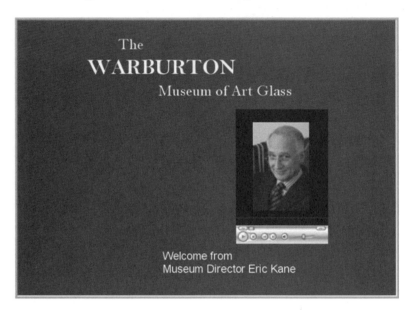

An Aside: Do You Really Need Video?

One of the most expensive undertakings related to e-learning is developing, recording, and editing custom video. This has improved with the availability of inexpensive digital video cameras and editing software like the free MS Windows Movie Maker. (Windows users with Service Pack 2 have this; if you didn't know it, check "Start—Programs" and look for "Windows Movie Maker" to see whether it's there.) Even if you don't have to rent equipment or hire professional actors, creating custom video can be a very time-consuming undertaking. As with animation, consider: What will the video add that still photos will not? Will the motion somehow provide instruction? Several excellent programs already mentioned in this book, shown again in Figures 9.21 through 9.23, use photos rather than video without affecting the integrity or effectiveness of the instruction.

Figure 9.21. "Nail Care"

Read care plan and consult with resident.

Previous   Next

Figure 9.22. "Gamekeeper's Conundrum

Source: Royal Veterinary College

Figure 9.23. Workplace Harassment

Source: www.Brightline Compliance

Adding Flash Objects

Flash software, from Adobe, is used for creating higher-end or custom animations beyond the reach of PowerPoint. As Flash files (these have .swf extensions) tend to be smaller than other multimedia files, I often also convert video and other media files to Flash. It's just a matter of opening the Flash software, opening the video file, and saving it as a Flash file. Flash objects are inserted via the Control Toolbox found under "View—Toolbars." Before you begin, make sure your .swf file is stored in the same folder as your PowerPoint show. Some basic directions are shown in Figures 9.24 through 9.27.

Figure 9.24. Insert Flash Object

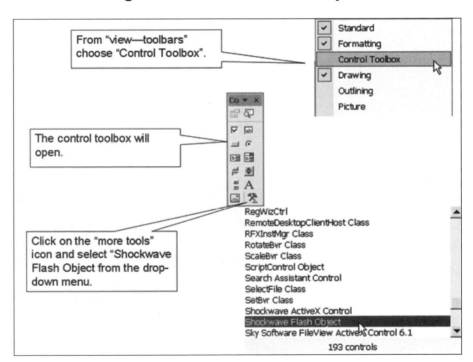

Figure 9.25. Draw Rectangle; Right-Click for "Properties"

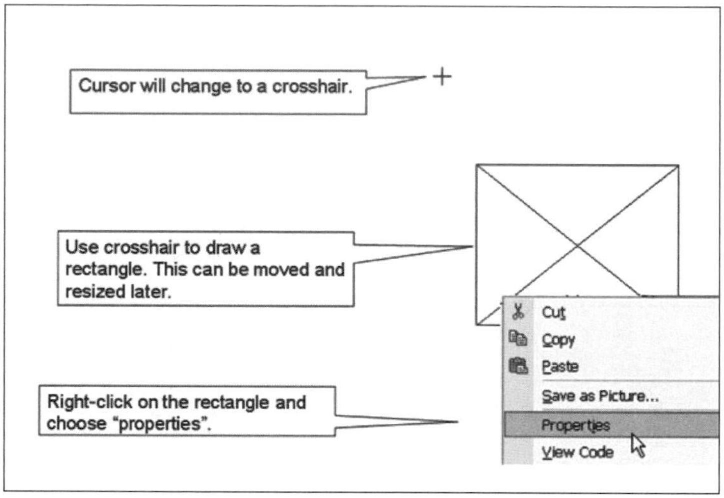

Cursor will change to a crosshair.

Use crosshair to draw a rectangle. This can be moved and resized later.

Right-click on the rectangle and choose "properties".

Cut
Copy
Paste
Save as Picture...
Properties
View Code

Figure 9.26. Type in the Name of the Flash file, Including the .swf Extension

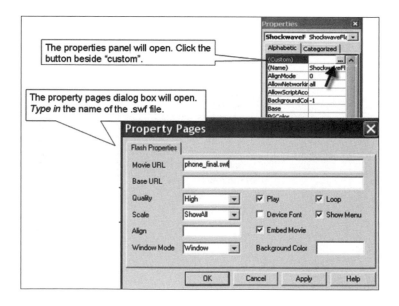

Figure 9.27. Flash Object in Context

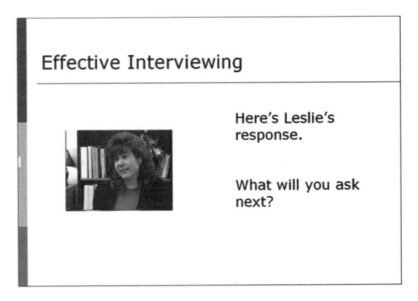

As you can see from the figures, you can resize and reposition the rectangle. The file will play when you open the program in Slide Show mode.

Summary

Well-considered narration and other multimedia effects can greatly enhance your PowerPoint-based e-learning program. Adding this material is the last stage in program development. Chapter 10 explores the end result of all your work: saving the final program and uploading it to the Internet for delivery to your learners.

Delivery and Support

Distributing Your e-Learning Programs

The final step in creating e-learning with PowerPoint is to put it on the Web. You may be working with your own internal information technology staff for this; if so, they will likely provide server space on which you can store your files and may be willing to do the file upload for you. Or, your IT department may assign you space on your organization's server so you can upload the files yourself. You'll need free FTP (File Transfer Protocol) software for this. Uploading is as simple as dragging and dropping files from your computer onto the server; just be sure to upload everything associated with the PowerPoint show, including audio clips and any external documents, such as printable handouts. What and how you upload may depend partly on how you choose to save the file. See the following for more information.

You may already have invested in a learning management system (LMS) on which to host your programs. That product will offer specific guidance in how to upload materials and in what format they should be saved.

Or you may have neither internal IT support nor an LMS and will need to acquire your own hosting services. You will be loading your programs onto a server hosted by an external company, so will need the free FTP software mentioned above. If you're new to this kind of technology, go with a provider who will help you start. Many now offer very user-friendly interfaces and tutorials. Also, before choosing a plan, gain an understanding of what you want to deliver and how many users you are likely to have. Large files with audio and video clips will require a good deal of server space, so you will need to think about how much storage space you'll need.

The other big issue is data transfer ("bandwidth"). This is the amount of data that is transferred from your account as learners access your e-learning programs. It's important that you have enough of both storage space and data transfer capability, so this is one time I recommend overbuying. Good news: hosting is increasingly inexpensive. As this book goes to press, a hosted site with 15 gigabytes of storage space, and 300 gigabytes of data transfer per month, is offered by several vendors for only US $14.95 per month. Apart from cost, when choosing a hosting service check references to find out about the company's quality. Ask around, for instance, about the frequency and duration of service outages and availability and competence of live help.

About Bandwidth

There is no such thing as "unlimited" bandwidth. Some hosting companies make this promise with the (realistic) assumption that most websites will never use all that much. Running e-learning programs is an entirely different matter and something your host may not have considered.

Saving and Uploading Your Files

As I've previously mentioned, there are four ways to save your PowerPoint-based e-learning program for distribution on the Web:

1. Upload as is

2. Save as a PowerPoint show

3. Save as a Web page

4. Convert it to a Flash (.swf) file

1. Upload It as Is

You can just save the file with the usual .ppt extension. Learners will see a pop-up box that looks like the one in Figure 10.1.

Figure 10.1. Pop-Up Box Appears

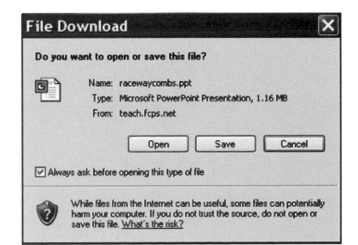

2. Save It as a PowerPoint Show (.pps)

The file will open as a full-screen PowerPoint show that learners can open or save to their own computers. Learners will see a pop-up box that looks like the one in Figure 10.2.

Note with both the examples that learners may be frightened off by the warning accompanying the pop-up box. You may want to send a preparatory email or otherwise communicate that the file is safe and they should open or save it.

Figure 10.2. Pop-Up Box Appears

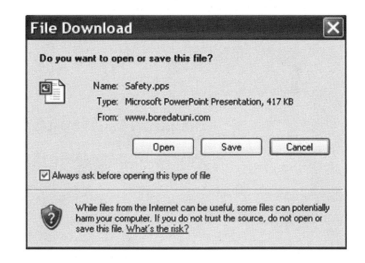

3. Save It as a Web Page (html)

The program will display in frames, with an outline view of slides to the left, as shown in Figure 10.3.

Figure 10.3. PowerPoint Show Saved as Web Page

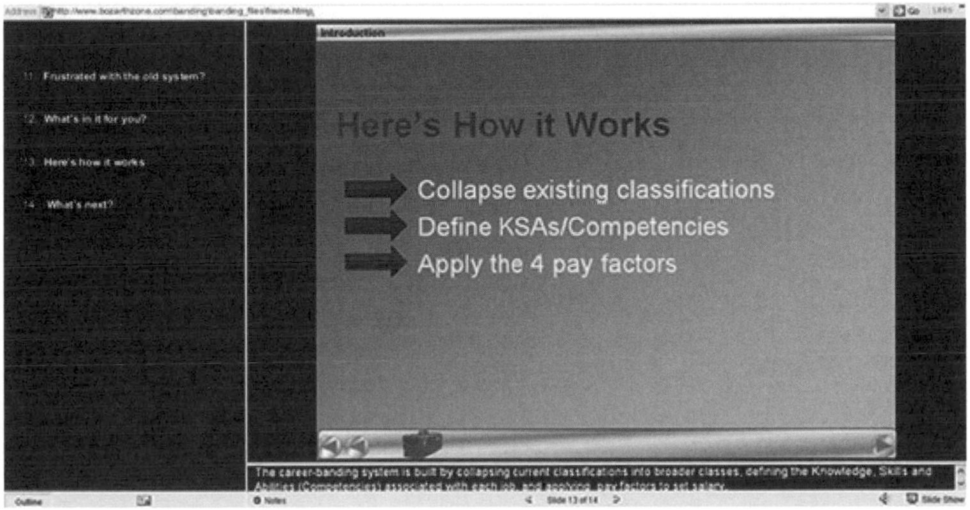

Saving as a Web page adds additional features and options, as shown in Figure 10.4, such as text notes below the slide, options for audio playback, and a slide counter.

Figure 10.4. Saving as Web Page Adds Items and Options

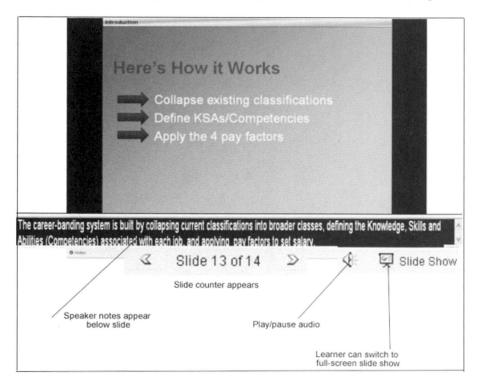

4. Convert It to a Flash (.swf) File

For most e-learning programs created with PowerPoint, this may be the best choice. Why? Because PowerPoint files, especially those with animation, narration, or music, are enormous. They can eat up bandwidth, and if saved with a .pps extension can take a long time to open, as the entire file must load before any screen is displayed. There are a number of low-cost (less than $500, and some less than $100) software programs that will convert the PowerPoint file to a smaller Flash file (which will have an .swf extension). Programs converted to Flash will stream more smoothly, take up less space on the server, and consume less bandwidth while running. Most converter tools create separate Flash files that load in sequence, allowing learners to access the beginning of the program before the end has even loaded. The Flash file will display properly on any screen, from large monitors to small handheld devices, and nowadays the free Flash player is nearly ubiquitous and already installed on most computers. And the products are usually very easy to use. (**Note:** You don't need to purchase or know how to use Flash software to use the converter tools. The converter tools only handle PowerPoint. However, you *will* need the Flash software, or access to it or a colleague willing to help you out, in order to do the conversion of video clips to Flash—.swf files—mentioned in Chapter 9.) Figures 10.5 through 10.10 show a conversion using the PowerConverter from www.presentationpro.com.

Figure 10.5. One-Click Button Opens the Converter

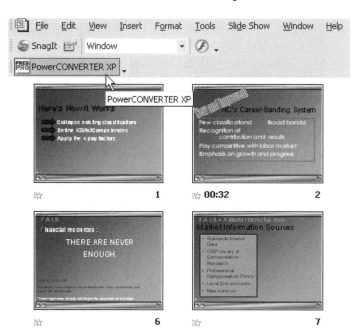

Figure 10.6. Choose Options for File Size, Image Quality, Etc.

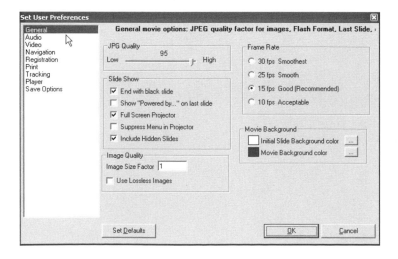

Figure 10.7. Choose Audio Compression and Playback Options

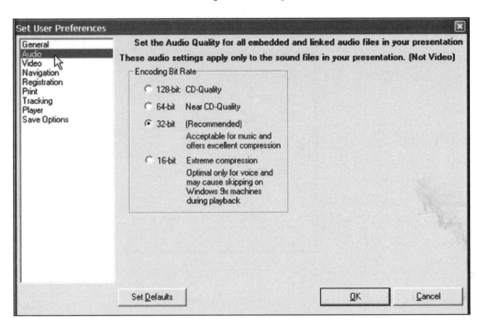

Figure 10.8. Choose Based on Typical Learner Connection Speed

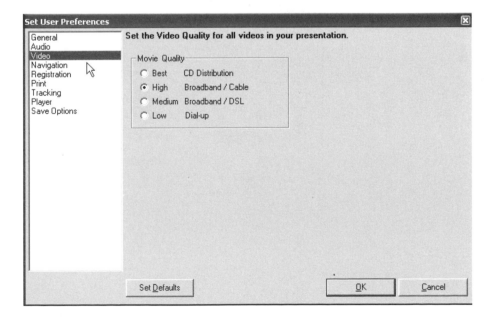

Figure 10.9. Convert to Flash

Figure 10.10. Save as Web File; Upload

Know your tool: While converter products are similar, each has its own quirks. Some animations are converted seamlessly by one and lost by another. Some converters automatically insert navigation buttons that can be difficult to override. Some inexplicably cost—and this is not an exaggeration—*one thousand percent* more than others—even though the functionality and quality are the same. (And remember: before you purchase anything, you need to be fluent with PowerPoint itself. Costs of converter tools are often run up by the addition of "features" that replicate something PowerPoint already does. See Choosing a Converter Tool: Some Advice on the following page.) Try demos and free trial periods to see the eccentricities of the tools you're considering, and go with the one that seems to do most of what you plan to for the most reasonable price. Some popular converter products include Presentation-Pro's Power Converter (www.presentationpro.com) and Impatica (www.impatica.com/). Companies such as www.articulate.com offer, by way of extending their converter tools, a suite of add-on products for building quizzes and tracking completion.

Lesson Learned

As you finalize and prepare to distribute your materials, be sure you are working with only one final copy of the program. Trying to edit multiple versions, or to keep up with different copies from different stakeholders or reviewers, will quickly prove cumbersome and create confusion.

Do It Yourself

While you can do the conversion from PowerPoint to Flash "by hand," it is a rather complicated affair and might be more than you want to take on. There are limits to the animations that will convert, and you will need to do a good deal of slide-by-slide manual labor on layers and shapes and inserting ActionScript. The directions for converting to Flash can be found in a Google search (try searching for "convert PowerPoint to Flash manually"), but really, if you are planning to create a lot of programs with PowerPoint, investing in a converter tool might be a better choice for you. If you don't already have the Flash software, you'll need to purchase it in order to do the conversion manually.

Choosing a Converter Tool: Some Advice

A converter tool will compress your PowerPoint files and make them easier to stream and push out to your learners and easy for your learners to access. They're great and I highly recommend using one.

And now about the hype: There are many PowerPoint-to-Flash converter tools out there, most of them just fine, and most backed by ad copywriters, a team of graphic and instructional designers, a big budget for gorgeous samples and demos, and a sales force in need of commissions. Sales pitches promise that "anyone" can (choose one) *effortlessly/ quickly/easily/rapidly* develop (choose one) *engaging/interactive/compelling* e-learning. True, some tools make some tasks easier. But there is no software into which you can input a big pile of text, or a bad PowerPoint show, and see it magically transformed into engaging, interactive, effective e-learning! Someone, somewhere, still has to create the instruction itself. Someone has to clarify objectives, select strategies, choose a treatment, create the decision tree for simulations, and craft good quiz questions. *No product will do that for you.*

In making a purchasing decision, beware of the seductive capacity of "featureitis." Many sales approaches tout features that PowerPoint already has: "Add narration and video!" "Provide a music soundtrack!" Or they push features that are of lower quality than the PowerPoint feature: "Phone in your narration!" Or they offer a $1,000 add-ons for a quiz feature that could be had via an external quiz engine for next to nothing (try www.quia.com, for instance, for $99/year). Or they're downright scary: "Your subject-matter experts can create their own courses!"

Be sure to buy what matters: How is the product's tech support? Does the price include upgrades? What animations don't survive conversion? How do multiple audio files (music, narration, sound effects) work on a single slide? Converters are great tools, but buy what you need.

Conversion is quite simple. Figures 10.5 through 10.10 were examples of conversion screens using the PowerConverter from PresentationPro.

Once PowerPoint converter tools do their work, content developers are able to use their authoring tools to begin building robust e-learning content through the addition of navigation, videos, graphics, audio files, interactive exercises, games, assessments, and links to resources.

A Recap

We've reviewed various ways to save your e-learning program and distribute it to your learners. Table 10.1 provides a summary of the pros and cons of different file types.

One More Option: Save as CD

While "e-learning" is most often defined as something delivered over the Internet, you do have the option of saving your programs to CD. You can save the files in several of the same ways you've seen them described for Web deployment (in their original form, as PowerPoint shows, or converted to Flash files). The advantages: file size will be far less a consideration, and bandwidth will not be an issue at all. The disadvantage, and it's a big one: if you need to make a change or update, you must locate and replace all the existing CDs.

Table 10.1. Pros and Cons of File Different File Types

Distribution Method	Advantages	Disadvantages
Save as PowerPoint file (.ppt)	Animations and events will upload intact	Very large files can cause download delays and consume bandwidth Learners must have compatible version of PowerPoint or the free PowerPoint viewer Learners can edit/alter the file Unreliable display in browsers other than Explorer
Save as Web page (html)	Easy to do Don't need to know html Files load separately, so download time is quicker Can be accessed via any browser Learner can resize display Speaker notes area can be used for delivering additional text Trigger effects will remain intact	Creates many files; hard to manage Most transitions and animations lost Audio and video, including narration, often lost Creates "messy," lengthy code Show appears in frames that may not display properly in all browsers
Save as PowerPoint show (.pps)	File will open in slide show mode Animations and trigger effects will work More tamperproof than saving as .ppt Program uploads as one file	Users need compatible version of PowerPoint or the free PowerPoint viewer Files size can be large Whole show loads at once, so download time may be slow

Distribution Method	Advantages	Disadvantages
Convert to .swf (Flash) Note: DOES NOT require purchase of Adobe Flash software	Smaller file Player is nearly ubiquitous Most animations, narrations, etc., will survive conversion Program will be tamperproof If using converter tool, ability to save as separate files greatly reduces download time Easy distribution on CD-ROM, if desired Those already using a learning management system (LMS) may have to upload in Flash format Depending on product used will be provided multiple output options: .swf file for Web upload, version for placing on CD, option for delivering by email, etc. Depending on product used, will automatically be programmed for SCORM compliance	Requires purchase of converter product (starts at about $300) or cumbersome by-hand conversion (and if by hand, also need to purchase Flash) Users need free Flash player All converters do not handle all animations and events: few, for instance, handle trigger animations

Content Libraries and Reusable Learning Objects

Be sure as you create material that you store it in ways that will help you retrieve and reuse it later. Images, video clips, narration clips, GUIs, storyboards, and screenshots are all items you might have use for at another time, either with a new program or an update to an existing one. If you have access to an LCMS (learning content

(continued)

management system), you most likely already have protocols and clear guidelines for doing this. See the note about SCORM and shareable objects. For those storing materials in "homemade" libraries, work to develop clear naming conventions and storage places, such as a shared file on your organization's intranet, so that materials can be located.

Tracking

"Tracking" is a hot-button word in e-learning. Where for years we've "tracked" participation by having learners sign attendance sheets, suddenly in the era of e-learning we feel we need so much more technology to accomplish this. You may already own a learning management system (LMS) to which you plan to link your PowerPoint-based e-learning program. If not (and this is especially important to those of you on tight budgets), consider: What are you really trying to track, and why, and what will you do with the data? Many sophisticated tracking systems produce ninety-six reports, and often none of them has exactly the information you need. Are you tracking for compliance? To protect yourself from lawsuits? Or because it's a habit? What do you really need to know?

- How many people accessed the course?

- Whether Jane accessed the course?

- Whether Jane started and finished the course?

- Whether Jane passed the test?

- Whether Jane. . . ?

- . . . .and so on

PowerPoint lends itself to several fairly easy solutions here. For instance, you can include a hyperlink to a completion form that the learner can save, forward, or print and submit to an administrator, as shown in Figure 10.11.

Figure 10.11. Printable Completion Form

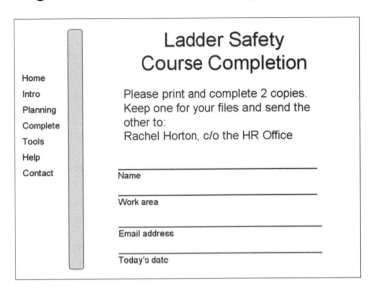

Figure 10.12. Completion Set to Auto-Email

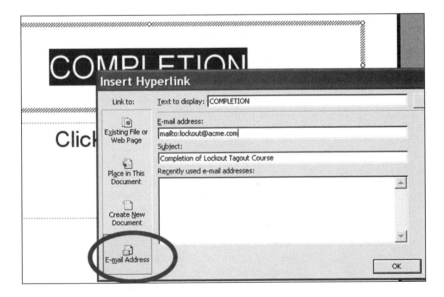

You can include an email link to an administrator or to a separate mailbox set up for completions by topic. An example is shown in Figure 10.12.

Or you can link to a hosted online form or a final exam using a tool available from an online survey or quiz engine like www.Surveymonkey. com or www.Quia.com, which can offer reporting functions similar to that of an LMS.

What Is SCORM and Should I Care About It?

SCORM is a term uniquely associated with e-learning and stands for "Shareable Content Object Reference Model." It establishes standards for "interoperability," that is, standards such that different components and products can "talk" to each other. In practice it's most often used to ensure that different elements of e-learning programs or programs from assorted sources (for instance, it's not unusual for an organization to have some programs developed in-house as well as some purchased from commercial vendors) will all run on any LMS (if the organization has one). A common metaphor associated with SCORM is that of the household electrical outlet: my coffeemaker and my waffle iron both have similar plugs that fit into the wall receptacle. A "shareable content object" can be a single item, such as an image or a quiz, a module from an online training program, or an entire online training program.

SCORM is especially important if you plan to run your PowerPoint-based e-learning program on an LMS (learning management system). There are many other ways to track learner data (see above), and items like job aids and performance support tools, because they don't need to be tracked, don't need to be associated with an LMS either. Even if you want your program associated with the LMS, you can just use hyperlinking for that. For instance, use the PowerPoint program as is, but link to a quiz or completion form that's handled by the LMS. SCORM requires use of a programming language called Javascript to communicate with the LMS. If you feel you need to make your PowerPoint-based e-learning programs SCORM compliant, you can use a PowerPoint-to-Flash converter tool that automatically handles the SCORM compatibility (such as Articulate Presenter) or find a programmer who can help you with inserting the code (it's included on the CD thanks to Ellen Meiselman of www.thedesignsource.net). There are also some products specifically designed for converting PowerPoint shows to SCORM-compliant programs; word of mouth is good on Wondershare (www. sameshow.com/index.html) and Thesis (www.hunterstone.com/).

Test, Test, Test—And Launch!

As noted throughout this book, ongoing testing is critical to a smooth and timely program launch. I am not a proponent of the old-school "develop whole program—pilot—revise whole program" approach. It's cumbersome and can create far more rework than just "tweaking" as you go. It can also be maddeningly lengthy. One advantage of e-learning is its capacity for a quick launch and just-in-time training solutions. As we've discussed in other chapters, you'll likely be most successful when you:

- *Develop storyboards and simple prototypes in PowerPoint.* Stakeholders— such as managers, sales staff, and customers—are likely familiar with the "look" of a PowerPoint slideshow. They'll understand the vision for the final program better than if they were shown, say, a script. Obtaining clarity and stakeholder agreement early will save time and rework later.

- *Involve end users—your learners—up-front.* Have them try out the GUI, the Jeopardy game, and the external quiz. They can give you very useful feedback as you are creating the program. Waiting until a finished product is ready will, again, put you at risk of rework that would've been easier if done sooner.

- *Sit and watch users as your pilot users interact with the program.* Pay attention to times they seem to hesitate or are unsure about what to do/where to go next. Notice what really seems to hold their attention and what they skim or skip through. Time them to see how long the quiz really takes.

- *Test the program on different machines and browsers.* Colors display differently from one monitor to another; interactions that work just fine in Internet Explorer may inexplicably misbehave in, say, Mozilla.

Your organization may have protocols in place for launching a program. You may just be loading your files to an LMS with which your employees are familiar. I have found that an email note to learners, telling them how to access the new program and letting them know what technology they'll need (such as Internet Explorer, the Flash player, or a printer) reduces frustration for them. The catalog that houses most of my e-learning courses has a "tech requirements" page that learners need to view before they can access any program.

If e-learning is a new endeavor for you and your organization, I'd like to add some encouraging words: I have been working with e-learning projects since 1999, in an organization with 90,000 employees from all employment categories and educational backgrounds. Despite what the literature sometimes rumors, I have experienced virtually no "learner resistance" to e-learning. Learners appreciate e-learning's "just-in-time" capability. They can access training when they need it, not when the training department has it scheduled. They can go back and revisit materials. They can control when and where they access the training. And they appreciate the fact that e-learning respects their time. They are not pulled from work (or, as is often the case, required to travel) to an eight-hour class that really covers only an hour or two of content. I do occasionally run into issues with employees, such as prison guards or hospital nurses, who don't have their own work computers. This has always been resolved by explaining that learners don't need their own computers, just access to one for a short while. (It's akin to explaining that each employee doesn't need his or her own photocopier.) The resistance I do encounter is more often from IT departments blocking a particular technology (usually something involving bandwidth, like video, which I can resolve by promising to launch to only a few learners at a time) and—from trainers. e-Learning is, unfortunately, perceived as a threat by some classroom trainers. This is the subject of my dissertation research; watch my website (www.bozarthzone.com) for results of that, and please contact me if you have experiences with this that you'd like to share.

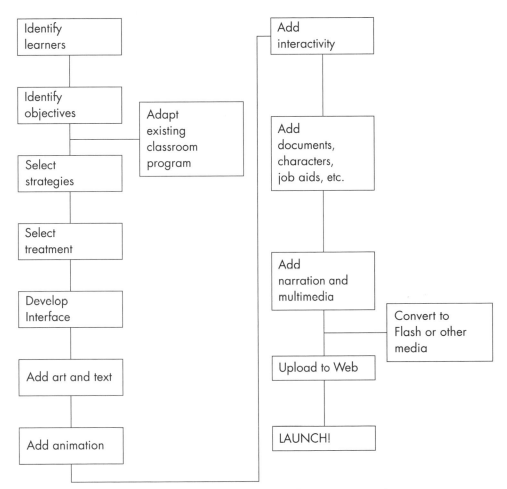

Creating e-Learning with PowerPoint

Summary

The decisions you make about distributing your PowerPoint-based e-learning program will affect decisions about design. Must you have trigger animations? If so, at least for now, you will need to deliver your program as a large PowerPoint file, likely made larger by the addition of media elements or narration. Must you limit file size? You'll either need to eliminate media and narration or deliver the program converted as a Flash file—which means no triggers. Working with your IT department, knowing the technology most widely available to your learners, will help you make good decisions about distributing your program, which in turn will help to ensure its success.

Author's Note

And this is the end of the book. In moving on to developing e-learning with PowerPoint, I hope you will take away the things I have tried to emphasize. Remember that e-learning is not an objective in itself. Determine what performance issues could be resolved through training, and then choose the training solution that will solve the problem. Look beyond what we may think of as traditional training solutions: Are there job aids, documents, or activities that would solve problems? Is there a game that teaches better than a "presentation"? Technology is helping us redefine "training." Marc Rosenberg, author of *e-Learning: Strategies for Delivering Knowledge in the Digital Age,* often uses the analogy of the railroad industry's failure to adapt to the advent of trucking: the railroad industry saw itself as being in the train business, not the transportation business. As training professionals, it's likewise important that we remember that training is not about the classroom, it's about performance improvement. Learn to use tools and approaches that will help your organization achieve that goal.

And remember: good e-learning is not about software—it's about design.

PowerPoint Basics

Creating e-learning with PowerPoint requires some skill at using the product. In this book, I assume that you have some experience with creating slide shows, including using basics of Word art, using AutoShapes, working with the drawing and picture toolbars, inserting and resizing clip art, and creating simple animations. A quick overview of PowerPoint tools and simple operations is provided here in two parts: the first, for those using PowerPoint 2002/XP/2003, the second, for users of PowerPoint 2007. Experienced users may choose to skip this Appendix; those with very rudimentary skills might want to practice basic tasks or seek out additional training. (Searching www.google.com for specific tasks, such as "how to create animations in PowerPoint," will take you to any number of tutorials.)

Here is a list of keyboard shortcuts. A printable version of this chart is included on the CD accompanying this book.

Table A.1. Keyboard Shortcuts

Insert new slide	CTRL+M
Switch to next pane	F6
Switch to the previous pane	SHIFT+F6
Duplicate current slide	CTRL+D
Start slide show	F5
Promote paragraph	ALT+SHIFT+LEFT ARROW
Demote paragraph	ALT+SHIFT+RIGHT ARROW
Apply subscript	CTRL+EQUAL SIGN (=)
Apply superscript	CTRL+PLUS SIGN (+)
Open font dialog box	CTRL+T
Repeat last action	F4 or CTRL+Y
Find	CTRL+F
View guides	CTRL+G
Delete a word	CTRL+BACKSPACE
Capitalize	SHIFT+F3
Bold	CTRL+B
Italicize	CTRL+I
Insert hyperlink	CTRL+K
Select all	CTRL+A
Copy	CTRL+C
Paste	CTRL+V
Undo	CTRL+Z
Save	CTRL+S
Print	CTRL+P
Open	CTRL+O
Move object behind another	Order, send to back
Bring object to front	Order, bring to front
Draw perfect circle	Shift+ drag shape
Nudge object by grid unit	Select object then nudge with arrow keys or spacebar
Nudge object by pixel	Select object, hold down CTRL while nudging

The remaining pages show a number illustrations of PowerPoint commands, toolbars, and assorted functions.

Part 1: PowerPoint 2002/XP/2003

Appendix Figure 1. 2002/XP/2003 Interface

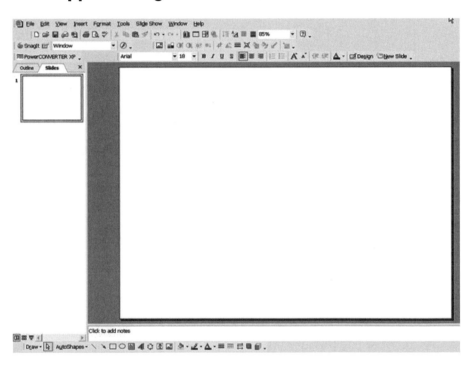

Appendix Figure 2. Commands

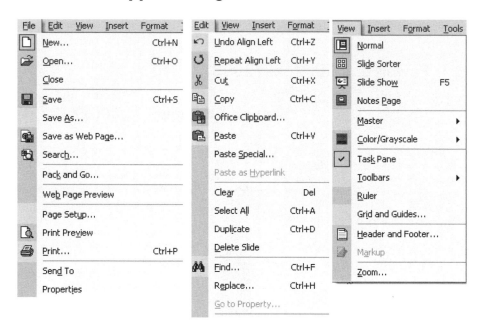

Appendix Figure 3. Standard Toolbar

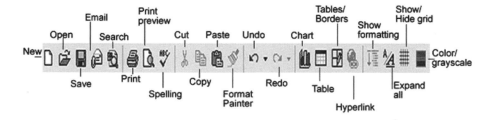

Appendix Figure 4. Drawing Toolbar

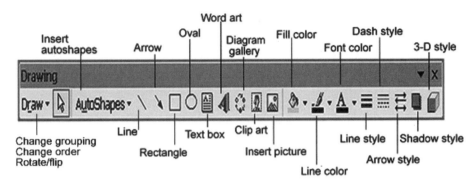

Appendix Figure 5. Select Objects

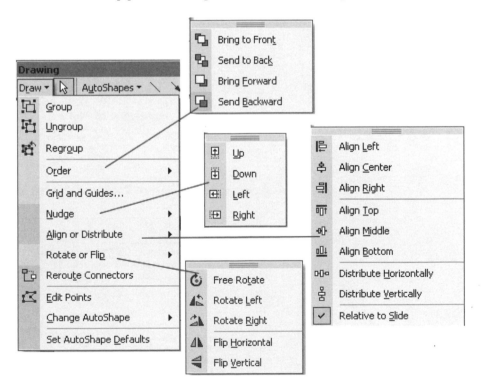

Appendix Figure 6. Autoshapes

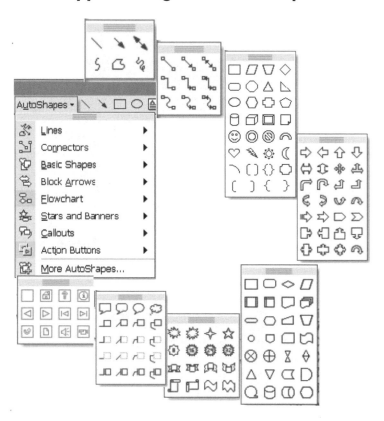

Appendix Figure 7. Modifying Autoshapes

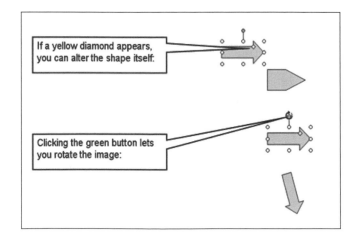

Appendix Figure 8. Word Art Gallery

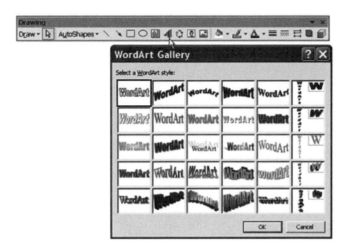

Appendix Figure 9. Diagram Gallery

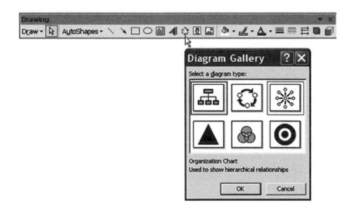

Appendix Figure 10. Fill-Color Palettes

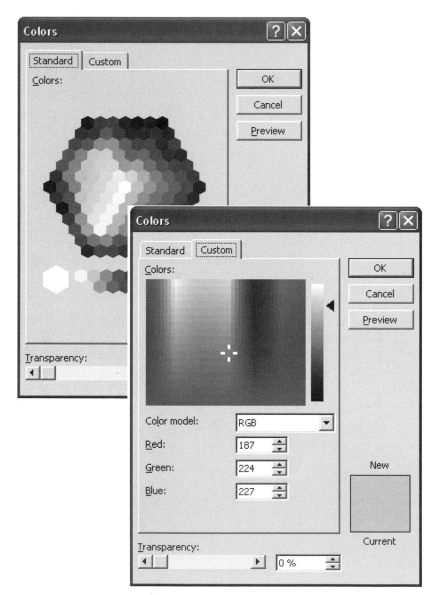

Appendix Figure 11. Fill Effects

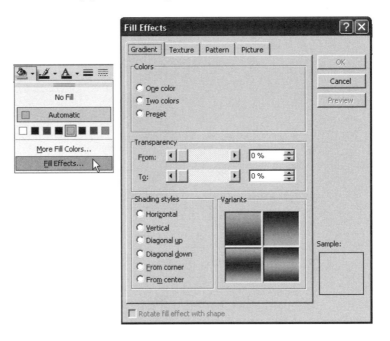

Appendix Figure 12. Line Color

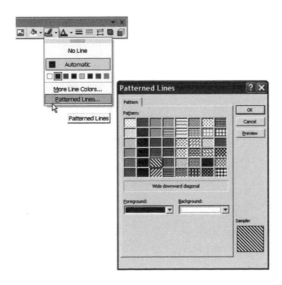

Appendix Figure 13. Fills for Autoshapes

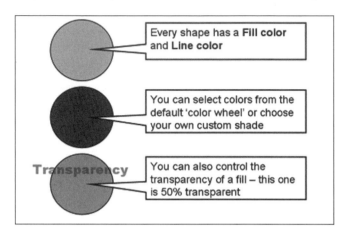

Appendix Figure 14. Types of Fills for Autoshapes

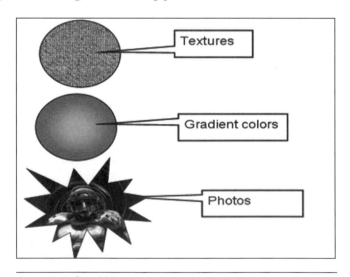

Source: Adam Warren

Appendix Figure 15. Line, Dash, Arrow, Shadow, and 3-D Styles

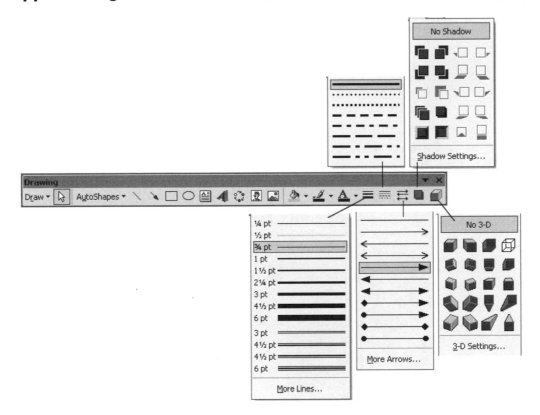

Appendix Figure 16. Picture Toolbar

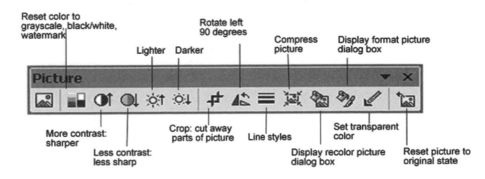

Part 2: PowerPoint 2007

PowerPoint 2007 introduced a new interface. Rather than working from different toolbars, users are presented with the new "ribbon," a series of command tabs across the top of the screen. Apart from the new interface, little of the functionality has changed—for example, there aren't many new animations or shapes. There are more options of accessing some common features—shapes can now be inserted in a number of different ways—and greatly expanded tools for art, particularly gradient colors, diagrams, and editing photographs.

Appendix Figure 17. PowerPoint 2007

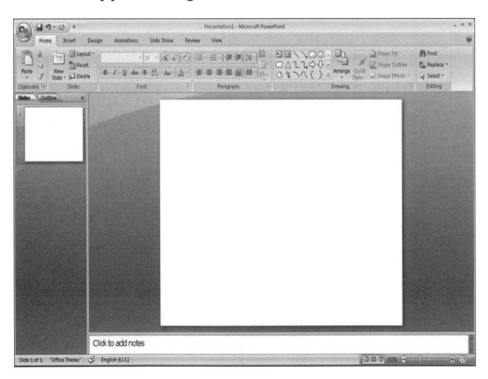

Appendix Figure 18. "Home" Tab

"AutoShapes" are now just "Shapes" and can be accessed via the "home" tab, the "insert" tab, or the drawing toolbar that appears after selecting an item. Action buttons are located with "shapes."

Appendix Figure 19. Shapes

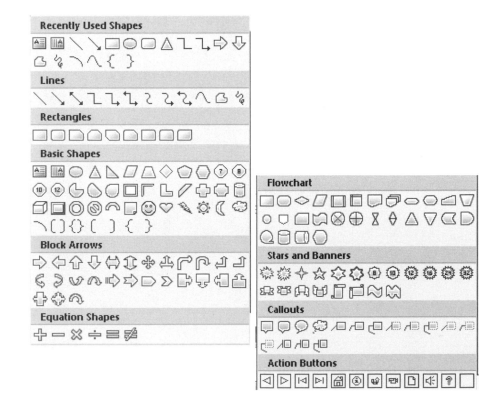

The "insert" tab provides groupings of items: tables, illustrations, links, text, and media clips. Text and shapes can also be inserted from the "home" tab.

Appendix Figure 20. "Insert" Tab

Appendix Figure 21. Photo Album

Appendix Figure 22. "Smart Art" Diagrams

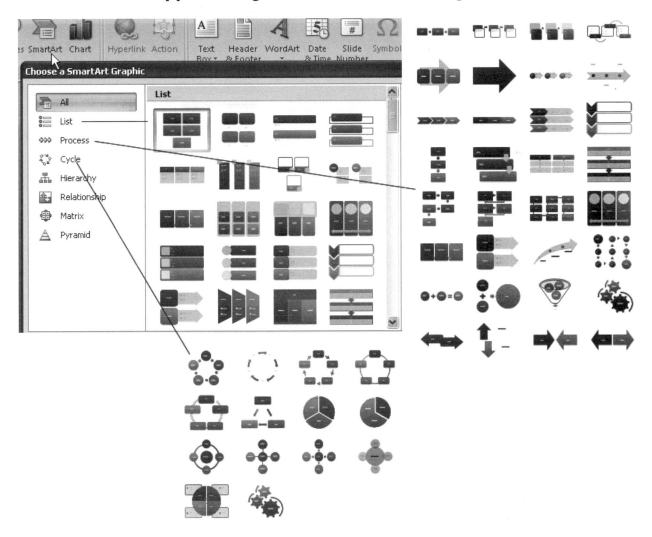

Appendix Figure 23. More "Smart Art"

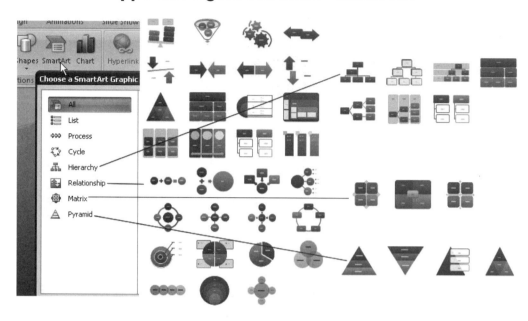

Appendix Figure 24. Charts

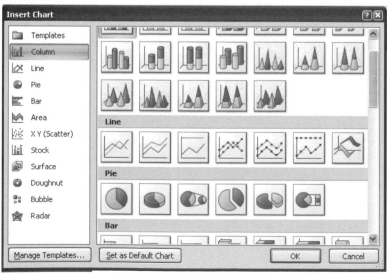

Appendix Figure 25. "Design" Tab

Appendix Figure 26. "Animations" Tab

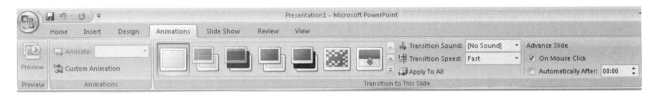

Appendix Figure 27. "Slide Show" Tab

Appendix Figure 28. "Review" Tab

Appendix Figure 29. "View" Tab

Clicking on a shape opens the "format" tab and drawing tools.

Appendix Figure 30. Drawing Tools

Appendix Figure 31. Shapes

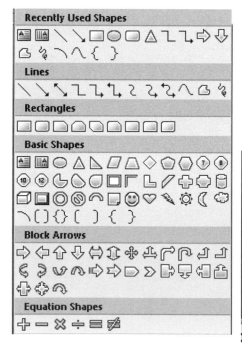

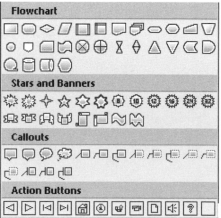

Appendix Figure 32. Modifying Shapes

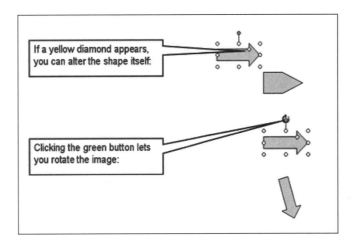

Appendix Figure 33. Arrange

Appendix Figure 34. Quick Styles

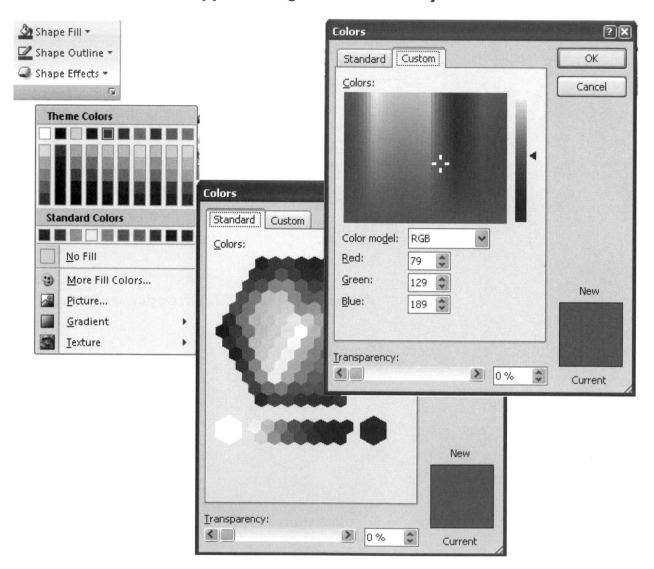

Appendix Figure 35. Shape Fill

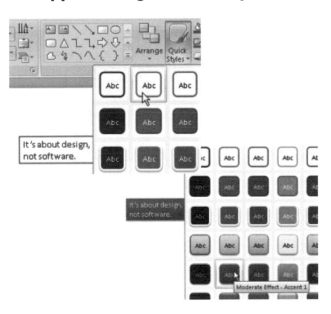

Appendix Figure 36. Filling Shapes

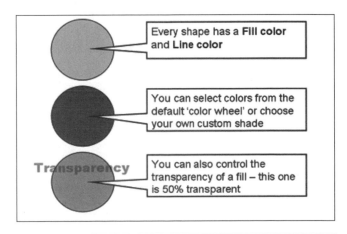

Source: Adam Warren

Appendix Figure 37. Types of Fills for Shapes

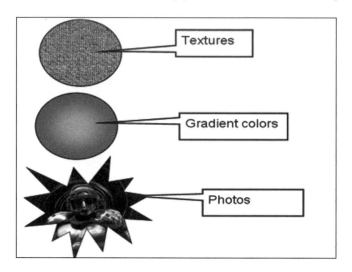

Appendix Figure 38. Shape Outline

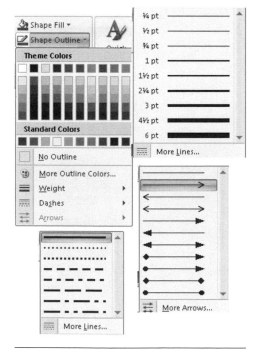

Source: Adam Warren

Appendix Figure 39. Shape Effects

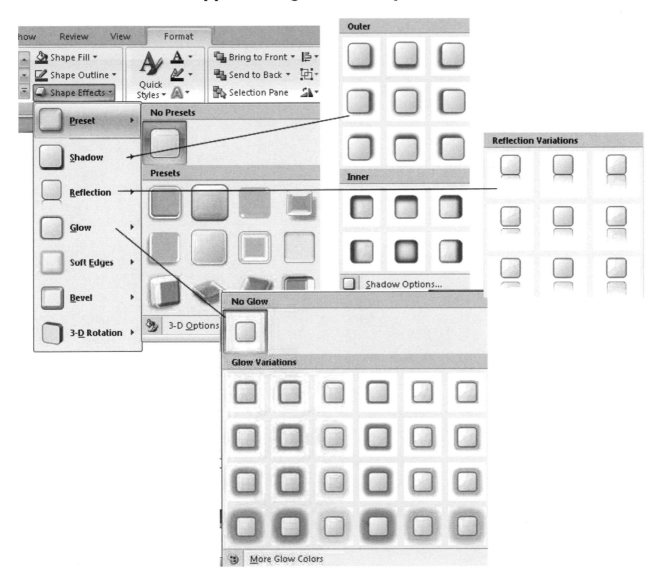

Appendix Figure 40. More Shape Effects

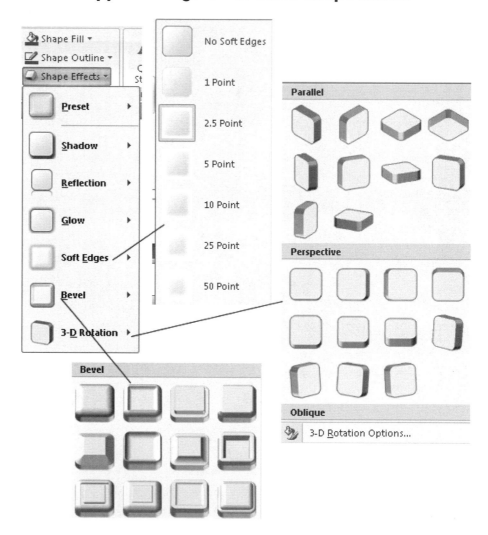

Clicking on a picture opens the "format" tab and the picture tools.

Appendix Figure 41. Picture Tools

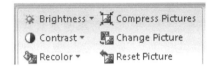

Appendix Figure 42. Add Frames to Photos

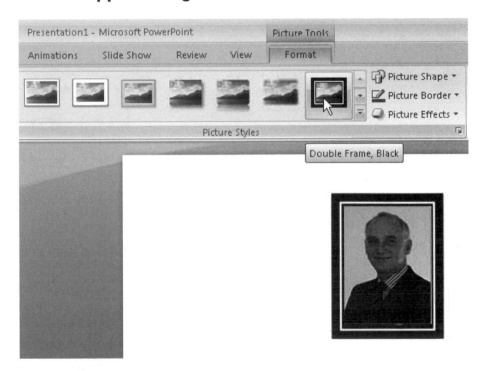

Appendix Figure 43. Add Borders and Other Effects

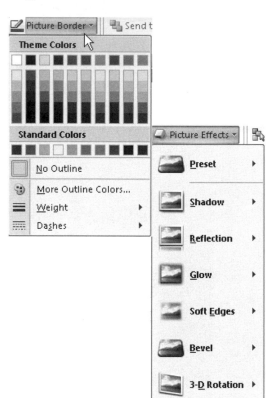

Summary

This supplement was meant to provide a quick overview of tools available in PowerPoint; familiarity with these will be helpful as you work to build e-learning programs. More sophisticated operations, such as editing clip art and recording narration, are included within their respective chapters, and many tasks are further explained on the CD accompanying this book. If you are not already a skilled PowerPoint user, you are encouraged to practice and learn as much as you can. Nothing in this book is technically that difficult, but proficiency will, of course, increase your confidence, enable your creative ideas, and reduce program development time.

REFERENCES AND RESOURCES

Books and Articles

Atkinson, C. (2005). *Beyond bullet points.* Redmond, WA: Microsoft Press.

Aust, R., & Isaacson, R. (2005). Designing and evaluating user interfaces for e-learning. Retrieved from http://elearndesign.org/papers/eLearn2005_Aust.pdf

Bozarth, J. (2005). *e-Learning solutions on a shoestring: Help for the chronically underfunded trainer.* San Francisco, CA: Pfeiffer.

Chapman, B. (2005). *PowerPoint to e-learning development tools: Comparative analysis of twenty leading systems.* Sunnyvale, CA: Brandon Hall Research.

Clark, R., & Mayer, R. (2002). e-Learning and the science of instruction. San Francisco, CA: Pfeiffer.

Clark, R., & Lyons, C. (2005). *Graphics for learning: Proven guidelines for planning, designing, and evaluating visuals in training materials.* San Francisco, CA: Pfeiffer.

Clark, R., Nguyen, F., & Sweller, J. (2006). *Efficiency in learning: Efficiency-based guidelines to manage cognitive load.* San Francisco, CA: Pfeiffer.

Culberson, R. (n.d.). Use of characters in e-learning. Retrieved from www.nurelm.com/resources.jsp?pageId=2161392210281162147507764

Driscoll, M., & Carliner, S. (2005). *Advanced web-based training strategies.* San Francisco, CA: Pfeiffer.

Finklestein, E. (2003). *How to do everything with Microsoft Office Power-Point 2003.* Emeryville, CA: McGraw Hill/Osborne.

Fried, I. (2005, September 20). Office 12 makeover takes on "feature creep." CNET News.com. Retrieved from http://news.com.com/Office+12+makeover+takes+on+feature+creep/2100-1012_3-5873597.html?tag=html.alert

Lowe, R. (2003). Animation and learning: Selective processing of information in dynamic graphics. *Learning and Instruction, 13*(3), 157–176.

Marcovitz, D. (2004). *Powerful PowerPoint for educators: Using VisualBasic for applications to make PowerPoint interactive.* New York: Libraries Unlimited.

Mayer, R. (2001). *Multimedia learning.* New York: Cambridge University Press.

Mayer, R. (2003). The promise of multimedia learning: Using the same instructional design methods across different media. *Learning and Instruction, 13*(2),123–139.

Mayer, R., & Moreno, R. (2002). Animation as an aid to learning. *Educational Psychology Review, 14*(1), 87–99.

McKenzie, J. (Ed.). *From now on. The Educational Technology Journal.* Available at http://fno.org/.

O'Day, D. (2006). Animated cell biology: a quick and easy method for making effective, high-quality teaching animations. *CBE Life Sciences Education, 5*(3), 255–263.

O'Day, D. (2006). How to make pedagogically meaningful animations for teaching and research using PowerPoint and Camtasia. Retrieved December 30, 2006, from www.techsmith.com/community/education/interview/odayanimationipsi2006.pdf

O'Driscoll, T., & Gery, G. (2005, February). Workflow learning gets real. *Training.*

Rosenberg, M. (2000). *e-Learning: Strategies for delivering knowledge in the digital age.* New York: McGraw-Hill.

Rossett, A., & Gautier-Downes, J. (1991). *A handbook of job aids.* San Francisco, CA: Pfeiffer.

Rossett, A., & Schafer, L. (2007). *Job aids and performance support.* San Francisco, CA: Pfeiffer.

Schank, R.C. (2005). Lessons *in learning, e-learning, and training.* San Francisco, CA: Pfeiffer.

Shank, P., & Sitze, A. (2004). *Making sense of online learning.* San Francisco, CA: Pfeiffer.

Silberman, M. (2005). *101 ways to make training active* (2nd ed.). San Francisco, CA: Pfeiffer.

Stolovitch, H., & Keeps, E. (2002). *Telling ain't training.* Alexandria, VA: ASTD/ISPI.

Sweller, J., van Merrienboer, J., & Paas, F. (1998). Cognitive architecture and instructional design. *Educational Psychology Review, 10*(3).

Toth, T. (2004). *Technology for trainers.* Alexandria, VA: ASTD.

Van Gog, T., Paas, F., & van Merrienboer, J. (2004). Process-oriented worked examples: Improving transfer performance through enhanced understanding. *Instructional Science, 32*(1–2), 83–98.

Van Wempen, F. (2004). *PowerPoint: Advanced presentation techniques.* San Francisco, CA: Jossey-Bass.

Wilson-Pauwells, L. (1997). Bringing it into focus: Visual cues and their roles in developing attention. *Journal of Biomedical Communication, 24,* 12–16.

Zull, J. (2002). *The art of changing the brain.* New York: Stylus.

Programs and Websites

Several programs are mentioned repeatedly throughout this book, usually due to their particularly creative and effective approach. Most are exemplars of thoughtful design, not gee-whiz expensive technology. Readers are encouraged to visit the sites below to view these programs in their entirety:

"A. Pintura: Art Detective" from Eduweb at www.eduweb.com/pintura/

"Electric Circuitry," by Simon Drane at http://ferl.becta.org.uk/display.cfm?resID=2509

"Hungerbanquet" from OxFam America at www.hungerbanquet.org

"Gamekeeper's Conundrum" and "Emergency Case Simulator," both from the Royal Veterinary College at www.rvc.ac.uk/Review/Cases/Index.htm or www.rvc.ac.uk/review/Pitfalls/pitfalls.htm

"Diversity Challenge" and "Keeping Safe," both from www.kwango.com. Examples available on the site.

Ellen Finklestein: www.ellenfinklestein.com. Repository of extensive instruction and information on PowerPoint, including tricks and tips.

Ferl offers an extensive, searchable resource bank of teacher-created materials, including hundreds of PowerPoint shows. http://ferl.becta.org.uk

Indezine.com: free PowerPoint information, templates, and backgrounds. Frequently updated; free newsletter.

Laura Bergell's www.maniactive.com site. Free templates and editable presentations.

PowerPoint Heaven: http://pptheaven.mvps.org/index.html. Shawn Toh's site for glitzy, high-tech PowerPoint ideas, tricks, and tutorials. Gallery of amazing games. Free access and downloads.

Downloads

"Sexual Harassment" from Brightline Compliance at www.brightlinecompliance.com/training/preventing-workplace-harass- demo.html

Godin, S. "Really Bad PowerPoint." Booklet available for free download from http://www.sethgodin.com/freeprize/reallybad-1.pdf.

"What If Lincoln Had Used PowerPoint for the Gettysburg Address?" Downloadable presentation from Peter Norvig at. http://norvig.com/Gettysburg/.

J
ane Bozarth has been a training practitioner since 1989. A graduate of the University of North Carolina at Chapel Hill, she also has an M.Ed. in training and development/technology in training from NC State University and is presently pursuing her doctorate in training and development. Jane's graduate work in online learning led to her current position as e-learning coordinator with the NC Office of State Personnel's Human Resources Development Group. Her specialty, finding low-cost ways of creating or purchasing quality e-learning solutions, led to the publication of *e-Learning Solutions on a Shoestring* in 2005 (Pfeiffer). A recipient of a 2005 LOLA award, a 2006 *Training* Magazine Editor's Pick Award, and NASPE's 2005 Rooney Award, Jane is a popular presenter and often appears at national events such as Nielsen Communications' Training and Online Learning Conference and Expo, the ASTD International Conference and Expo, the e-Learning Guild Online Forums, and many management and professional association gatherings.

She enjoys business writing, and in addition to her regular column in *Training,* Jane's work has appeared in trade and academic journals, including *The Creative Training Techniques Newsletter* and *The Journal of Educational Technology and Society.* Jane and her husband, Kent Underwood, live in Durham, North Carolina. She can be contacted via her website: www.bozarthzone.com.

HOW TO USE THE CD-ROM

System Requirements

PC with Microsoft Windows 98SE or later

Mac with Apple OS version 8.6 or later

Using the CD with Windows

To view the items located on the CD, follow these steps:

1. Insert the CD into your computer's CD-ROM drive.

2. A window appears with the following options:

Contents: Allows you to view the files included on the CD-ROM.

Software: Allows you to install useful software from the CD-ROM.

Links: Displays a hyperlinked page of websites.

Author: Displays a page with information about the Author(s).

Contact Us: Displays a page with information on contacting the publisher or author.

Help: Displays a page with information on using the CD.

Exit: Closes the interface window.

If you do not have autorun enabled, or if the autorun window does not appear, follow these steps to access the CD:

1. Click Start→Run.

2. In the dialog box that appears, type d:<\\>start.exe, where d is the letter of your CD-ROM drive. This brings up the autorun window described in the preceding set of steps.

3. Choose the desired option from the menu. (See Step 2 in the preceding list for a description of these options.)

In Case of Trouble

If you experience difficulty using the CD-ROM, please follow these steps:

1. Make sure your hardware and systems configurations conform to the systems requirements noted under "System Requirements" above.

2. Review the installation procedure for your type of hardware and operating system.

It is possible to reinstall the software if necessary.

To speak with someone in Product Technical Support, call 800–762–2974 or 317–572–3994 M–F 8:30 a.m.–5:00 p.m. EST. You can also get support and contact Product Technical Support through our website at www.wiley.com/techsupport.

Before calling or writing, please have the following information available:

• Type of computer and operating system

• Any error messages displayed

• Complete description of the problem.

It is best if you are sitting at your computer when making the call.

Pfeiffer Publications Guide

This guide is designed to familiarize you with the various types of Pfeiffer publications. The formats section describes the various types of products that we publish; the methodologies section describes the many different ways that content might be provided within a product. We also provide a list of the topic areas in which we publish.

FORMATS

In addition to its extensive book-publishing program, Pfeiffer offers content in an array of formats, from fieldbooks for the practitioner to complete, ready-to-use training packages that support group learning.

FIELDBOOK Designed to provide information and guidance to practitioners in the midst of action. Most fieldbooks are companions to another, sometimes earlier, work, from which its ideas are derived; the fieldbook makes practical what was theoretical in the original text. Fieldbooks can certainly be read from cover to cover. More likely, though, you'll find yourself bouncing around following a particular theme, or dipping in as the mood, and the situation, dictate.

HANDBOOK A contributed volume of work on a single topic, comprising an eclectic mix of ideas, case studies, and best practices sourced by practitioners and experts in the field.

An editor or team of editors usually is appointed to seek out contributors and to evaluate content for relevance to the topic. Think of a handbook not as a ready-to-eat meal, but as a cookbook of ingredients that enables you to create the most fitting experience for the occasion.

RESOURCE Materials designed to support group learning. They come in many forms: a complete, ready-to-use exercise (such as a game); a comprehensive resource on one topic (such as conflict management) containing a variety of methods and approaches; or a collection of like-minded activities (such as icebreakers) on multiple subjects and situations.

TRAINING PACKAGE An entire, ready-to-use learning program that focuses on a particular topic or skill. All packages comprise a guide for the facilitator/trainer and a workbook for the participants. Some packages are supported with additional media—such as video—or learning aids, instruments, or other devices to help participants understand concepts or practice and develop skills.

- *Facilitator/trainer's guide* Contains an introduction to the program, advice on how to organize and facilitate the learning event, and step-by-step instructor notes. The guide also contains copies of presentation materials—handouts, presentations, and overhead designs, for example—used in the program.

• *Participant's workbook* Contains exercises and reading materials that support the learning goal and serves as a valuable reference and support guide for participants in the weeks and months that follow the learning event. Typically, each participant will require his or her own workbook.

ELECTRONIC CD-ROMs and web-based products transform static Pfeiffer content into dynamic, interactive experiences. Designed to take advantage of the searchability, automation, and ease-of-use that technology provides, our e-products bring convenience and immediate accessibility to your workspace.

METHODOLOGIES

CASE STUDY A presentation, in narrative form, of an actual event that has occurred inside an organization. Case studies are not prescriptive, nor are they used to prove a point; they are designed to develop critical analysis and decision-making skills. A case study has a specific time frame, specifies a sequence of events, is narrative in structure, and contains a plot structure—an issue (what should be/have been done?). Use case studies when the goal is to enable participants to apply previously learned theories to the circumstances in the case, decide what is pertinent, identify the real issues, decide what should have been done, and develop a plan of action.

ENERGIZER A short activity that develops readiness for the next session or learning event. Energizers are most commonly used after a break or lunch to stimulate or refocus the group. Many involve some form of physical activity, so they are a useful way to counter post-lunch lethargy. Other uses include transitioning from one topic to another, where "mental" distancing is important.

EXPERIENTIAL LEARNING ACTIVITY (ELA) A facilitator-led intervention that moves participants through the learning cycle from experience to application (also known as a Structured Experience). ELAs are carefully thought-out designs in which there is a definite learning purpose and intended outcome. Each step—everything that participants do during the activity—facilitates the accomplishment of the stated goal. Each ELA includes complete instructions for facilitating the intervention and a clear statement of goals, suggested group size and timing, materials required, an explanation of the process, and, where appropriate, possible variations to the activity. (For more detail on Experiential Learning Activities, see the Introduction to the *Reference Guide to Handbooks and Annuals*, 1999 edition, Pfeiffer, San Francisco.)

GAME A group activity that has the purpose of fostering team spirit and togetherness in addition to the achievement of a pre-stated goal. Usually contrived—undertaking a desert expedition, for example—this type of learning method offers an engaging means for participants to demonstrate and practice business and interpersonal skills. Games are effective for team building and personal development mainly because the goal is subordinate to the process—the means through which participants reach decisions, collaborate, communicate, and generate trust and understanding. Games often engage teams in "friendly" competition.

ICEBREAKER A (usually) short activity designed to help participants overcome initial anxiety in a training session and/or to acquaint the participants with one another. An icebreaker can be a fun activity or can be tied to specific topics or training goals. While a useful tool in itself, the icebreaker comes into its own in situations where tension or resistance exists within a group.

INSTRUMENT A device used to assess, appraise, evaluate, describe, classify, and summarize various aspects of human behavior. The term used to describe an instrument depends primarily on its format and purpose. These terms include survey, questionnaire, inventory, diagnostic, survey, and poll. Some uses of instruments include providing instrumental feedback to group members, studying here-and-now processes or functioning within a group, manipulating group composition, and evaluating outcomes of training and other interventions.

Instruments are popular in the training and HR field because, in general, more growth can occur if an individual is provided with a method for focusing specifically on his or her own behavior. Instruments also are used to obtain information that will serve as a basis for change and to assist in workforce planning efforts.

Paper-and-pencil tests still dominate the instrument landscape with a typical package comprising a facilitator's guide, which offers advice on administering the instrument and interpreting the collected data, and an initial set of instruments. Additional instruments are available separately. Pfeiffer, though, is investing heavily in e-instruments. Electronic instrumentation provides effortless distribution and, for larger groups particularly, offers advantages over paper-and-pencil tests in the time it takes to analyze data and provide feedback.

LECTURETTE A short talk that provides an explanation of a principle, model, or process that is pertinent to the participants' current learning needs. A lecturette is intended to establish a common language bond between the trainer and the participants by providing a mutual frame of reference. Use a lecturette as an introduction to a group activity or event, as an interjection during an event, or as a handout.

MODEL A graphic depiction of a system or process and the relationship among its elements. Models provide a frame of reference and something more tangible, and more easily remembered, than a verbal explanation. They also give participants something to "go on," enabling them to track their own progress as they experience the dynamics, processes, and relationships being depicted in the model.

ROLE PLAY A technique in which people assume a role in a situation/ scenario: a customer service rep in an angry-customer exchange, for example. The way in which the role is approached is then discussed and feedback is offered. The role play is often repeated using a different approach and/or incorporating changes made based on feedback received. In other words, role playing is a spontaneous interaction involving realistic behavior under artificial (and safe) conditions.

SIMULATION A methodology for understanding the interrelationships among components of a system or process. Simulations differ from games in that they test or use a model that depicts or mirrors some aspect of reality in form, if not necessarily in content. Learning occurs by studying the effects of change on one or more factors of the model. Simulations are commonly used to test hypotheses about what happens in a system—often referred to as "what if?" analysis—or to examine best-case/worst-case scenarios.

THEORY A presentation of an idea from a conjectural perspective. Theories are useful because they encourage us to examine behavior and phenomena through a different lens.

TOPICS

The twin goals of providing effective and practical solutions for workforce training and organization development and meeting the educational needs of training and human resource professionals shape Pfeiffer's publishing program. Core topics include the following:

Leadership & Management

Communication & Presentation

Coaching & Mentoring

Training & Development

e-Learning

Teams & Collaboration

OD & Strategic Planning

Human Resources

Consulting

What will you find on pfeiffer.com?

- The best in workplace performance solutions for training and HR professionals

- Downloadable training tools, exercises, and content

- Web-exclusive offers

- Training tips, articles, and news

- Seamless on-line ordering

- Author guidelines, information on becoming a Pfeiffer Affiliate, and much more

Discover more at www.pfeiffer.com